DAVID FEHERTY

ALSO BY DAVID FEHERTY

A Nasty Bit of Rough

RuggedLand

RUGGED LAND | 276 CANAL STREET · FIFTH FLOOR · NEW YORK CITY · NY 10013 · USA

RuggedLand

Published by Rugged Land, LLC
276 CANAL STREET • NEW YORK • NEW YORK • 10013

RUGGED LAND and colophon are trademarks of Rugged Land, LLC.

PUBLISHER'S CATALOGING-IN-PUBLICATION
(PROVIDED BY QUALITY BOOKS, INC.)

Feherty, David.
Somewhere in Ireland, a village is missing an idiot / by David Feherty.
p. cm.
"A David Feherty collection."
LCCN 2002117819
ISBN 1-59071-009-6

1. Feherty, David. 2. Sportwriters--United States--Biography.
3. Sportscasters--United States--Biography.
4. Novelists, American--20th century--Biography.
I. Title.

PR6106.E37A3 2003   823'.92
QBI33-1154

Interior Illustrations by Victor Juhasz
Book Design by Hsu and Associates

RUGGED LAND WEBSITE ADDRESS: WWW.RUGGEDLAND.COM

Copyright © 2003 by David Feherty

May 2003

1   3   5   7   9   10   8   6   4   2

First Edition

To Keith Richards...

...who once told me to Fuck Off in Hampstead.

Contents

Foreword

"**I**diot."

This book sort of happened while I was in the bathroom, I think, which is in a way quite fitting, as a great deal of its content is lavatorial in nature. Therefore, it stands to reason that it should be read in small excrements.... Or maybe that should be "increments," I don't know. Three lines into the foreword, and there's the first poop reference. There goes the Pulitzer again.

Let me begin by saying that Rick Reilly, my friend and colleague over at *Sports Exaggerated*, is my hero. I know he has all the sports to work with, but still, how he has managed to write a column of such quality every week for the last half-century is totally beyond me. I know it's not that long, but I bet it feels like it to him. For just five years now I've been writing one a month, and these days the only way I can come up with a topic is by dressing up as a nun, sticking a fountain pen in each ear, and banging my head for hours on a wall map of Nigeria. It probably explains why only about half of the following pieces have anything to do with golf.

I have to thank a bunch of sick, twisted, and clearly dysfunctional idiots at *Golf Magazine* for giving me a forum, and the readers too, for their feedback. It's not all positive, but all of it is appreciated, because it tells me at least I'm being read. I'm just trying to make people laugh, and if I don't, then I hope they smile. If they can't smile, that's good too, because they're probably the assholes I was trying to piss off in the first place. Thanks too, to Leslie Moonves, Sean McManus, Tony Pettiti, Lance Barrow, and anyone else at CBS who has had the power to fire me over the last few years, but has so far resisted the urge. I suspect that the following will make such resistance no easier but, hey, if I ever stopped to think, I might never write or speak again.

Chapter One
Who Am I? And Why Am I Here?

The Guy on the Fairway

I feel it might be appropriate to introduce myself. I am David Feherty, a Ryder Cup player, twenty-one years a pro, with ten victories worldwide and about $3 million in earnings. (The whereabouts of the money remains a mystery, although I do recall having a whale of a time.) My parents think I may have been swapped in the hospital nursery, my liver is the size of Wyoming, my weight normally hovers between 160 and two hundred pounds depending on the time of the year, and for some time now I have had this strange feeling that I am turning into an announcer. I've been waking up in the middle of the night saying things like, "Yes, Kenny, it's a 5-iron," and, "No, Gary, we're back on Earth now." Fortunately, my wife, Anita, knows exactly how to unplug me.

I think it's fair to say, though, that if last year seemed like a dream, this year feels like the dream came true. I always enjoyed talking more than playing, and now CBS is paying me for what I do most! I never envisaged playing past the age of forty anyway, so at thirty-eight-plus and in possession of my first real job, the words "Welcome Home" have a special significance for me. It is a new challenge, however, and it takes a little getting used to.

As a player I never really thought much about how a golf telecast was put together. I figured people like Gary McCord and Ken Venturi just got up there and talked. Now I realize that there are about a thousand ways to screw up a show, including a couple of new ones that they've named after me. Hell, it's all I can do at the moment to avoid looking like a deer frozen in the headlamps when someone turns a camera on me and asks me to entertain or inform. But somehow our resident geniuses in the production trailer manage to turn a minute-long on-camera feature from me into something watchable without the aid of George Lucas.

As a foot soldier, there are so many things to remember, like keeping an eye on where your cameras are so you don't appear in the shot, staying downwind so you can't be heard or, for that matter, smelled by the players, and being politically correct so you don't get fired. The last is a constant problem for me as my brain has a long record of going on vacation and leaving my mouth in charge, added to which I have always been perfectly satisfied with just being ordinarily correct. In fact, this happens so rarely, I'm usually overjoyed. When I was twenty, I thought I knew everything, and then when I reached thirty, I realized I actually knew nothing back then. Now that I am approaching forty, I'm starting to see a pattern emerge and, as a consequence, I listen to Ken Venturi's advice very, very carfully.

It's almost like being a player in a game against the television critics. Just like a golfer, we don't get an eraser and our bogeys are the broadcasting burps that all of you get to read about the following morning. Yet so little is known about why some of these minor hiccups occur. Well, as I said earlier, I have been responsible for inventing a few new ones in my short tenure as a shot-jockey and, like it or not, I'm going to share a couple of them with you.

Every viewer is familiar with the unanswered question syndrome.

For example, Jim Nantz asks yours truly for a club or a yardage only to be rewarded with a pregnant silence. "How can this happen?" I can almost hear the few of you still reading this ask yourselves. Well, while Jimmy effortlessly smoothes over the wrinkle as only he can, I'm struggling in a Porta-John trying to put my RF (radio frequency) pack back around my waist without dropping the microphone into the can. It's like wearing a fifteen-pound python that just swallowed a corgi around your waist, with all the pressure on your bladder and lower intestine. I swear it's so effective they should sell the damn things at Eckerd's.

Also, picture this. I'm leopard-crawling toward Greg Norman through the long grass in my Ralph Lauren, CBS-standard-issue camouflage jumpsuit with plastic-cleat knee pads and matching inflatable Goodyear blimp ball cap when the evil McCord spots me from his comfortable perch above the green. As the great man sets up over the ball, I slither close enough to spy the club and, with a silent, weed-eating turn, start to retreat to a safe distance to call the shot. "What sort of shot does he have there, David?" blares in my right ear. Now I've got two options. I can say, "Well, he definitely can't miss this green to the right, Gary" and die almost instantly, or shut up and live. Go figure.

Out there on the links, I'm starting to be recognized by fans as the "guy on the fairway," in stark contrast to my playing days when I was known as "the guy in the rough," and I'm always being asked when I am going to play again. Hopefully, only when I have to. It took me twenty-one years to realize how small the hole is and what a tremendous stress buster it is when you don't have to aim at it.

The second most popular question is, "What's it like making

the transition from player to broadcaster?" Okay, well, the main differences I've experienced are as follows: First, somebody else pays my expenses; second, I never miss a cut (this used to happen); and third, I get paid every week (that never happened).

Otherwise it's been easy, what with getting to work with people I've loved listening to for years and getting to watch people suffer like I used to for years. It's been a blast, and the most unexpected bonus of all is that my golf has improved beyond all recognition since I quit. Heck, I watch players make mistakes these days that I would never make if I were in their position. Which I'm not. It almost makes me want to play again…. Almost.

The Hairy One

It's funny how our lives change. If, twenty years ago, someone had told me that by the turn of the century, I would be living in Dallas, Texas, and writing for a living, I would have laughed. I was twenty-two years old and I had a plan. I was a golfer, a pro, and I was going to make a fortune. I was right, but somehow I managed to spend one in the process. I played for a living for twenty years and never really got in front. However, in one way I did get rich. Friends come and go, but enemies accumulate, that's what they say. I'm sure I have a few of the latter, but they have always been outnumbered by the good guys.

Tuesday night I was ambushed by Sam Torrance, the European Ryder Cup captain, and former cellmate of mine on the European Tour. On his way back to London from Los Angeles, where he had been shooting a commercial, he parachuted into Dallas for a day to visit me, and Erin Torrance Feherty, a two-year-old girl whom he had never met. The whole thing was orchestrated by She Who Must Be Obeyed, and was a bonus for all involved.

Forgive me if this seems uncharacteristically melancholy, but I wish he could have hung around for a few days. As I write this on Wednesday night, he is heading east at high speed, undoubtedly snoring like a tranquilized rhino, in the first-class section of a British Airways jumbo. I've spent too many flights in the seat next to him to believe otherwise. Also, I slipped him a couple of Ambien for the trip. Life is too short to be awake on an airplane, especially when they put up that godawful screen with the little 747, that moves like Pac-Man in a Zimmer frame over the southern tip of Greenland. Everyone stares at the damn thing for hours, thinking the same thing. "I know the Earth is round, but that big curve can't be the fastest way."

Sam and I have had curiously similar lives, in a remarkably different way. We both turned pro shortly after birth, but he could actually play. He rolls his own cigarettes, and has set himself on fire on several occasions, whereas I do not smoke, and have only set fire to myself once—with his Zippo in the south of France, when I tried to light a fart. Actually, I suppose I did light it. I remember the ash in my shorts, and a couple of days later, a painful stubble. Ah, those were the days. Sam had an agonizing tabloid newspaper divorce, as did I, but during his, he didn't spend four hours in a rickshaw, and then at three o'clock in the morning, tearfully burst into my room in Singapore after drinking two bottles of vodka, wanting to talk. He listened. Sam has been spotted, in various hotels throughout the world, sleepwalking naked. I have been spotted a few moments later, partially clothed and usually panic stricken, searching for him. They say you should never wake a sleepwalker, but I suspect that's a load of crap. However, I can assure you, there is a case to be made that you should never wake a naked, Scottish sleepwalker. If you happen to be a sheep, don't even think about it.

Sam got married again, this time to the love of his life. So did I, except I married a different person. Both of these amazing, beautiful women risked their lives to have children for men who refuse to grow up, but exchange baby photos. Go figure.

If, twenty years ago, someone had told me that by the turn of the century I would see Sam Torrance only two or three times a year, I would have hated them for suggesting the possibility. These things happen for a reason though, of that I'm sure. I think of all the times I had to lean on him, and I look around me now, and I know that you don't always have to be there, to be in someone's life. You just have to be a friend. If I die with only one friend like Sam Torrance, I'll be happy. Of course, I'll still be dead, but that would mean within days, I'd be thinner than he.

The Invisible Man

Since I became a writer and broadcaster, I've always maintained that I have never missed playing golf for a living, Even back in 1976, when I turned pro at the age of seventeen, I said that I didn't want to play past the age of forty, which, of course, seemed centuries away. I suppose I've been lucky enough to find a substitute for whatever it was that gave me the high, but there is one thing I miss about competing: facial recognition. In twenty years of playing, I made the kind of money that would now qualify as a bad eight weeks for Tiger, but still, every now and then someone would recognize me and ask for my autograph, or make me feel big in some other way. No matter what anyone says, it feels really good to be famous.

Things have been a little different since I moved to this side of the Atlantic, though. You see, on the European Tour, there is an entirely new cast of characters, for whom the great David Feherty is not even a memory. I was history before half of these whippersnappers showed up, and as for most of the guys with whom I did play, I'm just another V-necked bad-hair-day photo on the wall in a clubhouse in Madrid, or Cannes, or Munich, or wherever. I defected to America, but apparently Europe is managing just fine without me.

Here's the strange thing: Everyone who knew me in Europe thinks I'm now famous over here, and everyone here thinks I'm famous over there. But in reality, these days no one knows who the hell I am anywhere! Sure, there are bunches of people who recognize the voice, but even they have a tendency to guess wrong. In the lobby of the Naples Hilton, at last year's Shark Shootout, an elderly polyester lady sporting a day-glo orange golf glove was one of the few that pegged me right. She stopped me, and, wagging an orange finger in my face, said, "You're that Feherty fellow on the TV, aren't you?"

"Yes," I said, heartened that someone had made a positive ID. "Nice to meet you!"

She looked me over with a sigh, then said, "You sound thinner," and walked off.

Thank you. Thank you very much. Apparently, TV takes ten pounds off your voice.

There is something to the theory that a disembodied voice renders its owner less recognizable. For instance, I was at DFW airport just the other day to pick up my parents, who had flown in from Ireland for a visit. (Dad drank so much on the plane, Mom had to pay duty on him to get him into the country, but that's another story.) Both of my parents were looking all about for their only son, but walked right past him as he opened his arms and smiled a "Welcome to the New World" kind of smile. Brandt Jobe, who lives here in Dallas and occasionally does recognize me, was also there, struggling to get a giant rolling sack of golf clubs off one of the carousels. We exchanged pleasantries as the wrinkly ones sailed past, and then my mother heard my voice and began to strenuously elbow Father. There followed a battle of wits and agility between my parents and a fully loaded "Smarte Carte." Eventually they got turned around and headed back toward me. I would have helped, but it was too entertaining. It was like watching two elderly starfish attempting to change the course of the *Titanic*. Brandt, sensing a tender family moment was imminent, ran away.

Dad had noticed I'd been talking to someone, and after much hugging, etc., said, "I see someone knew who you were."

Hmm, I thought. He's right. I used to be David Feherty.

My father is very proud of me, and is at that stage in his life when it's an achievement for him to know who he is, so I declined to point out that if he and my mother didn't recognize me, it would seem unlikely at the very least that a member of the general public would. After all, they were staying for three weeks; I figured they'd know who I was by the time they had to go home.

I suppose if I were to be honest, I really do miss playing golf for a living, at least a little. I remember after playing well what it felt like trying to make my way through a swarm of reporters, all of whom wanted a few words with the guy in form. It was fun to be the benevolent king: "Yes, my people, come to me!"

Now, I'm just one of the swarm, and it often seems like the king isn't as benevolent as I remember being myself. I hate getting the Heisman move from a player. The player's ego left in me wants to interview itself instead. "Hey, up yours, pal. You're lucky to be on TV anyway!"

It would work once, but then I might have to go back to playing for a living.

If there is a worst part to my TV job, it would be the interviewing. I seldom get to ask my own questions, and a lot of the time I'm talking to someone who really doesn't want to be there. Yeah, I can hear you all now: "That poor man, how he must suffer." Thanks, but it's okay. I'll pull through, because I still have my writing, which is the most satisfying thing I do. It's certainly the aspect about which I receive the most feedback. Well, it's kind of like running, I suppose, in that the nice part is having written. As long as somebody reads it that is. The actual doing is a bit of a pain, like a homework assignment, and my first book was the longest assignment in the history of homework. I mean, it could be measured in geological time. It was like being literally constipated for twenty years, and then suddenly discovering Mr. Ex-Lax, or "George Peper," as we call him round here. The first three chapters took nineteen years eleven and a half months, and the remaining fifteen took ten days. I have no explanation for the change, except maybe I finally realized that there were people out there who were willing to listen to what I have to say. All of a sudden, Mr. Ego got fully engorged! When you think about it, it's probably the only reason anybody ever writes a book.

You can get folks to listen to you, without ever having to talk, and therefore find out who you are. Hang with me here; I think I'm making a self-discovery. Ernest Hemingway managed to communicate with countless millions without any of them finding out he was a total mental case, so why shouldn't I?

At the end of the day, all of us want to be loved and told that we're special. A writer gets a fair idea of the regard in which he is held when he tries to get quotes for the dust jacket from other writers. My favorite came from my nine-year-old son, Rory. Upon being shown the book, his first words to She Who Must Be Obeyed were, "I didn't know my dad could write!"

There's nothing like your kids to keep your ego in check. It's like my dear old Dad always told me: "It's nice to be important, but it's more important to be nice."

Now buy the book, you swine.

Dinner Is Served

I do most of my writing on airplanes and nearly all of my thinking behind the wheel of a car. I used to do it the other way around, but I kept clipping curbs while driving, and on airplanes, I found that when I stared straight ahead and silently mouthed the kinds of things that appear in these pages, people had a tendency to assume I was a suicidal hijacker. A man can only take so many cavity searches before the novelty wears off.

I know that I'm incredibly lucky when it comes to travel. CBS flies me first class everywhere I go, and as I sit in my nice big comfy seat in the sharp end of the bird, I always feel pangs of guilt, as people who probably work much harder than I do shuffle past me into the back. Although I do get over it.

In fact, by the end of the season, I am usually in full-on, belligerent, pain-in-the-ass mode by the time I check in at the airport.

"Did you pack your bags yourself, sir?"

"Hell no! Smedley, my butler, always does that for me!"

"Have you left your bags unattended at any time?"

"Certainly not. I even took them with me into the crapper in the Admiral's Club."

"Has anyone unknown to you given you any packages?"

"No, I know everyone who gave me a package. I just don't know what's in the packages."

Of course, travel these days is a serious business, and there are good reasons for asking what might appear at first to be silly questions, which is more than I can claim after some of the interviews I've done this year. I am the Tiger Woods of stupid questions. But at the end of the season, as we approach the big white-bearded fat boy's time, it's a relief to be at home watching the poor sideline saps in other sports, and I often wonder if their lives on the road revolve around the same simple pleasure that sustains the CBS golf crew from one day to the next. Dinner, that is.

You see, after a long day of talking garbage about golfers and making up quotes because they didn't want to talk to you, invariably the thoughts of the average tired, pissed-off, old hack will stray toward supper, and I am no different. Being long-winded, pompous, and opinionated is tiring and thirsty work, I can assure you, so at the end of the day, a good restaurant with a good wine list and a hotel with a good bed are all-important to me.

Having said that, no matter how good the restaurant is, the last thing I need is a long-winded, pompous, and opinionated waiter. I know, it doesn't seem fair, but hey, that's show business for you.

Now I'm the kind of announcer who is very meticulous about his diet, and I believe that in a good day's eatin', all the major food groups should be represented. I like to start the day off with a bit of vigorous mastication in the fiber department, say, about half a box of All-Bran or a small wicker chair, and then I'll generally wash it down with about seventeen cups of coffee. So, now that I have my fiber and caffeine to get the day off and moving, all I have to worry about is whether or not I can ingest enough meat and wine (both red)—and, of course, Rolaids—before bedtime. This is not usually a problem, unless I run out of Rolaids.

Being a born-again Texan, I am naturally drawn to those Tour stops that are in the vicinity of great steak houses. I can hear you all now, muttering about how that shouldn't be too difficult in this country, but just hang on, there, pardners—I am a cowpoke of a different ilk.

After a hard day in Akron, ropin' bum steers like Kostis and Rymer on the Midwestern plain, I like to hop aboard McCord, grasp him firmly by the handlebars, and gallop sidesaddle down to the Diamond Grille to order me up a filet of cow with a mess of Willie's fries. I want that cow burned on the outside, pal, and let's have no pink on the inside, either. I want beef, the other gray meat.

You see, in a lot of supposedly good steak houses, the chef will look at an order like this, assume that the customer is a moron, and subsequently find a piece of ligament-riddled roadkill, which he will then cremate into a small asteroid and serve garnished with a sprig of charcoal.

In a really good steak house, like the Diamond Grille, while the chef might still assume the customer to be a moron (lucky guess, mind you), he will select a nice cut of meat from the center of the filet, and cook it exactly the way I like it. Then I will smother it in A-1 sauce and Tabasco, and eat it far too quickly. This, of course, would make the NEC Invitational at Firestone one of my favorite Tour stops.

But the clear winner for me is the Byron Nelson Classic in my hometown of Dallas, Texas, which is also home to the world's greatest steak house, III Forks. Whenever we can, She Who Must Be Obeyed and I mosey on down there for dinner. I, of course, will be wearing my aardvark Lucchese ropers, jeans four inches too long, a sixty-two-gallon Stetson hat, and a belt buckle the size of McCord's forehead. (Actually, a forehead that size is a fivehead.) With me looking like this, my wife, understandably, always asks for her own table, but I can cut that little cowgirl out of any herd. Yee-ha! (Sorry about that.)

Of course, a great restaurant is as much about people as it is about food, and Dale Wamstad, the proprietor of III Forks, is a giant in the cow-broiling business. He founded the legendary Del Frisco's before moving on to this latest and greatest venture, and, as always, he is omnipresent in his restaurant. There is nothing worse than a restaurant in which the first impression the staff gives you is that you are incredibly fortunate to have secured a table in the first place. At III Forks, this is your last impression. Dale has the ability to make everyone who visits feel special. For a while, I thought it was just me, but I've been there often enough now to notice otherwise. Also, he has been able to instill the same qualities into his staff, which I think is the real trick.

For example, his general manager, Rick Stein, is perfectly capable of holding a deep and meaningful wine conversation with the balding, mid-life-crisis businessfart at the next table who is trying to impress his date, a nineteen-year-old topless dancer.

Don't ask me how I know, I just do. They make a nice couple and are obviously in love. The man is droning on about the wine's "huge nose," and its "subtle nuances of tobacco, sawdust, and black cherry."

Rick nods, neglecting to mention that he has not yet opened the bottle, and the man has just gargled a mouthful of iced tea. He knows I am listening. He opens their wine and sidles over to take our order.

"Now, you have a huge nose," he says to me. Oh, ha ha ha...

Down here in Texas, you see, wine is treated with salsa-like reverence, as it should be. Anyone who knows anything about hot sauce is aware that the really good stuff makes your taste buds feel like they just burst into flower, and the only way to make your tongue feel any better is to have some more. Exactly like wine. If you do not humor your tongue, it is quite liable to make its way out of your mouth and into the bottle on its own. So I always say to Rick, "Bring me a bottle of that red one with the nice label," and he always does.

Black cherries, my arse.

I'm kind of old-fashioned, even a little squeamish about food, and the folks at III Forks know it. Don't even suggest Japanese; I am just not into squid chitlins, thank you. Once I've put food into my mouth, I don't want to have to take it out again for any reason. Trout is out, forget shellfish—especially if it has watched me enter the room—and if I get one stringy or fatty bit of meat, the meal is over. Even the menu can put me off my grub. To me, the description of food is like voice mail: If it lasts longer than about eight seconds, it gets deleted.

"Thinly sliced medallions of pork, in a raspberry port-wine reduction, served on a tower of crispy parsnip strips, nestled into a bed of wilted arugula, accompanied by tiny new potatoes and truffled pearl onions, with Chef Otto's own special pickled swine nuts in aspic."

Forgive me, but I'm liable to barf halfway through a description like that. And then of course...

"Would you like to hear our specials?"

"No, thank you, I would like you to go away and fry something, preferably your own left nostril."

Rick would never say anything like that, even if nostrils were on the menu, which they never would be.

All I want is a nice big steak, which, even though it's cooked all the way through, is tender and juicy, some kind of spuds, and plenty of elbow room. Once at III Forks, during a particularly excellent meal, I thought I'd bitten into a nasty piece of gristle. But as it turned out, it was the knuckle on my right index finger. Looking back, I don't blame myself for being overeager.

Like they say down here, "I wasn't born in Texas, but I got here as soon as I could." Merry Christmas/Happy Chanukah, pardners!

Chapter Two
Game Theories

Carrying On

I detest golf carts. I love to walk with the wind at my back and a faithful bag carrier plodding behind. Unless of course my faithful bag carrier hasn't showered for days, in which case I like the wind in my face. That way, I have more time to notice the sights, sounds, and smells of the countryside, rather than those of the faithful bag carrier.

The only wildlife you can see from a speeding cart is the roadkill that's been flattened by the one in front of you. It's true that carts won't show up late, give you the wrong yardage, talk too much, or demand a tip, but I'll still take caddies. I used to be one.

Growing up, I was the pro shop kid, always hanging around the workshop, learning how to replace the now-obsolete whipping around the neck of a wooden club. Or, I was changing grips, my hands sticky and smelly with double-sided tape and gasoline.

Come to think of it, I probably unwittingly lost billions of brain cells due to solvent abuse. No wonder I couldn't do my homework.

For the tidy sum of about a buck a round, I would pack the sack for the members. Sometimes, the club pro would take me to one of the local pro-ams to caddie for him.

During school holidays, I even got to go on road trips, thus gaining limited membership to the magical underworld of the Irish professional caddie. I say limited membership, because to them I was a snot-nosed little whelp who was doing one of them out of a living. I would have to wait some three or four years until I turned pro myself before I got any respect from this bunch.

There was one old bag-rat who used to terrify me. An obvious hedge-dweller, with one eye looking at me and the other looking for me, he was fond of a pint of cleaning products if nothing else was available. He looked like he'd had a fire on his face that someone had put out with a spiked golf shoe.

I later learned this was pretty close to the truth. He had burped while lighting a cigarette, igniting his beard like a bonfire. Apparently a Drano burp is highly flammable.

"Keep those bloody clubs quiet," he would growl at me as I clanked along, the bag bouncing on my hip with every footfall. He, on the other hand, shuffled along in slippery leather-soled shoes, the bag hanging silently from his bony shoulder like a baby in a hammock. Not one club touched another.

Good players and good caddies have a lot in common. A caddie needs a good grip (in reality because his player often doesn't have one). And, he needs a good stance (as in knowing where to take it).

This is why a great player never asks a "friend" to carry the bag during an important week. Give the average Joe the bag and even if he is a scratch handicap, compared to a good Tour caddie he'll look like Edward Scissorhands at his first bagpipe lesson.

To name but four: Steve Williams (Tiger Woods), Jim McKay (Phil Mickelson), Tony Navarro (Greg Norman), and Greg Rita (Scott Hoch) are captains of their industry. They have an intimate knowledge of the game and, more importantly, they have an intimate knowledge of their players.

It's an art to be able to tell whether your boss wants your opinion or confirmation that his own is correct. You have to be half caddie and half therapist. These men and others are going a long way toward dignifying a longtime maligned profession. I say maligned, largely due to the kind of lunatics who used to work for me.

I always hired caddies for their amusement value rather than their golf expertise and boy, did I have a few beauties. Every Tour caddie has a nickname and one of my early loopers on the European Tour was "Yorkie Bill." His best pal was "Jungle Jim," a Neanderthal with one tooth and a facial twitch that intermittently made his upper lip almost make contact with his right eyebrow.

These two derelicts traveled around Britain by rail, buying but one ticket between them. They would sit down close to the nearest toilet and wait for the first woman to go in. Then Yorkie would rap loudly on the door and shout, "Tickets, please."

"But I'm on the toilet," would come the mournful reply.

"Just shove it under the door," Yorkie would bellow.

It never failed. They would be sitting in the next compartment like cherubs while the unfortunate woman was emptied off at the next stop. I once asked him why he always picked a woman.

"Because the last thing I need is someone who stands to go to the toilet," he said. "They might open the door."

The man was a genius. Once, after losing sight of my wayward tee shot into a driving rain, I asked him as he sheltered behind my umbrella, "Where did that go?"

"Where did what go?" he replied.

When Bernhard Langer burst onto the European scene in the late 1970s, he had working for him a Scot by the name of Davey

"Captain" Kirk. The Cap'n had an unintelligible Glasgow accent, which made him a perfect match for Langer. They both spoke little English.

Then, there was "Rhino," so called because he was thick-skinned and charged a lot. One of my personal favorites was "Tiny," who was only four-foot-ten and weighed about eighty pounds.

Tiny didn't care who he worked for; he treated everyone with equal disdain. Routine questions like, "Can I get home from here, Tiny?" were answered with, "I don't know; where do you live?"

"Can I carry that bunker?" a player would ask.

"Not a chance, there's a ton of sand in it," Tiny would reply. He had more chance of reading a Chinese newspaper correctly than a six-footer, but he was worth a shot a round in entertainment.

In a strange way, I rely on caddies now more than I ever did. As a television foot soldier, my direct link to the player is the caddie. He provides me with much of the information I need to relay to the viewer—the yardage his player has left to the flag and the club he is about to hit. I could not do my job properly without them.

Alas, Yorkie, Cap'n Kirk, and Jungle Jim are dead and gone, but I often think of them as I receive a sly wink or stealthy hand signal from their modern-day counterparts. I grew up fascinated by caddies and I love their company still.

Caddie Firings and Stupid Rules

The Masters is over, and we're all back to normal at CBS, whatever that means. All I know is that a "normal" broadcast includes McCord, which of course makes it an oxymoron, but the truth is our show is just not the same without him. Don't tell him I said this.

The first thing that I noticed about Harbour Town was that there were gnot gnearly as many gnats gnawing at us as there gnormally are there. Glen Day's win in the MCI Classic was obviously brilliant and long overdue, but as usual I am going to ignore the headlines and take you swimming in the undertow, or rummaging through the Tour's dirty laundry if you like.

It's been a bad couple of weeks for the sack-draggers out there. Jerry Higginbotham and Mark O'Meara parted company on the same Augusta National green that they embraced upon the year before, and Lorne Duncan, also a veteran bagman who has worked in the past for such luminaries as Craig Stadler and, ahem, me, was fired by Jesper Parnevik in what appeared to be very peculiar circumstances. I didn't like the way it was reported.

A spectator reported to a Rules official that he had seen Jesper brush the line of his putt with his glove. After the round, when Parnevik was asked if this was true he could not recall the incident. Duncan, however, did remember his absentminded boss's slip-up, and Parnevik was subsequently disqualified. Duncan was immediately fired. Now, to the casual observer, this would appear like an act of mean-spirited retribution on Parnevik's part, but this was not the case.

I found out, upon digging further, that Duncan knew he was on the way out with Jesper anyway. He knew that this was to be his last week working for Jesper because there had been little conversation between the two for a couple weeks, and for a caddie, this is usually an indication that your days on the bag are numbered. Sometimes a relationship just becomes stale. Duncan is an excellent caddie who worked for an excellent player, and both of them will do just fine in the company of others. Both Duncan and Parnevik have well-deserved reputations of integrity. These are the facts.

The real problem of course, and I love to harp on about this, lies in the stupidity of the Rules of Golf. How about this one. You can brush your line with your gloved hand, but not with your glove. Apparently your hand has to be in the glove. But how much of your hand has to be in there? If only your middle finger is inserted, and you sweep away a leaf, would that be a penalty for rudeness? Presumably, you can stand on your hands and use your hair as a broom, but whatever you do don't pull a bunch of it out. You could use your hat also, just as long as your head was still in it.

A mentally disturbed gerbil could see that the book of Decisions on the Rules is becoming a joke. At six hundred pages and growing, soon we'll all need Johnny Cochran present just to make sure we don't screw up whilst putting the ball on a tee. While I'm on a rant, did anyone see McCord's Rules feature on the Sunday telecast? The Decisions book provides for relief from so-called "hazardous situations," such as an alligator in the vicinity of the ball, or a beehive, or rattlesnake or fire ants. This is garbage. I mean where's the fun in that? Personally, I'd like to see a player run screaming out of the woods punching himself in the head, and tearing his hair out, or hopping up the last hole with a one-shot lead, after losing a leg to a giant reptile. It would give me something other than the wind and the yardage to drone on about.

My Uncle Dickie was right. [To learn more about Uncle Dickie, read chapter eight, chapter nine, and Feherty's novel *A Nasty Bit of Rough*.] Play the ball as it lies, and the course as you find it. Throw in, "Without undue delay," and we're covered. Hit it and stop whining.

Hypocritical Headache
September 2002 b.m. (Before Martha)

This month, I'm going to do something really, really stupid. [Editor's note: We didn't gasp in disbelief, either.] (Writer's retort: You're all assholes.)

I'm going to write about some of the differences between men's and women's sports, or at least what I think those differences are. Furthermore, I'm going to tell you why they are different. I'd like to/have to start off by saying that the editors, publishers, and owners of *Golf Magazine* (most of whom are idiots) do not always share the views represented in this column. Hey, to each his or her own. But they're still idiots.

I'm going to blow off one toe at a time here, so let's start off on a sport with which I am fairly familiar: golf. Generally speaking, women are not as good at golf as men, but, for the record, making a golf swing is harder to do if you happen to be the owner of a pair of breasts. (I'm anticipating the heckling to start right about here, so here's my reply to the first burst of outrage.)

On the contrary, ma'am, I do know what I'm talking about, because over the course of my twenty-year playing career, my weight yo-yoed between 155 and 220 pounds, and at the tubby end, I had quite an impressive cleavage. All I can tell you is that my pair definitely got in the way of my backswing. And yes, they were real, not that it's any of your business. If I'd had them enhanced, I might never have left my hotel room.

Also, it would seem to me, that most of the world's top female golfers are closer to "A" than "D" when it comes to the other cup size. It might be a coincidence, but I suspect not. They don't help.

Of course, it's very unfair and downright idiotic to compare the women of the LPGA to the men of the PGA Tour in the first place. One of the great misconceptions in golf is the notion that a woman's short game should be as good as that of her male counterparts. Physical strength off the tee and out of the fairway is an obvious advantage for the men. But out of rough and heavy sand around the green, men have an even bigger edge.

In order to play a lot of the high flops and spinning sand shots we see these days, a player has to be able to rip the clubhead through heavy sand or long grass, without allowing it to turn over. Most women simply don't have the strength to do it. They play a different game, that's all.

At this point I should probably share with you that I have been suffering from a chronic and seemingly incurable form of male chauvinistic swinery, which manifests itself most clearly in my sports television viewing preference. In short, the only female athletes in whom I have any interest are the scantily clad, good-looking ones. But at the risk of appearing in the crosshairs of a weapon wielded by Gloria Steinem or one of her followers, I would respectfully suggest that this doesn't make me a bad person.

Every living creature on the planet is driven by two basic, primal urges—the need to eat and the need to mate. If we lose one of them, we're extinct. While such a result would undoubtedly be the best possible outcome for every other creature on the planet, they're going to have to wait a while yet, because we, the morons at the top of the food chain, aren't done eating and mating yet.

Actually, when I pause to think about it, mating was probably the first contact sport. I mean there's no question about the competitive nature of it, is there? Oh dear, now I'm thinking about it. I'm flying over Yellowstone as I write, so let's take the elk as an example.

The males who eat the most become the biggest and have a decided advantage in the rut, when they butt heads with the others. The rut is the tournament in which the first prize is the best females, who show no interest whatsoever until a clear winner emerges, at which point they become even less interested. This seems familiar.

So far, the only obvious difference I can see between elkind and mankind is that once the elk are finally ready to mate, it's the male who has the headache.

In fairness to my sports-watching brethren, I think that underneath it all, most female sports fans are kind of the same as we are. When it comes to men's sports they are interested primarily in the ones where the guys are kind of hunky and wear skin-tight uniforms. When Jason Sehorn leaps into the air and pulls down that pesky inflatable bladder, I think, "Wow, what a catch!"

Meanwhile, the ladies are thinking not only, "Wow, what a catch!" but "What a set of buns!" as well. My friend Donna Caponi, who is an LPGA Hall of Famer, has confirmed this for me. Donna is a keen sports fan and a self-confessed bun-lover.

Women like boxing (almost naked guys), track and field (muscles, spandex, and the ubiquitous slow motion bouncing package—don't tell me you don't love it, you lying vixens), and any other sport in which guys pose, check, strut, or thrust. Good for the ladies, I say!

As for me, and every other red-blooded male I know, we like women's figure skating, beach volleyball, track and field, and gymnastics, although the balance beam totally weirds me out. I can't watch those girls cartwheel into the straddle without having a full body spasm and an involuntary attack of yodeling.

Oh, oh, oh, and I love women's tennis! Yes, Anna Kournikova may never have won a damn thing, but I'd like to go on the record as saying I don't care, and I'd rather watch her losing in slow motion than any man winning at regular speed.

Women's soccer is completely unwatchable (but, then, so is men's soccer), as is the WNBA (and the NBA), and for me, women in auto racing are rather like women in the priesthood, in that gender doesn't matter at all because I'm not paying any attention.

I have to admit though, I was a whole lot more comfortable with my cynical male attitude to women's sport when I was just the father of four boys. Then came a bombshell in the shape of my daughter, Erin, otherwise known as "The Small Person Who Must Be Obeyed."

Erin was four in June and will start school in the fall. I don't know what it's like in other cities, but here in Dallas, a lot of private schools have a bad attitude. Or maybe it's me, but I figure that a school that accepts only the brightest of children has no right to brag about its academic results. You see, even though I wasn't an honor student, (in fact, I didn't graduate) I think I can figure out if the kids were smart when they went in, then they should still be smart when they come out.

Show me a school that takes the slower kids and turns them around, and I'll be impressed. Recently, I did the parent interview thing at one of these private institutions, so that they could determine if my daughter was "the right fit." Right fit, my arse, pal.

It was a disaster, and She Who Must Be Obeyed has now barred me from any future altercations with prospective future school principals. I went with the attitude of, "Is your school good enough for my child?" rather than the other way around, and apparently it wasn't the way to go. The funny thing was, I found myself laying down all these criteria that I felt a school should have to meet if it was going to be lucky enough to get my girl, one of which was no cheerleading.

I want my baby on the field competing, not on the sidelines jumping up and down and cheering for a bunch of sweaty, zit-ridden boys. I want her to have as good a chance to be an athlete as the boys, and then I'll be the one on the sidelines, thank you. Then, I remembered, I'm only interested in the sports where the women are scantily clad and beautiful.

Like cheerleading. Damn!

But she's my daughter, and…well, you know….

Oh, God, I think I'm getting a hypocritical headache. Stick a fork in me, because just the other day in our upstairs play room, Erin grabbed a plastic golf club left hand below right (as most kids will), and made a perfect golf swing. I about dunged myself.

None of my kids has shown the slightest interest in any sport, never mind golf. "Where did you learn that?" I asked her. She looked at me like I was an idiot and said, "On the television, Daddy."

So maybe that's where all those women's sports fans come from! Because this daddy will tell you this: If his girl turns out to be a golfer, he'll watch every swing she makes. I'll be the grumpy old fart in the crowd, poking young people out of the way with a furled brolly so I can get a better view. "Get out of my ass you wayholes, that's my baby!"

Don't get me wrong, I love my boys, but my baby girl rules my world, and it makes me wonder why the women aren't playing for more money on the LPGA Tour. I'm in television, so I know all about some of the reasons, like ratings, advertising revenue, image problems, etc. But don't the CEO's of Fortune 500 companies have daughters too?

And don't they look at them the way I look at mine? I was on a plane the other day, not really listening to the captain's welcome on the PA, when the moron next to me removed his snout from the *Wall Street Journal* and said moodily, "Oh, great, the pilot's a chick."

I told him I always felt a little safer when a woman was at the controls, because in order to get the job, she probably had to be a damn sight better than the men. It's tough for women to get through that glass ceiling, and if they do, they have to work with men looking up their skirts. Needless to say, the guy beside me didn't have a daughter.

I was tucking Erin into bed the other night, and as usual she was playing me like a three-dollar violin. "One more kiss, Daddy," then, as I was heading out the door, "One more love, Daddy." I went back to the bed and lay down facing her with my head on her pillow, and pulled a long, brown ringlet of hair out of her eyes. It was dim, but I could see the ear-splitting grin on the naughty face as she reached with a damp, chubby, little hand and grasped my ear.

"Your ears are freezin,' Daddy," she said, as I gently scratched her back.

I asked her, "Are you gonna be a golfer when you grow up, baby?"

"Girls can do anything, Daddy," she said, curling up in a giggling ball, waiting for the tickle. "Girls are tricky."

"Oh, yeah, girls can," I tell her, "especially the tricky ones like you," and she explodes into a writhing, squealing, little piglet when the tickling begins. We both end up in tears, hers of laughter, and mine of unsurpassable joy and indescribable love, mixed with an aching sadness, for I know she is only on loan to me, and I wish this moment would never end.

When she's old enough, I'll tell her about a bumper sticker I saw once before she was born. At the time it meant nothing to me, but because of her, I get it now. It read: "Ginger Rogers did everything Fred Astaire did, backwards, in five-inch heels."

Annika Sorenstam reminds me of Ginger Rogers, because if she were a man, she might be famous.

That Was Ugly

I set out this week to write about the Presidents Cup, but first, there's something else I'd like to float out into the crisp, clean air of Cyberville. Sorry, but it's fairly smelly. In fact, now that it's more than a week old, it's positively ripe.

I was watching the afternoon football game, Sunday before last, when my phone rang. I hate it when my phone rings. This was interesting news, however, about something weird going on at the Solheim Cup. I flicked over and caught the tail end of an interview with European team captain Dale Reid, none of which I understood, except for the fact that the Europeans had won. Jolly good, I thought …well done…whatever…back to the game. No offense, ladies, it's just at this time of year, I've had enough of golf. Yesterday, somebody told me that Duval won a couple of weeks ago. I guess he's feeling better…whatever…back to the game.

The following day, I read what had happened. Annika Sorenstam had played out of turn, chipped in, and then Pat Bradley, the American captain, intervened with a protest which was eventually successful, forcing Annika to play the shot again...and I can't even be bothered to finish this sentence. It looks just as stupid and pointless on the page as it must have done on the golf course. What bothered me was my telephone, scumbags, all wanting an opinion.

I didn't see it happen. I only heard about it. I didn't have anything to do with it, honestly. It wasn't me, and I don't want to talk about it. I wasn't even there when I didn't do it, and I don't have an opinion on it either. Go away.

Then, darn it, I saw the tape. It made me wonder if stupidity might be a virus. You know, like herpes? It gets you when your defenses are strained to the utmost, like in a Ryder Cup or Solheim Cup.

This latest outbreak marred what should have been a celebration of sportsmanship, or sportswomanship, or whatever the hell we're supposed to call it, in these days of political correctness. (That reminds me—boy, do I miss Dave Marr.) I know, I know, it's not politically correct to call anyone stupid these days either. How about this then: I think that many of those involved in the outbreak exhibited what could best be described as "a low threshold of understanding."

Nah, I know what you're thinking. "Stupid" still sounds better, doesn't it? For some reason, international team golf events seem to bring out the worst in some people. And the best of course, let's not forget that. However, let's concentrate on those who seem to lose seventy-five points off their IQ the minute they pull on the official team shirt. Generally speaking, they are much more entertaining.

For as long as I can remember, in the game of golf, if it was in any way hard to decide who was away, if one player was off the putting surface, they would go first. It's just common courtesy, and it evolved from the fact that the player off the green usually left the flagstick in the hole. Also, it has always been part of the etiquette of the game that if a player sees a rule about to be broken, he or she would give their opponent the benefit of this opinion, before the next shot was played. Like, "Hang on there, Annika, I think I'm away." You either say something like that, or you say, "Hey, good shot, Annika!" One or the other. Anything else is going to look petty, mean-spirited, pointless, witless, or at best, really, really weird. On the other hand, this altercation was strangely entertaining, even though I can't figure out why. Probably for the same reason that those videos of horrific car accidents are so popular.

Maybe I'm alone, but to me, these things look even worse when the protagonists are female. That's probably hideously sexist, but forgive me, I really believe that women are smarter than men. I just can't imagine my mom making that kind of move. My daughter, maybe, but she's only two years old. I mean, when a bunch of men get into a pointless sports argument, I usually just shake my head and think, "Well...whaddaya expect?" Unless, of course, I'm involved in the fracas, in which case (owing to the fact that I'm always correct), I usually display a kind of incredulous indignation toward the sort of moron who would disagree with the likes of me. Like most males, I'm like this about all sports at which I consider myself an expert, including driving a car. And like most males, I thought this was one of our last bastions of superiority over women. They play all the sports like us now, but I thought we still ruled when it came to the asinine unsporting behavior department. And now they're kicking our butt in that one, too.

So what if the dugouts empty, and a mass brawl erupts at home plate. Hey, it's just a bunch of guys on creosote, or diabolic 'roids, or whatever they call that stuff. Who cares? I don't like it, but it doesn't make me feel any weirder than usual. The outbreak at Brookline was a knee-jerk reaction, which ultimately didn't bother me either, but in the latest Solheim affair, the female culprits appeared to have time to consider a plan of action. "Let me see, should we do nothing, and run the risk of looking classy, or behave like a headless chicken and give everyone a laugh?" My god, it was like a point you'd see brought up in a really bitter divorce.

Which is entertaining. Granted, it's weird entertainment, but then so is *The Simpsons*. Now, bring on the Presidents Cup. I was beginning to think the Ryder Cup was the only one worth watching. Not that Kenny would make a mistake like this one, but he might start a fight. Kenny and Peter Thompson in the pressroom. Grumpy old pros. One thing is for sure, though; there would be no low blows with those two guys. They both know what it means to have the honor.

Members of the Club

One of the things I like most about American golf is the atmosphere in the clubhouse and the feeling that the management has hired the right people for the right jobs. Most clubs here have a casual feel, with no sense of a class system within the membership.

Golf clubs in Britain and Ireland can be considerably stuffier. Many have separate men's and women's lounges and the hallways and fairways are patrolled by the dreaded committee members.

Golfers can be reported for such crimes as not replacing divots, using more than one towel in the shower, or—heavens to Betsy, surely not!—even taking a hand towel onto the golf course. (This hideous act is one of the most serious breaches.)

As soon as an ordinary member is invited to be a committee person, he becomes bloated and drunk with power. Mild-mannered people can turn into opinionated, pontificating windbags in an instant. (Come to think of it, that describes me perfectly. Except I'm correct.)

I believe I have to go back to the origins of the game to determine the exact cause of this dreaded metamorphosis, and you're coming with me whether you like it or not.

Now, not a lot of people know this, but the game of golf was invented by the Irish. In fact, there are a lot of things for which we are responsible that might surprise you.

Take the kilt and the bagpipes, for examples—and keep them. You're quite welcome.

Both are Irish inventions and were originally to be used as weapons. Anyone who has seen *Braveheart* will be aware how the kilt was used in warfare. Anyone who has been awakened at dawn by the skirl of pipes will know they are certainly instruments, but of torture, not music. But, I digress....

A long time ago, when there were only two kinds of people—the filthy rich and the filthy poor—the cleverest man in Ireland, heavily disguised as a daft old shepherd, sat on a grassy mound on the useless piece of land that lay between his lordship's farm and the sea.

His faithful old Irish sheepdog (a breed now more commonly known as sheep) lay contented in the crook of his arm. All of a sudden, a seagull overhead suffered a massive coronary and crash-landed onto a rabbit, killing it instantly. (This is true, honestly.)

For a while, the old man pondered what all this might mean and eventually figured it must be lunchtime, so he ate the seagull. Then, it struck him.

He thought to himself, "If I took a piece of that rabbit skin, stuffed it with those seagull feathers, and sewed it up, I bet I could hit it a fair lick with this crook of mine."

He did, he could, and the game of golf was invented. The first technological breakthrough came some months later when he worked out that the ball would go even farther if it was sewn up with the fur on the inside.

The clever Irishman was obsessed and, although his sheepdog left him, he continued to practice and was soon drawing a large crowd at the eighteenth green, which was, strangely enough, located right outside the village pub.

Of course, in those days, anything that was any fun was usually made illegal, unless you happened to be one of the filthy rich, in which case you could do whatever the hell you liked.

As it happened, the well-to-do townsfolk did like the game and forbade the peasants from playing. The well-to-do did, of course, need the peasants to carry their bags, and so the talented poor began caddieing for the talentless rich, a tradition that lives to this day.

The golf club was invented and those who were members wore wigs and silly red jackets and felt thoroughly superior to those who were not in the club. Eventually, staff people were hired to carry out the wishes of the members who formed their own inner groups to make sure the other members kept up the standards that set their honorable company apart.

I believe somehow this evolved into the semi-farcical situation in which a lot of British and Irish golf clubs now find themselves. A captain of the club, elected annually, is surrounded by his council. Then, we have the various cliques, my favorite of which is the greens committee, whose job it is to oversee the maintenance of the course.

For some unknown reason, the greens superintendent, who—you could be forgiven for thinking—might actually know something about the subject, has to answer to the chairman of this committee, who might be an expert in proctology. Now, there's a scary thought.

I was once fond of playing at a club where this relationship was particularly bitter. (As always, the names have been changed to protect the guilty.) Flanagan was a good superintendent with a sound knowledge of his turf and how the game should be played.

Mr. Bulstrode, on the other hand, was a pompous old goat with a 23 handicap who, if given a flashlight and the use of both hands, would have great difficulty finding his own backside.

He had one of those hideous little drop-kick dogs—you know the type—like a Maltese poodle crossed with an albino cockroach. It was snow white in the middle, but stained at both ends. It had the sort of yappy little face that you'd never get tired of kicking. The vile little rodent would regularly leave Flanagan a present in the middle of the fairway.

Because Mr. Bulstrode played golf in seventy-five-yard sideways increments, he believed a golf course should be devoid of all rough, but felt the occasional flower bed with a rockery and a scowling garden gnome was nice.

More than once, Flanagan had threatened to insert one such

gnome into Mr. Bulstrode after the malignant old duffer had instructed him to perform some ridiculous task that went against his grain.

Fortunately, Mr. Bulstrode had a change of heart—which didn't like him, either—and he croaked. It transpired that he wanted his ashes scattered over his beloved golf course. In a curious twist of fate, the task befell his old adversary—Flanagan the greenkeeper.

Mr. Bulstrode arrived at the maintenance shed in a generic container (he was also cheap) where Flanagan, with tears of heartfelt mirth, fondly mixed him with weedkiller and took Mr. Bulstrode out to his favorite rockery/flower bed where, in an even layer, he laid him to rest.

The following morning everything in the area was in a similar condition to Mr. Bulstrode except for the garden gnome, which had been mysterious replaced by one sporting a broad grin. I love happy endings, don't you?

There was a point to this story when I started. I think what I am trying to say is the next time you stride into the club lounge leaving a trail of wet grass and mud from your nicely manicured golf course, be thankful that the management has had the good sense to employ professionals. Let them get on with providing a service for the members.

Most importantly, the barman will fill your glass with ice, sometimes even all the way to the top. I like it here in America. I think I'll stay.

Try This Silly Season Event

Well, the Skins game is over and thank heaven for that.

I have to admit I'm not sure about the new format, but then again, I didn't even like the old one. Or maybe it's just the participants, I don't know, but it's all downhill from here. I remember writing about this a couple of years ago, but I'm working on the principle that most of you don't remember what I wrote a couple of weeks ago, and therefore I'm going with it again. A more interesting Skins game would be between four suckers that really needed the money. Norman needed another million like I needed another three-year contract with *Golf Magazine*, but we both got what we didn't need.

What none of us needs is more Silly Season golf. There should be a federal law against televising golf in the off-season, like shooting quail in August. Last week was the Father/Son Challenge, for God's sake. In my house, that means my nine-year-old's math homework, not members of the Lucky Sperm Club hacking it around with their incontinent parents. For a start, where are all the daughters? I mean, if we're going to have to suffer this kind of stale off-season queso, it should at least have a little entertainment value. The regular season is like reality TV, so the off-season should be at least as silly as your average daytime soap. Or wrestling.

How about the Vicious Ex-Wife vs. Current Topless Dancer Girlfriend Challenge? A few of those women who spent most of their lives dutifully trudging after their husbands—sitting in crappy motels, trying to get four-footer-induced skid marks out of threadbare boxers, or doing homework, wiping runny noses and arguing about bedtime, now find themselves replaced by newer, more pneumatic models since Dad finally made it to the Grateful Nearly Dead Tour and is making real cash. Ooh, you know there is some righteous indignation out there, and that makes for good TV.

Of course, not every male professional golfer's ex-wife has been callously tossed aside in favor of fresher meat, and there are two sides to every story. But the other side is likely to be boring and involve some tanned and buff twenty-something closet florist with a rose clenched between his teeth, in hiking boots and a one-piece spandex jumpsuit unzipped to the scrotum. Anyone who is interested in that side of the story is reading the wrong magazine.

First, the ex-husband would have to caddie for the new model. The ex-wife could use her attorney, and, wait a minute, maybe she could use zipper-boy's. Anyway, there should be a very public weigh-in, so we can generate the maximum amount of animosity. (I don't know how we're going to keep that human toilet-brush Don King out of this picture.)

Of course, everyone should be armed. Nine-millimeter, rocket launcher, whatever. Maybe we could have the ex-wife of one of the players who had a really successful regular tour career in here. You know, some bitter witch with millions who's had nothing better to do for years but eat Twinkies and watch CNN. Someone who, if they lose a couple of holes early, can afford to call in air support.

Wait, this is too good for the network. It should be pay-per-view and there should be a mediator behind every green, dressed in a big purple Barney suit so that every participant would have somebody to kick the crap out of on the way to the next tee. Hey, these people need some kind of therapy.

It has everything. From the classic cliché of the pro showing the leggy blonde how to hold the club to the ex-wife committing a brutal double homicide with a sand wedge, only to find out that her new love has fallen for the guy with the hairless Chihuahua who did the window treatments in the ladies' locker room. It could be the lead-in to one of those like-life-isn't-crappy-enough-for-most-people-already courtroom dramas.

Alternatively, you could have been watching the Father/Son Challenge.

Going Mad

I know I've said this somewhere before, but that "everything in moderation" deal says to me that you should be moderate in moderation. Otherwise, it would say, "almost everything in moderation."

In other words, everyone should be allowed to go berserk every now and then, especially on the golf course. It's been ages since I've seen a really good temper tantrum. You know—the kind where one of your playing partners goes double postal after a string of rotten shots.

I'm not talking about simple club abuse or course molestation, either. I mean a full-on, Rottweiler-on-angel-dust, foaming-at-the-mouth, running-full-tilt-into-an-oak-tree, profanity-riddled seizure. For a start, it's great entertainment for everyone else. I have been guilty of such outbursts myself; granted, not for a while, but only because these days I just don't care where the ball goes.

At least these kinds of psychotechnics show that the offender has some interest, some passion. For me, the hardest part about witnessing such an event was always the struggle to keep a straight face. While the creator of such a self-inflicted mental misdemeanor is invariably left feeling stupid and humiliated, for some reason, those who stand by and watch are curiously cheered up by the whole grubby affair.

The spectacle of a fully grown man (I have never seen the female version of this phenomenon—at least, not on the golf course) setting about an inanimate object, such as a golf bag, invariably reduced me to tears of laughter in a "there but for the grace of God go I" sort of way. While most people wouldn't condone such behavior, I think it's safe to say that those of us who play can at least understand the reason for it.

Golf has always had its fair share of hotheads. Tommy Bolt, for instance, whose clubs were on a frequent flier program, was always one that the crowds loved to watch; and, my pal Steve Pate, even though he has mellowed with age, is still liable to erupt every now and then, usually at the U.S. Open. Speaking of which, when John Daly whacked his moving ball back up the slope last year at Pinehurst, he was simply doing exactly what every other player in the field would like to have done at some stage that week.

I think my favorite mind-loser, though, would have to be Zimbabwean Simon Hobday, who has brightened up the Senior PGA Tour for the last few years. Always a crowd favorite, Hobbers was prone to taking off his clothes and swimming across snake-infested water hazards and doing his laundry in the bathtub, stirring anti-clockwise with his laminated wooden driver. Golf needs more people like him.

Even as a young man, Simon looked like he was holding an electric eel by the tail when he was putting, but as a ball-striker he was without an equal at the opposite end of the scale. Add these two properties together, and you have a recipe for severe, upper-level mental disturbances on the golf course. Fortunately, Simon's sense of humor is also legendary. Once, he turned up on the first tee wearing a giant sombrero. He horseshoed out from four feet on the first green, turned his face heavenward and screamed, "So you still recognized me, huh?"

Another real beauty is Tony Johnstone, also a Zimbabwean. (There must be something in their water.) A regular on the European Tour, Tony was the original red-haired, flaming nut case when things went awry, and like most golfers who wear their brains on their sleeves, was completely sweet-natured off the course.

On one occasion in the mid-'80s, he was drawn with the genial Englishman Carl Mason and me at the Lancôme Trophy in Paris, which is—some of you may not know—just outside France. On the fourth hole, he took severe exception to a small spruce tree, which he felt had deliberately diverted the course of his downswing, causing him to miss that which he had been aiming at—i.e., the ball.

Carl and I looked on somewhat bemused as Tony started with a tirade of abuse, directed at the tree, which he immediately accused of being French, among other things. Actually, it was Japanese, but at the time I felt it wise not to point this out.

Selecting another club, our rabid partner quickly chipped out sideways and then set about reducing the unfortunate plant to matchwood, and he was well in front in the bout until suddenly the tree caught him with a recoiling branch right across the side of the head. He staggered back, holding his head in his hands.

This was enough to send Carl and me running for the bushes to find a safe place from which to watch—and soil ourselves. Then, Tony took his sweater off, and we thought this signified the end of the contest, but no. With renewed fervor, he started flailing again, only stopping when he realized he lacked the strength to dig out the stump.

Breathing heavily, he marched across the fairway, quickly slashed his ball onto the green, and walked past our hiding place, saying, "It's all right, boys. You can come out now!" By this time, Carl had lost half his body fluid through his tear ducts, and I had pulled a muscle in my stomach.

Personally, I think it's kind of sad that this kind of behavior is dying out in the professional game. There is a kind of sterility to the atmosphere when everyone behaves perfectly, an unreal calm if you like, and I think that one of the unique aspects of the game of golf is that the best player in the world sometimes feels just as frustrated as the average hacker. I suspect that it's a source of comfort to a lot of people to see evidence of this.

As for my own greatest moment of madness, after a particularly ill-timed bogey in Belgium, I once sank my putter into the bottom pocket of my bag, breaking three shafts under the grip in the process. On the next tee, my caddie delved deep for a new ball, only to find I had also made solid contact with my Rolex, and a tube of Preparation H, which had spurted out all over every new ball I had left.

On the upside, the watch—which had never kept time—was dead-on twice a day, and after about ten minutes, I found the golf ball considerably less irritating and somewhat smaller, which of course meant I hit it farther.

Instead of anger management counseling, I think judges would be well advised to sentence people to eighteen holes a week instead, with a "Destroy One Tree, Plant Ten" clause included.

Hey, the venting is therapeutic and the gardening is relaxing. What do you think?

The Kingdom of Fandom

I have just celebrated my first anniversary with *Golf Magazine*, and I'm delighted to tell you that editor-in-chief George Peper, in his infinite wisdom (or another act of lunacy), has decided to give me another chance.

I've written for a couple of other publications in the past, but I've never enjoyed the artistic license or leeway that I've been allowed here. So, I'd like to thank all of you who have been kind enough to write with your comments. Well, nearly all of you.

Speaking of you, I'm going to now turn my attention in your direction and examine the many different varieties of spectator/fan that line the fairways on tours around the world.

In my travels, I've noticed there is no such thing as "the average fan." Each one is different and these variations become more obvious as we travel from country to country. For example, the European spectator has about one hundred different subspecies. The American variety has about half that many, which are at times a little more outrageous, if not more original.

Take Greensboro, North Carolina, for instance. In the 1994 Greater Greensboro Open, I had occasion to ask a fan, who was obviously slightly on the Anheuser side of Busch, to be quiet. He turned around, dropped his drawers, and mooned me.

Seldom one to be stuck for words, I replied, "Fair enough. At least that end of you is quiet." Sadly, it wasn't for long and there is no answer to that.

One of the most interesting breeds of European spectators is the Swede. The Swedish golf fan is one of the hardiest in the world. Sweden gave us the spiked Wellington boot (even though we didn't want it), so a little wind and rain is unlikely to scare them off the golf course.

Swedes wear their ball caps so tight that even when the wind blows hard enough to invert the bill, it never blows off their heads. This, of course, cuts off circulation to the brain, so incredibly tight trousers must be worn to equalize the pressure (see Jesper Parnevik). Otherwise they'd faint at the top of the backswing. And you thought it was merely a fashion statement.

A little farther south we find the Germans, who are some of the most disciplined fans in the world. They always obey the rules whether it be on the golf course or on the highway. If you hit a good shot at the German Open, they are wildly enthusiastic, and if you hit a bad one, they almost seem puzzled by your lack of efficiency.

However, do not be fooled by that seemingly rigid exterior. Beneath that shell sometimes beats the heart of a true maniac. Once, at the BMW International in Munich, I was driven from the hotel to the golf course by a very pretty young German woman in a very fast BMW. She asked me if I was a nervous passenger, to which I, of course, replied in the extremely macho negatory mode.

Sixty-three miles and twenty-four minutes later I stepped out at the golf course. You do the math. At one point, we were nudging the underside of 280 kilometers per hour. (I'll do the math for you this time—180 mph.)

Needless to say, I chatted casually on the way, too cool for words, but I can assure you if someone had slipped a lump of coal between my buttocks before we left, it would have been a diamond by the time we arrived.

We Irish are almost the exact opposite of the French in that we dress badly, can't cook, can't stand each other, and love everyone else. (I hope I'm offending every nation equally here.) So, it was always interesting for me to play the Lancôme Trophy, just outside Paris.

It felt like a huge fashion show, with a golf tournament as a sideshow. The crowd came out to view each other, but even this was less weird than the Madrid Open, which I was lucky enough to win in 1992, in front of a crowd of, ahem, members only, please.

I wouldn't have minded but the Real Club de Puerto de Hierro has more bunkers than members.

Playing in Australia is always an experience and particularly when one is paired with Greg Norman. Once in Melbourne, he was jeered and booed by a small group of placard-waving, egg-throwing, anti-apartheid demonstrators, who objected to his visits to South Africa. (Presumably they were content with the plight of the Aborigines in their own country.)

A group of the gallery, bless their cotton socks, took the time and trouble to climb the fence, chase the idiots down the street, and beat the crap out of them. The moral presumably is that sport, beer, and politics don't mix in Australia.

But enough of this nonresident nation-bashing. What about the average American fan? Sorry, you don't exist, either. This country is just as diverse as Europe, even though we only speak a couple of languages here.

If my flatulent friend in Greensboro weren't enough, I was exposed to another underwear event in that fair city. Later that same week, I was standing on the fringe of the putting green, chipping and answering questions of a nice elderly gentleman who stood behind me.

After some minutes, I turned to sign his hat and noticed that his voluminous drawstring shorts were around his ankles. Worse than that, he was wearing a pair of antique Fruit of the Looms that had been rendered more "O" than "Y" in front by the passing of, among other things, time.

When I pointed this out, he calmly bent over and hoisted his shorts up to just below his armpits. He tied the drawstring into a lovely bow, straightened his cap, thanked me, and sauntered casually away, leaving me in what felt like the Twilight Zone.

Now, picture this: In Orlando, I was asked for my autograph by another elderly gentleman, thankfully, this time, fully clothed. Apparently, the autograph was for his grandson (who has to be forty if he's a day).

I signed my name on a Rolodex card and handed it back. He looked at it, turned it over, signed his name in an elegant hand, and gave it back to me.

"What's this for?" I asked.

"It's my autograph," he says. "You can read it, can't you?"

"Yes, I can."

"Well, I can't read yours, so I don't know who the hell you are, and you can keep your damn signature until you learn how to write."

Well, excuuuuuuuuuse me, and I'm back in the Zone.

Playing in Boston for me is like playing the Irish Open, except there are more Irish spectators in Boston, all of whom had one thing in common during the 1994 Bank of Boston: They all wanted to get me hammered.

Fortunately, only seven or eight of them succeeded. I was eventually beaten into second place by the evil Kenneth Perry. I think he was run out of town by a shillelagh-waving mob.

I often wonder what would have happened that week if I could have remembered who I was. I probably would have missed the cut.

Next stop: New York and the lovely Westchester Country Club, where the fans have a tendency to conduct conversations across fairways at the top of their lungs—and at the top of your backswing.

"Hey, Joey! Where in the helluvya been?" Combine that with the beefed up security that follows Tiger Woods these days and you get the rent-a-cop who has watched too many Steven Seagal movies.

Last year at Westchester, I was patrolling the park with Tiger, wearing my customary CBS cap and carrying my mike flagged with the CBS logo. Assuming I was a heavily disguised spectator, the would-be Mr. Seagal attempted to physically remove me from the premises while I was trying to answer an unusually intelligent question from Gary McCord. I don't think this would have happened in California.

Of course, not all golf fans remotely resemble those I've just described. Some are dedicated, intelligent, polite, clean, thrifty, brave, and reverent. (No, that's the Boy Scouts.) It's just that the ones who get noticed are the same ones who tend to gravitate toward me.

And, they say opposites attract. Hmmmm. I don't think so.

Neither Wind nor Rain

Now that I don't play anymore, I think it's about time that the Tour in this country had some rotten conditions. I'd like to see it get really tough for these guys with their air-conditioned locker rooms, free buffet, free ice, and the ability to turn right on red in their courtesy cars. They even have a fitness trailer to warm up in or in case they pull a little muscle. In my day, laddie, you had to pull at least one muscle in order to get your heart started in the morning. Hardship gives you backbone, that's what I say, so it's disturbing to me to see so many of my former colleagues defecting to these cushy conditions.

Take the weather. You can't seriously call it a challenge over here. I live in Dallas, and I'm sick of good weather. Down here the definition of an awkward hole is "one with a heat rash around it." We've been lightly sautéed here for months and, frankly, you can stick a fork in me because I am well and truly done.

I want to look out the window and see a day so cold and lousy that there is absolutely no chance of anyone else being on the TPC at Las Colinas. Those are the days I play by myself because it reminds me of Ireland in the summer. Back home, we get nine months of absolutely ghastly weather and then winter sets in. We Irish are famous for our red hair and freckles. This has nothing to do with genetics. It's rust. Where I was born, in Bangor, County Down, on a clear day you could see Ailsa Craig, the giant rock that sits in the sea by the golf course at Turnberry on the west coast of Scotland. If it was visible, it usually meant that it would rain soon. If it wasn't visible, it meant that it was raining already, but that didn't keep people from playing golf. They played anyway, seemingly oblivious to the conditions. If the rain fell gently, it was called a "soft" day. If the wind blew, driving the rain into your face like ack-ack fire, it was a "hard" day. Simple really. If it didn't rain or blow it was called an "extremely unusual day."

There was nothing to compare with a hard day at Royal County Down, the world's most beautiful golf course. Waves of 40-mph squalls would come in across the steel-gray Irish sea, making "one-under" a hard-fought eighty-nine. Playing in these conditions was always exciting for me as a young whippersnapper. My friends and I used to giggle gleefully in anticipation as the car was buffeted by huge gusts on the drive to the course. Hitting three woods and a wedge to the par-5 eighteenth was a common occurrence and a horror story that could be embellished afterward. There was always some drunken, strawberry-nosed old fart lurking in his gardening clothing by the bar waiting to tell the bedraggled that it was only a "wee draft" compared to yesterday. It amazed me that he could wear a pair of DNA-encrusted cavalry twill trousers and an egg-stained club tie over a frayed plaid shirt, but I couldn't wear a pair of blue jeans. "We have to keep up appearances." Okay, pal, in that case lock the old boy up in the broom closet.

In the late 1970s, I was a fledgling pro and I played on the Irish pro-am circuit, often in vile weather and for meager prize money. On many occasions, first prize was less than one hundred dollars and the amateurs were die-hard golf idiots who dressed like the crew on a Norwegian prawn trawler. You know, oilskins and parkas. I once witnessed one of my partners, in the days when penalty drops were taken over the shoulder, drop his ball into the hood of his anorak. It took him five minutes to find it. The rest of us couldn't resist the opportunity to help him look, all the time paralyzed with laughter.

"Damned if I know where it went, Frank. It must have gotten a hell of a bounce!"

I once played in a pro-am with a big man with a short swing who couldn't hit the ball more than about 120 yards. Later in the round, the sun came out and the temperature rose about thirty degrees. He took off his jacket and five sweaters and it turned out he was a wee man with a long swing who could hit it about 240!

Finally, for those of you who enjoy your shower after riding in a cart for five hours and perhaps have the occasional cold one afterward, consider this. Imagine how good it feels after a three-hour route march through a blizzard over mountainous sand dunes. (Yes, three hours! Golf is supposed to be exercise.) After an invigorating lukewarm shower in a freezing cold, spartan locker room (the shower feels roasting because your body temperature has fallen to forty degrees), there is no better feeling in the world than cozying up to the warmth and intoxicating scent of a peat fire, holding a hot Irish whiskey filled with brown sugar and cloves. You can gaze out the rain-lashed window at the windswept links that has just kicked your ass and succumb to the gradual warming as you descend into that age-old euphoric trance that says, "Now that, my friend, was a real round of golf."

If the old fart at the bar tells you it was worse yesterday, you can engage in another time-honored tradition and tell him to "bugger off!"

Girls in the Boys' Club

I've been doing a lot of soul-searching recently, tossing and turning at night, you know, trying to work out where I stand on the girls-in-the-boys'-club issue.

All right, all right, give over already. I know most of you read right through me. So what if I've always known where I stand on it? The real issue for me has been whether I should be dumb enough to write about it. Evidently, I should.

As all men know, there's no real upside to arguing with women, because even when we win, we lose something, or at best end up paying more than retail. I achieved the terminal stupidity required to write this when She Who Must Be Obeyed (who has right to remain silent, but not the ability) told me I should go ahead and scribble down that which she told me I was right to believe in.

I love that woman enough to end a sentence with a preposition. She does all the heavy lifting in my life, so it was fitting that she came to this conclusion for me. You see, for a while now, I have been polling my female friends (all of whom, uh, like, have a life). I wanted their opinion on the matter and so far I haven't been able to find a single woman who would object to a group of men having their own club.

All right, so the married ones might feel a little differently, but no matter what anyone says, this is about a single principle, not a single club. Nor is it about black or white, Jew or Gentile. It's about an extra chromosome and a missing rib, which makes it a different matter entirely. It's sex, man, and the undeniable truth that while opposites attract, they're still opposites. There may be a thin line between love and hate, but there's a stripe the width of Texas between a man and a woman, and in this case it's even wider.

Regarding the moral matter, She Who Must Be Obeyed says the case against me closes with a bang right there, as I'm a self-confessed immoral swine. But even I know I can't get away with the simple truth like that. I'm led to believe that at the crux of the problem, a lot of insider business stuff is going on in those clubhouses to which women are not allowed access.

Well, it occurs to me that there's a lot of business stuff going on in boardrooms too, and women don't have access to some of those, either. Some they do, and some they don't. Some golf clubs they do, and some golf clubs they don't. (Please, please don't tell me I'm the only one that's noticed this; I couldn't stand to be that damned clever.)

But there's that nasty little word, "moral." I hate that word. Remember the Moral Majority? The lovely and talented Reverend Jerry Falwell and his merry band of better-than-the-rest-of-us blowhards? Like the principal antagonist in this debate, Reverend Falwell's uncommonly high sense of morality proved to be the perfect antidote to common sense, which is the nemesis of every narrow-minded person.

For real-world feminists, who thankfully tend to concentrate on serious issues like teen pregnancy, equal pay, and domestic abuse, it's better to shut up, let the militants amuse themselves with trivialities, and hope they do as little damage as possible. At this point I think it's important that we males remember that the vast majority of women would love for us to be so successful that we might become a member of one of these clubs. (And it's equally important to remember that virtually none of us ever will.)

Let me reassure every American that theirs is not the only country whose people are sometimes deafened by overzealous, self-righteous trumpeting. Having returned from the Ryder Cup, it seems to me that the British are just as susceptible to the occasional attack of blinding stupidity from out of left field.

At the moment, a debate is raging over the future of hunting with dogs, in which a small minority of city-dwelling animal-rights activists has succeeded in convincing, with skewed logic and misinformation, the horribly chinless and liberal members of the ruling Labour party to ban the practice. These are people who visit the countryside only on weekends in their Suburban Assault Vehicles, wear nasty pullovers crocheted out of their own armpit hair, and whose objective is to protect the cute little foxes (which are about as endangered as the Queen of England's corgis) from those nasty country folk on horseback with their packs of baying hounds. "Tally ho! Toodle Pip! Chin-chin old boy, lovely day for a snifter, what?"

You get the picture. They're idiots too, but the fact is, they do no harm whatsoever, unless you're a fox. And if you are, and you're cunning enough to be reading this, you ought to be able to escape from a bunch of smelly canines and a posse of tweedy old duffers whose mode of transport is the most neurotic animal on the planet, shouldn't you? But here's the kicker, which has the real-world animal lovers in a schizoid tizzy. If these city-dwelling animal-rights activists get their way, for every fox saved, one healthy horse will have to be shot, and three dogs will go to the pound. In this case, for "go to the pound," read "shot," because at the pound these dogs are invariably held in cages marked:

"This is Basil, a flea-ridden three-year-old nutless lurcher who has all his shots and the temperament of a hairy piranha. He's an irrepressible howler, not particularly brilliant around old people, and even with constant training, he'll mark his territory in your laundry basket then hump the living daylights out of the nearest small child."

Not surprisingly, these dogs can be a little difficult to shift. You see, they're bred to hunt and nothing else. They won't sniff the arse of the poodle next door; they'll tear it off and bury it for later. The Nigels claim they have the support of 72 percent of the population—a number, if indeed true, leaves me wondering if any of those polled were supplied with the less than pretty facts.

For genuine animal-rights folk, this is clearly not a good situation. On one hand, it's sort of awkward for them to support a pastime in which fuzzy little foxes are being torn apart by packs of woofing mad canines; on the other, the whole dog and horse firing-squad thing makes them squeamish, too—although I think they blindfold the horses (or maybe that's steeplechasing). But you know it makes them wonder if complaining about the problem was a good idea in the first place, as ultimately it would seem that the actions of the lunatics on the fringes of their organizations would do a great deal more harm than good. Sound familiar? Thought so.

The real aftermath of this appallingly pretentious stand by high-minded women on what is supposed to be the moral high ground is the impression left that they are in the majority. I don't believe it for a moment.

Still, fair play for those who want to fight for what they think is their just reward, which in this case is access to worse bridge partners. As Patton once said: "That is all."

I think I understand why most women don't want to be bothered with this pointless debate, but the thing that really jerks me around is the way most of us men have taken the virtual fifth, as if there was something to be ashamed about. Any man who refuses to be bullied and is willing to speak up in defense of the only female-free territory we have left is a hero to me.

Why have so few of us stood up to have our nuts counted here? Talk about being emasculated. Television is filled with women demonstrating their intellectual and moral superiority over their male partners and friends. There isn't a night of sitcoms that goes by without some hapless guy getting a slap upside the head or a kick in the pants from his daughter, girlfriend, wife, or the gay guy. He always takes it like a man, too, which these days seems to be lying down. Turn it the other way and there would be an outcry from the estrogen police. Commercials regularly portray the male of the species as stupid or misinformed, yet those of us with any sense never complain about it either.

If you ask me, the fact that we're comfortable with our misinformed stupid selves, or at least the fact that women think of us in that way, is a credit to us. If you find our shortcomings funny, rather than crying foul, we'll laugh along with you. The legendary anthropologist Margaret Mead was something of an expert on our species, a visionary who once said that male-only clubs served a useful purpose.

She was right. So I wonder which modern-day television show she would consider to be doing more of a disservice to women. A golf tournament or *The Bachelor*?

I think I know the answer, but just to be sure, I'm going to check with the wife.

Chapter Three

My Less Than Finest Hours

Queasy Ryder

The Concorde rolled to a stop at the end of the tarmac at Charleston not-very-international airport. There were hundreds of cars parked along the perimeter fence and thousands of people lining the road. It was at that moment I finally realized the magnitude of the event I was about to take part in. Sam Torrance, the man who was to be my hairy Scottish crutch all week, sat beside me. I mentioned to him that I couldn't believe how many people had turned out to welcome us.

"They're here to see the bloody airplane, you moron" was his tactful reply.

He was right, of course, but, nonetheless, it was quite an experience for a Ryder Cup rookie to walk off the world's most beautiful aircraft and into the media maelstrom that had by then become a rivalry of cross-global proportions. It's like childbirth—it doesn't matter how many times it's described to you, you still have no idea of what it's actually like, and I, for one, was blissfully unaware. Torrance, on the other hand, had almost lost count of how many he'd played in. (His golf had always been better than his math.) He and I were destined to be matched against Lanny Wadkins and Mark O'Meara in the last match of the first morning's fourballs.

Kiawah was so difficult in 1991 that it was possible to drop a shot between the locker room and the first tee. The greens were harder to hit than Oscar De la Hoya's nose. Sam and I were good friends with both Lanny and Mark, but for the next five hours we had to be enemies, and I had a problem with that. It's hard to act like a tough guy when every part of your body is shaking.

The introduction of the players to the crowd on the first tee is like no other experience in golf. When you introduce patriotism and pride, national ego and genuine animosity into the equation, you are greeted with a roar that says, "Win, and you are the supreme beings in all the universe. Lose, and may the fleas of a million rodents infect your every orifice."

I held up okay until I got to the first green. By then it became obvious that putting was going to be a problem. I could get away with flinching my bigger muscles into something that resembled a golf swing, thus fooling most people into thinking that I was cool, calm, and not quite hysterical, but when it came down to controlling the smaller motor impulses, there was obviously a rogue neuron in charge somewhere. On my first attempt with the flat stick, my muscles came to an almost unanimous decision: Everything moved except my bowels (and believe me, it was damn close).

On the way to the next tee Sam, always the diplomat, comforted me with the words, "If you don't pull yourself together, I'm going to join them, and you can play all three of us, you useless bastard." I was understandably galvanized.

Over the course of the next few hours, we threw the match at them and they threw it back at us until we reached the eighteenth, one down. In the gathering gloom, all four of us played the difficult par-four as if it were completely dark outside and, somehow, I ended up with a twelve-footer to win the hole and halve the match. I had read the greens like a Russian newspaper all day, so I asked Sam to aim me. To his eternal credit, he said, "Hit it firm on the left edge," in a manner that made me feel he was completely positive. (You know he wasn't.) Somehow I made a controlled spasm and the ball rolled into the center of the cup. The crowd roared; I almost fainted. Sam and I had made my first Ryder Cup half-point!

Later that evening, after two beers and a Valium, I wondered to myself what it was all about. I had won tournaments and contended in majors, but never had I felt such mind-bending, gut-churning pressure—and worse than that, there was no money involved! I was used to playing my own ball, making my own mistakes, and being in sole charge of my own success or failure. After all, that's the nature of the game that we play. Now, all of a sudden, eleven of the players that I most admired were baring their souls in the team room, the veterans exposing their soft underbellies for the first time just so the rookies could find some comfort in the fact that the Ryder Cup makes everyone human. It breeds a rare generosity in an otherwise selfish game.

I narrowly missed the team in 1993 and was heartbroken. I went to The Belfry and sat with the players and their wives behind the eighteenth green, gnawing the bark off that massive oak tree as every match came in. I just had to be there. Once you have played Ryder Cup golf, you feel the call, you feel the anguish and the euphoria of the current players. I only played one Ryder Cup, but I know still that I am one of them.

However, lest any of you think after that mushy bit I may have become less of a cynical son of a bitch, here's a poem—my ode to the Cup (I didn't write this, someone broke into my house and left it on my notepad—honestly!):

In southern Spain, they'll feel the pain
when they fight for that Ryder Cup.
It's hard to play when you're so far away
and the food makes you want to throw up.

I can't honestly explain that point when your brain
feels like it's about to implode.
But that's not the worst thing, your lower intestine
might spontaneously decide to unload.

It adds completely new meaning to that uneasy feeling
as you squeamishly consider your shot.
Try making a putt when the cheeks of your butt
have tied themselves into a knot.

So give them a break as you watch their knees shake.
For the losers there will be no shame.
But you won't cheer them up if they've lost the cup
by saying, "It's only a game!"

Passages, Port-l-lets, and Pepto-Bismol

I have a confession to make. Last Saturday at the Kemper Open was not a good day for me. I had ingested some slightly dubious Italian food on Friday night, and when I woke up on Saturday morning I knew it was going to be a tough day on the links. It was to be Port-l-let city for me. Later that day, I strapped my RF (radio frequency) pack around my waist (which didn't help), put on my headset and strode manfully out to work. But the day was going to feel like a long one, if the rumblings in my stomach were any kind of prognosis.

My first problem, however, was to be with my equipment. For some unknown reason I was picking up air traffic control at Washington's Dulles Aiport on my headset. At one stage, somone asked me for my height and position, so I told them I was five-foot-eleven and in the middle of the eighth fairway.

Inevitably, I hit a patch of intestinal turbulence near the twelfth green while Rich Beem was in the middle of making a double bogey. The Port-l-lets were agonizingly close on the other side of the creek, about twenty yards away, but the nearest bridge was over the back of the green, and I had to wait for Rich to putt out. Alas, dear readers, the end result was, how shall I put it, a trouser tragedy that resulted in my mysterious absence from the broadcast for about ten minutes, and a pair of brand-new jockey shorts had to make the ultimate sacrifice.

You could be forgiven for wondering why I would share such a personal passage with you, but here's the rub. The following day, when I joined the young man who had led the Kemper all week on the second fairway, he told me that he had something for me. He rummaged in his bag, pulled out a bottle of Pepto-Bismol, winked and then went on his winning way. Apparently, he had got wind of my trouble the day before. Or perhaps that was downwind. The mere fact that he thought to stop in at Eckerd's on his way to the golf course that morning for my benefit is an indication of the strength of the man's character.

Rich Beem is an interesting young man. He led the tournament, but for about ten minutes in the third round, for all four days, but found time to talk to me in between almost every shot. It was also a great comeback for Steve Duplantis, Jim Furyk's former caddie, who is a single parent and travels with his three-year-old daugher, Sierra. Along with Stuart Appleby's recent win in the Shell Houston Open, this was another tournament with a feel-good ending.

Scratching an Itch

Whenever one of the victims of my on-course reporting finds a tree between his or her ball and the hole, I often identify the leafy offender for the benefit of the folks at home. Occasionally, I am asked why. Having spent rather more of my career than I should have in the trees, it's no small wonder I recognize so many of them. But a few years ago, there was one incident in particular that sparked my quest for arboreal knowledge. It felt like a mishap at the time, but seems like a blessing these days.

Like many of my stories, this one is lavatorial in nature, but this one, for a change, has more emphasis on the nature than the lavatory. I was playing the Buick Classic at Westchester and was called upon by the aforementioned nature, whose timing (as usual) was appalling. I was in my flaming downward spiral toward mediocrity, then to the relatively safe haven of broadcasting after completing the round, and had just thrown a hat trick of bogeys at the grand old course. I found myself pondering this great misfortune and my trouser-shrouded ankles at the same time, while in a players-only porta-potty on the inward half. With my elbows on my knees, I massaged my temples with both hands, and let out a heavy sigh. The chance of making the cut was down the toilet, my career in ruins. How, I wondered, could it get any worse?

A few moments later, after discovering an empty toilet roll holder, I knew the answer. I weighed all the obvious options, none of which were any good. I needed three birdies, had only one glove, and wasn't wearing a hat. At this stage, one dead birdie would have helped. Then, a shaft of sunlight burst through a crack in the door, illuminating my solution with a ray of hope. On the floor, there were three leaves, attached to a slender green stem. Not great, and they could have been drier, but better than nothing.

At least it would have been better than nothing, if I had only known what poison-freaking-ivy looked like. Here is the official description from the *Peterson Field Guide*, along with my own translation:

"Poison ivy grows as an erect shrub, trailing vine, or climber." It might not get you in the woods, but it's perfectly capable of chasing you down the fairway. "Leaves may be stiff and leathery, or merely thin, somewhat hairy or not, shiny or dull, coarse-toothed and wavy edged, or neither." We haven't got a clue what it looks like, either. If you're reading this, hunkered down somewhere in a quiet woodland moment, stay completely still and look around you for a rock. A smooth one, preferably...no, actually, never mind, just tear out a few pages. This book is about as useful as a broken bottle in your situation.

(While I'm on the subject, I remember a colleague of mine who, some years earlier in Africa, had found himself in a similarly nightmarish position, and thought he had found his salvation in the form of a label from a nearby beer bottle. Unfortunately, there was a tiny sliver of glass still attached to it, and I don't want to talk about it any more. I'm sorry I even brought it up.)

I felt like an idiot when I realized what I'd done, and as I recall, for some considerable time afterward. Today, though, I realize that I shouldn't have, because virtually no one knows what poison ivy looks like! Of course, I believe the average dolphin is probably one hundred times smarter than the cleverest human, which is probably me. Dr. Kevorkian is in jail, and Dr. Laura isn't. No dolphins were involved in that process, I noticed. Meanwhile, we humans are still trying to figure out what bears do in the woods. I have no idea, but I'd be willing to bet there has never been one dumb enough to wipe his arse with poison ivy.

Anyway, after that day six years ago, I vowed to educate myself on the subject of any growing thing I might encounter between the parking lot and the scorer's tent. If I live to be one hundred, I might get through the *Peterson Field Guide*, by which time I'll have forgotten the names of everything and everybody, but I won't care. Golf courses have become more fascinating and beautiful places to me since I started to notice the gorgeous, living things that burst from the ground upon which they are built.

Now, before any of you start calling me a shrub-hugger, let me elaborate.

Okay, so I'm a shrub-hugger. I'm coming out of the woodshed, and I feel better about myself already. From this day forward, I'm going to hug my shrubs in public! Now, if I can just get some of these golf course designers to join me around the campfire, perhaps we can address a problem that, unfortunately, many of us will live to see. I'm talking about the wrong trees, and the amount of them that are being planted on many new golf courses.

Most developers have the desire to see their property look as pretty as possible, as quickly as possible. Only natural of course, but it's kind of a quick fix if you ask me. Which you didn't, but then again, I have the pen. High-dollar developments are usually planted with great stuff, but on some golf courses, I'm seeing more and more fast-growing, closely planted, butt-ugly triangular conifers, in places that deserve slow-growing cedar elms and walnuts, or ashes and willows and oaks. These are trees that will eventually grow into graceful giants, with showy canopies, that might fill twenty to fifty yards of space and have plenty of room underneath for idiots like you and me to find our ball, and then take another ill-conceived swipe at it.

All great architects try to design around the great trees that are already there, but sadly, economic pressure is sometimes the greater force, and for the sake of a better hole, a plant that has been rising slowly and relentlessly from the dirt for centuries is lost. This always makes me want to barf, especially when the hole is filled with something like a ratty bald cypress, or a clump of doucheberries. I mean, don't get me wrong: A bald cypress is okay, in fact they are very beautiful when rising from a swamp, but when a tree has knees, it's just that I prefer them to be covered in brackish water, thank you.

The other major problem I see is that very few golf clubs invest the amount of time or money to properly care for the good specimens they already have. The problem isn't confined to golf courses, either. Just take a look around your neighborhood, and you will likely see great trees slowly dying from neglect. In Dallas, where I live, as I drag my ghastly corpulence around on the dreaded morning jog, I notice that virtually every cedar elm I lean up against is also gasping for oxygen.

They are being choked to death by mistletoe—parasitical clumps of it—clinging to every limb. I hate mistletoe. Good neighbor that I am, I was going to show the guy down the street how to get rid of the stuff with a couple of shells from my trusty 12-gauge, but after seeing me standing on his front porch grinning, he barricaded himself in and called the law. I tell you, some people have no sense of gratitude. I don't think that guy's from Texas, either.

The thing to remember here is how some of our great old golf courses looked shortly after they were built. Old photographs of Winged Foot, Augusta National, and Riviera, to name but three, show what would appear at first to be pretty ordinary-looking places, with a few small trees and some stumpy-looking bushes.

When I think of what they look like now, I'm thankful for the men who had the foresight, the patience, and the generosity to plant and nurture these great giants, which they knew they'd never live to see. Most great artists leave their masterpieces behind them. These men left them in front, for us to enjoy, and presumably, to give poison ivy somewhere to hide.

Letting Loose

Well, with Shigeki Maruyama's fine win at the Nelson in Dallas this past weekend, the first half of a two-week home stint is over for me, and next it's over to Colonial in Fort Worth, Texas. Dallas and Fort Worth are two different towns, believe me. That's evident when you're landing at the airport, which sits pretty much in-between them. If your pilot is a local, you always know from where he or she hails, because you're welcomed to one or the other.

The Nelson and the Colonial are two different golf tournaments too. At the Nelson, we have the famous party tent, the Pavilion, where thousands of pseudo golf fans congregate each afternoon to admire a vast array of silicone spectator mounds and their owners, who are only too pleased to display them. Hey, it's spring after all, and most mammals in the area are doing exactly the same thing.

Certain events on the PGA Tour are famous for these meeting places. Phoenix has the Bird's Nest, Hilton Head the Quarterdeck, but there is nowhere quite like Dallas, where everything is bigger, including the number of people willing to get hammered, sunburned, and risk incineration by lightning, all in the name of love or, at least, lust.

Now, there are few games with a wealthier demographic than golf. Yachting perhaps, but there is a much stronger possibility that the commodore of the average yacht club already has someone who is willing to dress up like a nurse and change his diaper. This is an objective piece, of course, and I do have a master's degree in human stupidity, so don't call me sexist when I say that at the Nelson, there seems to be a higher ratio of slim, beautiful females attached to fat unattractive males than at any other event.

The side show at the Nelson is usually more entertaining than the golf. As the afternoon goes on, more and more of these incongruous, liquored-up, not-quite-mates-for-life venture out of the Pavilion and onto the golf course, so that the male can continue to impress the female with his brightly colored plumage, a coyote turd that someone told him was Cuban, and knowledge of a game about which she knows and cares nothing.

But by hardly sweating at all, preventing her plastic puppies from escaping their spandex tube kennel, and staying upright on the sodden turf in pole-dancing pumps, the female also tries to impress. It's a fascinating mating ritual, but completely unlike that of the whooping crane, which achieves the same result by leaping up and down, flapping its wings and yelling in birdspeak, "Dear God, but I'm horny!"

I would say that about 60 percent of those who attend the Byron Nelson do so with the sole purpose of getting laid, and the other 40 percent are there to watch them try. The remainder, which amounts to me, does his best to do television which, given the distraction factor, can be tough. After the third round on Saturday, I did a piece for our local CBS affiliate's evening sports roundup with former Cowboys quarterback Babe Laufenburg. We were set up behind the second tee, facing a vast swarm of fans making their way back to the Pavilion. I suspected there had been some drinking done, as a bunch of them stopped behind the cameras, made silly faces, and shouted, "Hi, Mom!"

The key word in that last sentence was "behind." Like, you'd need to be "in front" of the camera for Mom to see you, no? But it was Mother's Day, so Babe and I gave them the benefit of the doubt and carried on as if they weren't there. Then, a leggy woman with black-and-tan hair that had no doubt started the day fully inflated, teetered to a halt on mud-encrusted five-inch heels, and held out her arms sideways with her fingertips outstretched, like a diver with her toes over the edge of the ten-meter springboard.

By this stage of the festivities her mascara had started to run, and she looked like she was wearing a dead Afghan hound on her head. There was some minor jostling as the crowd behind her wingspan stumbled to a halt. Laufenberg was in the middle of asking me a question, but I was preoccupied with what I saw out of the corner of my eye. I could almost hear Scotty in the engine room of the *Starship Enterprise*: "Ah canny hold her cap'n, ah think she's goin' tae blow!!"

Then she blew, and I think her boyfriend must have set her choke wide open, because she let fly with a projectile burst of chunks, most of which would have finished out of bounds on the widest hole at the TPC. She might have been a golf fan too, because before the twenty or so folks in front had time to realize their backs had been pebbledashed with a lumpy puree of cheap chardonnay and franks, she'd reloaded and blown a provisional!

It was a staggering performance, and alone worth the price of a ticket. People were yelling, rolling around on the ground, and dry-heaving, as best of all, she sailed like some majestic icebreaker, through the sea of bodies off toward the Pavilion, and presumably, another drink. I mean, something like that'll leave a bad taste in your mouth. And, like I said, the cameras were pointing at us. Bummer!

Oh, well, there's always this week, where the same crowd will show up. Overnight infatuations seldom last, especially when most of the time people wake up the following morning. If you don't like the one you hit on at the Nelson, you get to hit on a mulligan at the Colonial.

Oh, yeah, and the golf is great in both places too.

Out-of-Mind Experiences

What makes a player choke? I should know, for in truth, I did it as often as anyone. Although to give myself a little credit, I generally had the good sense to do it before I got into contention. That way it was considerably less embarrassing.

No, what I'm talking about is why a man suddenly spasms and snatches defeat from the jaws of victory, so rendering himself incapable of remembering who he is or where he lives until he is back, safe in the arms of inadequacy.

The land of failure is a comfortable place because you have so much company. Successville, on the other hand, is a ghost town filled with responsibility and further expectations, and is inhabited by only the selfish and the brave.

Well, I've been selfish a lot, but only occasionally brave, and in those rare moments when I have overcome my anguish, it seems as if I have suffered some kind of selective memory loss.

I wish a different kind of amnesia to Jean Van de Velde (whose name, ironically, means "John of the Fields"), who butchered the British Open by spending most of his week in Scotland hitting the wrong club, in case you hadn't noticed. He pulled out his driver when other people were making tentative passes with their middle irons. So perhaps what appeared to be an incredible brain fart at the seventy-second hole was merely a continuation of the policy that got him there in the first place.

Whatever way you look at it, that bloody Sunday was a perfect example of why this is the world's greatest game. What theater! We had a playoff among three players, two of whom felt like they had won the lottery just by being there, and one who had the winning ticket under his beret, but threw his hat in the air by mistake.

But to be fair, we have to talk about Carnoustie, which was set up by people who should be put on some kind of medication for the rest of their lives. The reason there were so many odd names on the first couple of pages of the leaderboard was that the course was, to say the least, pretty odd, too.

Carnoustie, without a blade of rough, is a magnificent test of golf, and that is an inarguable fact. The way it was set up, with goat-choking weeds and fairways narrower than Adolf Hitler's mind, it was a test of how much of the Barry Burn you could swallow without throwing up. You have probably read a load of crap about the great players in the world and how they whined about the conditions, but the truth is, they had a very good point. Jack Nicklaus once said that golf wasn't meant to be fair, but I believe that it wasn't meant to be stupid, either.

That last bit was mine, not Jack's. But I digress, as usual. The worst I ever felt with a golf club in my hand was on the seventeenth tee of the Ocean Course at Kiawah Island on the Sunday of the 1991 Ryder Cup. I was two-up with two to play on the then-U.S. Open champion, but I had lost two holes in a row.

Payne Stewart had hit a fabulous shot onto the green, which to me by this stage looked about the size of my ball. The club felt incredibly light in my hands, and I experienced giddiness as I teed the ball up. I remember that every message my brain tried to send to my hands was intercepted by a mysterious pair of gonads, which had somehow taken up residence on either side of my windpipe.

I can honestly say that I have no recollection of the swing I made. I don't remember how it felt, how the ball flew, or for that matter, how I even made contact. No, the only thing I remember is turning around to see European captain Bernard Gallacher, his arms outstretched toward me and former captain Tony Jacklin, who was facing backward with his hands over his eyes.

Apparently he had even less faith in me than I did. The ball finished about thirty feet left of the hole and I won the match 2 and 1. That much I do remember.

Good players teach their bodies how to perform and then when the curtain rises, they somehow find the ability to switch off the old gray matter and allow their bodies to take the stage.

This was one of the few times I was able to perform such a feat. The other occasion I felt such horror and helplessness was also in a team event, the 1990 Dunhill Cup, in which I had the honor of captaining the notorious Irish side. In the finals, we played England, the old enemy, and after a tie, yours truly went out to play Howard Clark for all the marbles in a sudden-death playoff.

We halved the first and second at St. Andrews and then headed to the dreaded seventh hole. Howard found the left semi-rough off the tee and I hit a heely scunge that somehow found the left edge of the fairway. After Howard missed the green short and left, it seemed unlikely he could chip it close to the hole, which was cut directly behind the world's most awful bunker.

I was left with just over two hundred yards into a right-to-left wind, and I knew that one good swing would probably win it for Ireland. There ensued a violent struggle between my brain and my body. Neither had said a word to the other for the entire week and, as a result, I had managed to play extraordinarily well.

But on this occasion, my brain felt the need, like some idiot CEO, to take charge at this crucial moment. Somehow, body found the courage to tell brain to go empty the garbage or something and while brain's back was turned, body made the swing.

Again, I don't remember it, but that's probably because my mind was over by the water cooler. My 3-iron shot soared majestically at the center of the green and was wafted gently toward the hole by the breeze. It bounced softly and came to rest about fifteen feet behind the hole.

The crowd roared. My brain turned around violently from the water cooler and was just about to fire every muscle in my body when it realized that the bottom line had just been improved. Naturally, during the acceptance speech, it took all the credit.

I have always felt that if you want to be a great golfer, it is a tremendous advantage to be either really, really smart like Mac O'Grady or dumb as a rock like Gary McCord. Either you use your superior intellect to quell your self-doubt and anxiety, or you don't realize you are in contention until somebody hands you a check. Anything in between and you are probably buggered. Van de Velde was like most of the rest of us—that is, in between.

It wouldn't have mattered where he drove it off the tee on the final hole of regulation or what he hit for his second shot. He was going to find a way to lose because deep down inside, he didn't want the responsibility that comes with being a major champion. This does not make him a bad person.

Paul Lawrie, on the other hand—and here is the really sad story—did want the responsibility. I say it's a sad story because after the impossible drama of Van de Velde's seventy-second hole and the following farcical playoff, one of the greatest shots in major championship history was forgotten.

Lawrie was faced with 225 yards of terror, with out of bounds to the left and a little claret jug behind. He found the courage of the man who wants to be champion. What he does with the responsibility is up to him.

I just hope that he, unlike me, can remember the greatest swing he ever made.

A Very Bad Day

We all have the occasional bad day now and then, where nothing seems to go right from dawn to dusk. I had a beauty this past Sunday, at the final round of the LPGA Championship. Like most of these experiences, it was triggered by something small, of my own doing, and then snowballed as the day dragged on.

I don't normally drink very much when I'm on the road, but for some reason—insanity possibly—Saturday night was a belter. I held court majestically at the bar in the Hotel du Pont and, like one of the tall ships visiting Delaware waters, I swayed and creaked elegantly back to moor myself to the mattress in room 932, shortly after midnight. All was well, until I awoke at 8 a.m. wearing nothing but a black sock on my left foot, and a large blob of congealed toothpaste stuck in my chest hair. This in itself would not have been so mysterious had I not been wearing sandals without socks the previous evening.

Not to worry, thought I, as I stumbled to the bathroom to brush my teeth and chest; stranger things have happened. On the way, I realized, as one does, that at some stage last night, I had drunk at least one ashtray, and was dealing with a formidable hangover. In a stroke of genius, I decided to nip up to the twelfth floor for a brisk run on the old treadmill. Sweat it out, just the ticket.

I nodded toward a couple of spandex types in the corner, started the belt up to a feverish six miles an hour, and broke into a blubbery jog. After about forty-five seconds, it became apparent that it was not having the desired effect, so I ejected to the safety of the carpet, which, to my horror, seemed to be moving only a little slower than the belt. I was keenly aware of the stares from the spandex sisters in the corner, as I bumped into a pillar, then stumbled over to the water cooler just in time to barf violently into the trash can. I immediately felt much better, and looked over at the gallery, who by now were gaping. I said, "You make me sick!" removed the trash bag, and headed back to the safety of my room to plan my next move. Into the shower, and off to work. By now, the heat index is close to one hundred, and I am clammy. I can hardly wait to strap on my radio pack and for the batteries to steam up the small of my back, sending a river of sweat southward. I use a whole bottle of Gold Bond Medicated Powder and, feeling nothing from the waist down, set off to be wired for sound. I'm walking past the Port-o-lets when one of our cameramen exits. The door is caught in a gust of wind, and slams open, into the bridge of my nose, sending me reeling backward, right onto my posterior, which fortunately, as I mentioned earlier, is already numbed up. My proboscis, though broken three times previously, is altered once more.

Four o'clock, and the bell rings. I join Julie Inkster and Wendy Ward on the tenth fairway. I trudge around manfully, trying to stay downwind of them, as they are both having a tough enough day without getting a whiff of me. I want to get home, and I've got a tight connection to make at O'Hare, so I've got to make the flight from Philly. The only thing that can shrink my berries any smaller is a playoff.

Which happens, and lasts until 6:40 p.m. I am in my rental car at 7 p.m. driving toward the City of Brotherly Love. Get out of my way, you buttholes, I smell like a polecat with dysentery, and I'm wearing golf shoes. I get there with about twenty minutes to check in, and my flight is....canceled. Now I'm upset.

Back in the rental car, I'm heading for the scene of the crime, the Hotel du Pont. Unfortunately, I-95 is closed going south, and I don't realize that I have been diverted onto I-495, and somehow I end up on a bridge that is taking me to New Jersey. I hope there is an early one from Newark, because from here on in, I am acting like I'm doing this on purpose.

Warning: Stoned Hippos

The word *safari* in Swahili means "arduous journey," so the Safari Tour is aptly named. Leave it to me to never take the easy way when a difficult one is offered.

Besides, the word also means "adventurous expedition," according to *Webster's Collegiate*, and I was of the age where I craved adventure. Actually what I craved was to be away from the frozen ground and the freezing wind of a Northern Ireland winter. Today, I consider any place without bellmen, room service, and at least forty channels of cable to be an "arduous journey." But I digress.

Many of the venues on the Safari Tour are in rural, hotel-free areas of Africa, which is to say most of Africa. The mining town of Mufulira in Zambia is one such place. The entire population (of 225,271) waits eagerly every year for the return of the pros to play in the Mufulira Open.

The members of the host club provide accommodation in their modest houses, which due to the fact that most of them have been hired by the mining company on a short-term contract basis, are pretty spartan. No one invests in luxuries—such as carpet, air conditioning, or furniture. Basically they are camping out in the bush for years at a time, which, of course, can make anyone crazy. In at least one case, it did.

A couple of years before my visit to Muff, as it is known, a young English player named David Moore was billeted with his good friend, Gary Smith, in the home of a middle-aged couple. One night the husband came home from the club with a skinful of beer, accused David of sleeping with his wife, loaded up his .45 and chased both boys around the house. He emptied the gun through the locked bathroom door, mortally wounding David. Overcome with remorse, he then turned the gun on himself.

Having been told this story on the bus from the airport to Mufulira, I was very careful not to make eye contact with any kind of female all week. This journey was way too arduous for me, so I missed the cut and headed farther south once more, this time to South Africa.

In most places in the world where golf is played in rural areas, there is an outstanding chance that the surrounding fields will be inhabited by the kind of things you might be eating after your round. You know: cows, sheep, pigs, chickens, etc. In Africa, it is quite the other way 'round. Before you make the turn, you might be the main course at lunch for some of the creatures out there.

In northeastern South Africa, there is a golf course called Phalaborwa, which is separated from Kruger National Park by an electric fence. I used to think that this fence was placed there in order to keep the dumb animals off the golf course, but once I'd played there a few times, it became apparent that it was considerably more necessary to keep the supposedly intelligent humans out of the park.

The fence was regularly breached by the local elephant population, and this allowed all kinds of other herbivores access to the nice green grass. Naturally, the carnivores, who liked to eat the herbivores, followed suit. All this wildlife led to one of the strangest of golf hazards. Every morning, the entire golf course was covered in dung.

Rhino poop, gazelle pellets, jackal jobbies, warthog woopsie, buffalo stools, and elephant armchairs, you name it, it was all over the place. If you had a morning tee time, you had to pick your way through a veritable minefield, but by lunchtime it was all gone, thanks to that sanitary little scarab, the African dung beetle.

Every single morsel was rolled up into a golf ball-sized sphere with an egg at its center and buried under ground. This ensures that when the egg hatches, the little beetle (would that be a dunglet or a dungling?) has enough food to get it off and rolling.

The African dung beetle is without question the creature for whom the phrase "It's a dirty job, but somebody has to do it" was coined.

The whole survival of the fittest, eat-or-be-eaten thing is not something you normally have to worry about on a golf course, but at Phalaborwa you had to expect the unexpected. One of the members' favorite stories was of a foursome out on the back nine, where one of the ladies' tees nestles in the shade of a large Maroela tree.

One of these ladies set up over her tee shot and took her first look down the fairway, only to feel a warm, wet spot on her left shoulder. A red, warm, wet spot.

She looked up into the tree for the source, straight into the glassy, dead stare of a Thompsons gazelle draped over the thick bough, blood dripping from its muzzle. Standing over the carcass, looking down in an "I think your left-hand grip is too strong" kind of way, was a four-hundred-pound lioness.

In a situation like this, the experts will tell you not to turn your back on a lion, but to walk away slowly backward, until you're out of the area. I have no idea what the lady in question did, but I can assure you of this. If it had been me, I would have turned my back on that lion and made sure that I ran away faster than at least one of my playing partners, and I wouldn't have stopped running until I was out of the country, never mind the area. Also, the following morning, the dung beetles would have had a new item on their menu.

I know I have said this before, but caddies are my favorite people. African caddies are no exception, and although they spend a lot of their time working for people who consider them to be nothing but ignorant savages, I have found this to be untrue.

Most of them are honest, speak our language, and at least three or four others. I still struggle with English. Also, none of them are dumb enough to be chased by an angry hippo. The seventeenth hole at Phalaborwa was my favorite area of the golf course. Just short of the green on the left-hand side there was a pond inhabited by a group of hippos.

You could hear them snort and watch their ears splash, as they eyed you suspiciously from their muddy hollow. These animals are maybe the most misunderstood in all of Africa, and among the most dangerous. Every year without fail at the Phalaborwa Classic, some idiotic professional golfer would mix up the term "National Park" with "Theme Park" and saunter down to the water's edge to throw rocks at the big fat silly animals.

Hippos for the most part are docile, and they rarely leave the water except at night. They do, however—and this is where would-be Ace Venturas make their mistake—possess the ability to deflate their massive lungs, sink to the bottom and run, really quite quickly, toward the shore. It's like watching a freight train come out of the water. They can also bite you in half like a Twinkie. "Hey, where's the cream filling?"

As I said, despite all the warnings there was at least one "hippoccasion" every year at the Phalaborwa Classic. Fortunately, no one ever got seriously hurt, but it was always easy to pick out the culprit in the bar afterward. You just had to look for the whitest person in the room who would have an expression like a pregnant nun, and would be trying desperately not to spill a large brandy on himself. A look at the scoreboard would reveal, no matter how well he might have played the first seventeen, a triple or worse at the last.

Players like Nick Price, Mark McNulty, Tommy Tolles, John Daly, and Tom Lehman can verify these Phalaborwa stories and tell you plenty of their own because before they were kings, they all played in Africa.

I realize that the dark continent isn't on everyone's top-ten destinations—for either a holiday or beginning a career as a professional golfer. But if you're looking for an adventure, arduous or otherwise, there's no place I'd recommend more highly.

Besides, I'd much rather drink cold beer in warm bars than vice versa.

Working Vacation

At this time of the year, we of the CBS golf crew don't have a lot of golf going on, so some of us take a break from the vacations that are our careers and go on what is supposed to be a real vacation. I forget about golf for a week and head for the beach in Grand Cayman with She Who Must Be Obeyed, and our five kids.

To avoid Miami International Airport, which is a refugee camp with runways, you have to jump on a charter tour jet. You've seen the travel brochures with the tanned and buff twentysomethings, strolling hand-in-hand along a deserted white strand, or giggling together over a tropical cocktail, forehead to forehead, while the moon shoots a strip of silver across the shimmering sea behind them. It's lovely.

At least, it might be if there wasn't a gaggle of little breadsnatchers waddling along behind. What you actually get is a cramped flying RV, filled with other people's snot-ridden whining brats (and your own), followed by a few days spent smearing sungrease on everyone but yourself in approximately one thousand degrees Fahrenheit, over a beer that gets warm in about eight seconds.

Of course you never get to drink it, because you are too busy washing sand out of the wazoos of your assorted offspring over and over again all day long. Here I am trying to forget about work for a few days, and my youngest boy blunders into the condo, and takes off his swimsuit. Apparently, he has a pothole bunker up there somewhere, because about a ton of sand falls out of his backside and onto the carpet. I could drop a Strata and play an explosion shot into the master bedroom if I'd brought my clubs, though I doubt it could result in there being any more sand between the sheets. It's like trying to sleep in that scene from the movie *From Here to Eternity*, but without the water.

Since we've been here, She Who Must Be Obeyed has divided

most of her time between loading the washing machine, shoveling sand out of the washing machine, and asking me to shave, "for once in my life," whatever that's supposed to mean. Oh, deep joy, I'm on vacation.

If it snowed in July, I'd be up a hill somewhere, showering to get warm, and whining like a 747. People who travel for a living can find something to complain about anywhere. Oh, oh, oh, another thing, while I'm on the subject of misleading advertising, which I'm not, I've been reading some of the magazines that people have left in the condo down here. I discovered a copy of *Men's Health*, for a start. There is always a picture of some square-jawed hunk with knotted veins and a rippling six-pack on the cover, so naturally, I never, ever buy it.

"Drop those last ten pounds!" it exclaims. Yeah, screw the first twenty.

There was a survey in this edition that caught my eye. It described how to go about finding your perfect sex partner, so, since I am sharing a bed this week with my three-year-old daughter, who refuses to fall asleep unless she is holding She Who Must Be Obeyed's index finger in one hand, and mine in the other, making the exercise pointless, I decided to go for it. As I suspected, after twenty-five years on the road, the survey confirmed that my perfect sex partner is me.

I've become so desperate to spend a week away from what's normal, I even started to read *Wine Spectator*, which I think is the most perfectly named magazine on the planet, as most of the wine experts I know spend more time looking at the stuff than they do drinking it. Like all magazines, it is best read from back to front (ha ha) and I'd got about six pages into it when I came across a review of a wine that for some reason reminded me of McCord, and his golf swing.

Before I knew it, I'd been dragged back into the realm of golf once more. Fittingly, the reviewer's initials were B.S. It went something like this:

"It would be a good idea to take this bottle to someone else's house and leave it there. It has a vaguely amusing nose, but a leathery body, it's not very well rounded, and there is a distinct twang of elderly fruit on the finish. Probably should be put down, and left there."

Oh yeah, that's my buddy. There's no avoiding him either. We have cable down here, and he's playing with the wrinklies somewhere, I see his name on the bottom of the screen. Hubert Green is playing okay, and that reminds me of something. A couple of weeks ago, I saw that retrospective piece about the last time they played the U.S. Open at Southern Hills, and the threat on Hubert's life.

It struck me as strange that nobody mentioned, in 1977 or whenever it was, Hubert Green was so thin, that most people would have missed him from point-blank range. Hell, If he had put his hands up in surrender, he might have fallen through his own shorts and into his Sansabelts.

You see, that's why I don't work for NBC. I'd last about ten minutes.

Taking Complete Relief

I don't know about any of you, but I have a low threshold for pain. I am not the strong, silent type; I am the weak, noisy type.

I'll yell like a toddler until somebody gives me something strong enough to take away the pain.

I remember one particularly nasty shoulder injury that I was forced to play through due to my unfortunate financial circumstances at the time. In my infinite wisdom, I decided I would "numb it up" and then go whack a few to see how it would hold out. Now, this was not an Advil or Tylenol situation, no sir. I'm talking about enough Percodan to make Donny & Marie seem painless. Anyway, that morning I found out why they warn on the bottle that you shouldn't operate heavy machinery while under the influence. I swear, I could have made Arnold's tractor fly.

My shoulder was perfect, but unfortunately for four hours, I felt like an intergalactic space fairy from the planet Nad. Judging by my first few divots, I had been sent to Earth on a turf-collecting mission.

Once I got used to the lightheadedness, though, I hit the ball really well. But for the life of me I couldn't imagine trying to compete like that. I can hear it now: "What the hell happened to Feherty?"

"I've no idea, sir. He shot sixty-six, signed the card, 'Batman,' and then threw himself off the clubhouse roof. Funny thing is, it didn't seem to hurt him."

I'm not alone in this kind of behavior. Golfers have always played through their injuries, and these days it's getting easier to do, what with all the facilities on Tour.

The fitness trailer is staffed by expert therapists and stocked with bandages, lotions, potions, and ointments for, as my Auntie Jean used to say, "Colds, sore holes, and pimples on the willy." I have no idea why she used to say that, but I digress.

Actually, now that I come to think of it, maybe she had a point.

Some of the more common golfing ailments are the ones you never hear about.

You'll read about Freddie's back or Greg's shoulder, sure. But what about the guy who's been up since 4 a.m. playing the bathroom bugle? I'm sorry to bring up such an indelicate subject, but hey, one dodgy oyster and it could be you. In fact, the chances are you've been that soldier.

I could tell you horror stories about the Safari Tour, as could anyone who ever played it. Zambia, Nigeria, Kenya, and what was then Rhodesia were my first experiences of foreign golf and very foreign food. It's a whole new golfing experience trying to play golf in hundred-degree-plus temperatures when you have cold sweats and projectile diarrhea. Every swing is an adventure.

I can remember one round where I walked all eighteen holes in the address position because that was the only way I could ensure that nothing below my waist would touch anything else. I would have given my left nostril for a tube of Auntie Jean's ointment, but then, the Safari Tour is a whole other column.

Unfortunately, the slightest physical defect can affect a person's golf swing. A split fingernail, a minor neck crick, or a sprained eyelid can play havoc, but such is the delicate nature of the game. Most golf injuries are sustained during the course of play or practice, but not all of them.

Take the case of Loren Roberts, a man who at his angriest looks like he might be capable of tearing a piece of toast in half. He recently broke two ribs with a self-inflicted sneeze.

What immediately sprang to my evil mind was this: He was lucky. If it had been a fart, he might have shattered his pelvis.

Sam Torrance, veteran Ryder Cupper and my dear old roommate in Europe, was, and probably still is, the world sleepwalking champion and captain of the Scottish synchronized sleepwalking team. During the 1993 Ryder Cup at The Belfry, Sam was snoozing peacefully in his hotel room beside his lovely wife Suzanne.

Suddenly, he sat bolt upright in bed and stared around the room. He was fast asleep with his eyes wide open and in full ninja mode (try to picture Chris Farley here). He mistook a medium-sized potted Yucca tree for a masked intruder, tackled it, broke his toe, and his heart, for alas, it caused him to miss the final-day singles matches.

For months afterward, he was unmercifully ribbed by his colleagues. Every time he hit it into the trees, someone would say something like, "Careful, Sammy. It's a jungle out there."

Even Ben Crenshaw pulverized his foot after applying it to a trash can. It must have been a very naughty receptacle to make Gentle Ben lose his head like a hot bottle of Guinness.

I don't care what anyone says, we're always going to hear about bad backs, wrists, and elbows, and we're never going to hear about bad fronts, even though there are a number of them out there.

However, the most commonly pulled muscle on the golf course is between the ears. I know the ego resides in there somewhere, surrounded by thick bone, but somehow it still manages to get bruised.

This, of course, leads to all kinds of ailments of the cerebral kind. The most common of these is WMS, or Why Me Syndrome, also known as the Whining Flu. This affliction affects the temporal lobe so that sufferers are under the delusion that they receive ten times more bad bounces than does the average golfer. They think they are being victimized by some greater power, which of course they are, just like the rest of us.

The only cure for this all-too-common malaise is for the patient to be dragged up an alley by his most frequent playing companions and beaten severely about the head and shoulders with a blunt object. An old persimmon driver works nicely.

It worked for Woody Austin, who is back on the PGA Tour after taking the cure at Harbour Town almost two years ago. And, it worked for me (you see where I am now).

As luck would have it, the source of most of our problems is also the answer to them. Every great champion has, from time to time, benefited from a bout of this malady: the superiority complex.

Ben Hogan, Arnold Palmer, Jack Nicklaus, Tom Watson, Seve Ballesteros, Nick Faldo, Colin Montgomerie, Tiger Woods, and David Duval, to name but a few, have in their finest moments believed themselves to be just plain better than everyone else.

This is a trait they shared with me, for I, too, believed them to be just plain better than I was. I found this to be comforting in a way.

A very strange way, but what would you expect from the likes of me, a man who also finds it strange that injuries never affect good shots. I don't ever see anyone doubling up in agony after hitting one to three feet. But I have been sent hobbling off into the woods after clanking one off the bottom groove or near the hosel.

That's why I could have won the '94 British Open but for a ruptured gornacle (don't ask).

Walking Wounded

I had knee surgery this morning, so I'm feeling a little small and clumsy. Not that it makes much difference at the moment, as I'm trying to write this on a beautifully corrugated concrete stretch of Interstate 45 in the back of a Suburban, which is making my laptop behave like a breast implant on a vibrating trampoline. Spell Check will probably explode after the first few paragraphs, unless there actually are three sixes and a percentage sign in the number 45.

I'm on my way to Houston to do a corporate outing for AT&T and Nokia, at the TPC at the Woodlands. A clinic in the morning, followed by one hole with each of their eighteeen foursomes, and a wee speech at the prize-giving. Simple as that.

At least it would be if it wasn't for the knee. Up until a week ago, I thought the meniscus was an extinct Olympic track and field event, but then I learned I'd split mine. I'd had a sore knee for a couple of months, and had been dealing with it in my usual manly fashion—painkillers, Grey Goose, and some pathetically exaggerated limping. But no one even noticed the limping, so I bit the bullet and went for the last resort—a visit to Dr. Racanelli in Dallas. Next thing I knew I was scheduled for surgery.

I don't know about any of you, but I'm not fond of the thought of someone slicing into my personal self, and grinding, sucking, or scraping at my insides. I've been a professional golfer for twenty-six years and I'm proud of the fact that up until this morning, the only surgery I'd had was my circumcision. Most men have no memory of this procedure, but mine is burned into my frontal lobe like a cattle brand, as I was thirty-six years old at the time.

It's enough to say that this was a part of my anatomy that didn't need to be shortened. I remember waking up in the recovery room, and taking my first peek at Little Davey. He was a pretty impressive sight at first, kind of like a tennis ball on a piece of string. I had eighteen stitches and I remember wondering if it might be possible for the doctor to take away the pain, but leave the swelling.

As it turned out, the doctor told me that unfortunately, just the opposite was liable to happen, and he handed me a bottle of pills with instructions to take one each night before going to sleep. Dubious, I looked at the bottle. The pills were female hormones, which was too much for me to get my mind around.

"Hang on there a minute, doc," I said. "Let me get this straight. First, you lop a half-inch off the mast on the old wedding rig, and now you want me to grow a pair of knockers? What the hell are the female hormones for?"

The doctor looked down his nose at me sternly, and took off his glasses. "Mr. Feherty," he said with an exasperated sigh. "You have the equivalent of a small barbed-wire fence around your todger. This fence will not expand. Therefore, it would be a very good idea if you were to ensure that the property that it currently encircles does not grow any bigger either, at least for the time being. My advice to you is to take the female hormones as prescribed."

That night, I swallowed two of them, watched *Oprah*, and took up knitting.

Okay, you're probably thinking, what the hell has this got to do with knee surgery, and a corporate outing in Houston? Well, nothing really, except for the fact that after both my surgeries, I had to get straight back to playing golf. In other sports, injuries such as these would put players on the day-to-day list at best, and maybe have them sitting on the bench for weeks. A pitcher gets a little blister, and he's out, but if a golfer has eighteen stitches concealed in his underpants, he'll be walking eighteen holes just the same. We are the true iron men of sport, and tomorrow, I'm going to prove it at the Woodlands. Over and out, we're pulling into the hotel parking lot. I'll talk to y'all tomorrow.

Fourteen hours later:

Well, I'm guessing that Dr. Racanelli injected my damaged wheel with some kind of anesthetic, which wore off while I was asleep. When you factor in the fact that I had to share a room with Terjesen, my idiot agent, who snored like a chainsaw half the night, it's safe to say I was a little stiff and grumpy this morning. Still, after two Vicodin, a Vioxx, a bagel, and twelve cups of coffee, my one-legged clinic went well.

The best part about it was that everyone felt so sorry for me. I was careful enough to leave the black marker, "No Cut," on my good knee too, for added sympathy. The carts had to stay on the paths, but not for yours truly. It's good to be a temporary cripple!

Everyone is so nice to you. Nobody cared that I hit six inches behind the ball a few times, and I couldn't drive it more than two hundred. At the prize-giving and speech, people laughed harder than usual, and everyone said how good it was of me to come and do this, even though I was so badly hurt. They all seemed to forget I was getting paid.

Damn. When the left one heals up, I hope the right one explodes!

Humanity Stripped Naked

I was playing the other day in one of those corporate outings in which I give a clinic to start off and then play a hole with each of the lucky groups to see how much they have benefited from my extraordinary coaching expertise.

Judging by the general ineptitude this bunch displayed, I think I may have missed my vocation. A group of apparently intelligent people have seldom been so confused, I felt, without first having suffered the words of a politician.

Anyway, this one guy hit a shot off the first tee that rocketed into the ball washer with a deafening clang, shot backward—narrowly missing the rest of his foursome—and skipped about eight times across a little pond to the left before coming to rest in about an inch of water.

It really was a remarkable little shot, so totally pure in its absolute awfulness that it made me ache over the lack of anything remotely similar to talk about at work. No such luck. All I get these days on my job is a succession of high and handsome white streaks, homing in on a trembling hole. When I am working for CBS, I'm surrounded by flagstick molesters. I want to see a few duffs for a change, some hacks, shanks, and whizzers, and, maybe the rarest of all the miscues since the advent of steel shafts, the ancient scunge (pronounced skundge), which is a shank that never gets off the ground. Okay, I just made that up, but I think we've all hit the shot.

It seems like only yesterday that T. C. Chen was playing keepie-uppie with his sand wedge when his chip bounced twice off the face from just off the edge of the green at the 1985 U.S. Open at Oakland Hills. He was called "Two-Chip" Chen for the rest of his career. That was entertaining, at least for the rest of us, but I have one better. In the early days of my career, I was playing in an Irish PGA

Section tournament at Bundoran, way up northwest in Donegal. It was one of those days where there was a wind that pinned your ears back, accompanied by the occasional refreshing frozen rainsquall off the Atlantic. It was easy to stay awake, shall we say. I was playing with a great old Irish character named Andy Murphy, who had a head full of slamming doors at the best of times, but he hit a shot that day, the likes of which would have confused the best of Rules officials.

He was in a deep greenside bunker, playing into a vicious squall, when he took a swipe at the ball, which clipped the lip of the hazard and shot straight up. With the wind whipping back into his face, Andy staggered back and raised his arms to shield his eyes from the sand, just in time to hit the ball once more—this time with the butt end of the grip, which deflected it right onto the end of his nose.

This, of course, deadened the impact somewhat, and the ball fell straight downward into Andy's rain jacket. The whole episode probably took about three or four seconds, but the Ruling, which I have no intention of trying to either recall or work out again, took considerably longer. I do remember, however, that Andy was told to drop the ball in the bunker, which he did, neatly into one of his own giant, blundering footprints. I bought him a pint afterward, telling him the story would one day be worth a great deal more than that to me. Cheers, Andy, wherever you are.

There must be something in the water in Donegal because another of the strangest things I have ever seen on a golf course also occurred there on a delightful little seaside links called Narin & Portnoo. I was playing a practice round with Peter Hanna, a friend of mine who, like me, was an assistant pro and an aspiring Tour player. We all called him "The Banana," due to the scything left-to-right shape of his game.

At Narin & Portnoo all the greens are surrounded by little electric fences that are supposed to keep the sheep, which wander freely, off the putting surfaces. It was a lonely, late afternoon, and The Banana and I were out on the ninth hole, miles from anywhere, with not another soul in sight. I was hitting a few practice chips when I noticed The Banana over on the other side of the green, facing away from me, out to sea.

He flexed his knees, fumbled with his zipper, and moments later a little leprechaun waterfall tinkled quietly out. Quietly, that is, until the moment it made contact with the fence—that unfortunate moment in which about eight thousand volts came pulsing through.

The Banana let out a bloodcurdling banshee wail, as he said in his own words some time later, "It felt like me plums lit up like Christmas tree ornaments." I bought him a pint, too, although he was shaking so badly, I think he spilled most of it.

Sadly, these classic blunders were never recorded on film, unlike that which was probably the greatest faux pas ever seen in this game. Jean Van de Velde's incredible last hole at the 1999 Open Championship at Carnoustie was the kind of bungling idiocy that this column is all about. There is nothing more magnetic, or morbidly entertaining, than the sight of someone who is supposed to know what he is doing in the process of behaving as if he has mysteriously swapped heads with a chicken that has not yet hatched—especially if he can make the wreck last for thirty minutes, and even then, not manage to end it. Jean's debacle was made even more hideously attractive by the fact that he still had the opportunity to recover after it wasn't over, if you know what I mean.

I think ordinary people identify in a special way with this

kind of humanity stripped naked, particularly when it is displayed by someone who is meant to be above stuff like that. Such a dreadful mistake makes one who is exalted seem all at once like an ordinary person, just like you and me, and in Jean's case, because of the grace and honesty he showed throughout and afterward, he immediately shot straight back up in the estimation of everyone who witnessed the scene.

People went from admiring him, to laughing at him, to feeling for him, to feeling with him, and back to admiring him again. Now that's a trip worth taking. Hell, Jean Van de Velde would be considerably less popular today if he had hit driver, then 3-wood to six feet, and made the putt. Mark my words: Jean will end up in television over here and make a great job of it.

Now, as for my own worst moment on the golf course, I have a sneaking suspicion I may not have had it yet. But I hope I have. The one that stands out so far was so embarrassing at the time, that even as I type I can feel my ears turn red. It was years ago in the South of France. I was playing in Cannes, and had been drawn with the great Seve Ballesteros for the first time in my career.

Naturally, I had taken the precaution of soiling myself in the locker room, to get that bit out of the way, and what's more, I birdied the first hole to his par so I had the honor on the second, which was a brutally difficult uphill par-3 of about two hundred yards. Around the tee, there was a big crowd of French people, most of whom thought I was a caddie. I unsheathed my trusty 2-iron and set up over the ball. After a stylish waggle, I made a graceful swing and clean-socketed the ball straight into the middle branches of a beautiful willow that guarded the seventeenth green. There was a loud "THOK!" and the ball disappeared. The crowd craned their necks upward, hoping to trace the path of such a delicious disaster, but to no avail. The ball had simply vanished into thin air.

Now Seve was always inclined to barge right onto the tee behind you, into your personal space, as if to urge you to get out of his way, and on this occasion, I was still holding my follow-through position and scanning the sky in horror for my missing pill, when I caught a whiff of the great man's garlic.

Then there was a faint hiss, and a sudden "THWOP!" as the ball plummeted to earth and embedded itself in its own impression about six feet behind the spot from whence it had last been smitten. Seve and I were now standing shoulder to shoulder, staring at this sight, as if a meteorite had just landed. He looked at me, gave me one of his famous shrugs, and said, "Escuse me, Doug, you're away!" and backed off the tee.

I was Doug for the rest of the day, and I kind of preferred it that way. It was as if I had peed my pants, and somehow it was kind of comforting to delude myself that somebody else had done it.

Of course, I prayed for the ground to open up and swallow me, but alas, we were in France, where even the dirt is used to fare far superior than a hacker such as moi. If it had swallowed me, it would most likely have barfed me right back out. Even to this day, when I recall the incident, I shudder.

But then, perhaps that's why the game builds such intestinal fortitude. In golf, as in life, what matters is not what you are served, but whether or not you can hold it down, and it's obviously fun to watch people trying.

Chapter Four
The Wages of Idiocy

We Media Types Are Full of Stupid Questions

For the purposes of this column, I am assuming Phil Mickelson didn't win the Masters. Even though it would make most of the following even more redundant than usual, I hope he did, because it would mean I'd no longer have to ask him the same boring, asinine, please-don't-sink-a-FootJoy-into-my-groin questions when I interview him.

I like Phil, although I do admit I have a problem relating to his clubs, which I think are kind of gauche. You know—awkward looking? I'm probably just a right-handed homophobe, but left-handed clubs have always made me feel kind of weird. Don't get me wrong; in most other areas I have managed to transcend the stereotypical views of the chubby, white, right-handed victim of the Irish curse.

I probably won't remember to do it, but the next time I visit my therapist, I need to ask her if the left-handed thing might possibly have anything to do with the incident in 1969 when Luigi Esdale, the assistant pro at Bangor Golf Club, sent me to the hardware store to pick up a left-handed hammer. I was only eleven, but now that I think of it, when he asked me to get a can of tartan paint as well, it should have been a dead giveaway. Ah, the memories.

But if you want a real example of someone who has grace, dignity, stoicism (which is a word with no right to exist), and who has endured a barrage of stupid questions, you should look no further than Mickelson.

In my short stint as a course reporter, I've asked enough stupid questions to be able to spot one when it's asked by someone else, believe me, and it was no surprise when earlier this year Phil finally tossed his head back and gave us all the full Miss Piggy. Lucky no one got a slap in the kisser, because they probably wouldn't have seen a right hook coming.

First, let me say this: The media has an obvious obligation to ask questions, the answers to which readers, listeners, and viewers have a right. It wouldn't take a genius to figure out what most people would like to know about Phil. The thing is, if you believe everything you hear, then evidently you know more about Phil than Phil does.

For a start, seven years ago in Vegas, he placed a $700,000 bet at 1,500-1 odds on a football team that at the time didn't even exist, to win the Super Bowl six years later. Or something like that. Bingo, the man is a genius! Shortly thereafter, he backed Gonzaga to make the Sweet Sixteen within the next decade, the All-Blacks to defeat Australia in the Rugby World Cup, and Denzel Washington to play the role of Stephen Biko in a movie within three years.

Who knew that he could forsee all that?

More to the point, who should care? Like most people, I flick through the occasional supermarket tabloid bum-rag on my way through the fifteen-items-or-less lane, and while the checkout clerk wonders how one man could possibly need this amount of personal lubricant and beef jerky, I'm never seriously considering that there was actually a three-legged female figure skater competing at Salt Lake City.

Or maybe there was. Strange things happen in Utah. I remember a Canadian colliding really hard with one of the Russians, but I can't imagine it left one person with three legs. In Utah, they definitely had that guy on welfare who had eighteen wives, although I think he's in jail now—presumably finding out what it's like to have eighteen husbands. Either way, we're paying for it.

I digress as usual, but it's all about too much information. I couldn't care less whether Phil wins or loses a bet. Well, actually I'd prefer him to win, but it's his own business. He has been the first to admit he's been too free with personal info, but the media has been so eager to cast him as the guy who has won everything except for that which he really wants.

I dunno about any of you, but it looks to me like he has a bunch of things that most people would really want. Let's see, a beautiful wife and two beautiful daughters, all of whom love him. That would do for a start, and never mind the material stuff, of which he obviously has an ample sufficiency. Dear God, I can hear it already: "Can't skirt the issue...majors are the only things that matter at this stage...never be a complete player...don't run with those scissors, you'll put your eye out, blah, blah, blah..." I mean, can't we think of anything else to ask him? How about this:

Fat course reporter looking into hand-held camera: "Thank you, Kenny. This is Desmond Bulgeflirter, down behind the eighteenth green with an obviously disappointed Dick Trickelson." (Turns to player, who looks less than happy to be there.) "Dick, yet again it looked like you'd captured that elusive first major, until that bastard Ed Fiori holed a 3-iron on seventeen and then, wouldn't you know it, he gets it up and down off the back of Miller Barber's head for par at the last. I mean, what are the odds?"

Trickelson: "I called my guy in Vegas on that one before the round, Des, and believe me, he gave me a hell of a price. I wish I'd have taken it now, but having said that, at the last I really thought the guy was dead."

Reporter: "Who, Miller Barber?"

Trickelson: "No, Ed Fiori."

Reporter: "Well, it occurs to this announcer that you may have heard this question before, but how does it feel to be the best player in the world who's never won a major?"

Trickelson (now glaring murderously): "I'm sorry, can you repeat the question?"

Reporter (after short, thoughtful pause): "No, I think that was the last one of those I had in me. How about this, though: In your opinion, who is the worst player in the world ever to have won a major?"

Trickelson (with astonished look): "Whoa! It's a while since I got asked that one!" (Scratches his chin thoughtfully.) "Hmmm...I suppose that would have to be Old Tom Morris."

Reporter: "But surely a comparison there is a little tenuous. I mean, if Tom Morris had access to the kind of equipment you're playing with today—."

Trickelson, interrupting: "He would have sucked, Des, largely because he was right-handed."

Reporter: "Dick, I know you want to get back to your family or maybe go and kick the crap out of Colin Montgomerie's dog, but is there any chance you could give us an idea of who you think'll be in the Final Four?"

Trickelson: "Des, if I were you, I'd bet the farm on Ball State, Grambling, Texas A&M, and the Harlem Globetrotters."

Call me old-fashioned, but I think Phil Mickelson is a much better player than a lot of people, some of whom have won more than one major championship. I also think he will win one. Occasionally, because of the missing hardware, I'll read that someone doubts the strength of his character. "He's too soft," or, "Look, his shoulders have slumped."

Pssst! Hey, Einstein! Let me whisper this in your ear: HIS SHOULDERS WERE THAT SHAPE WHEN HE GOT OUT OF BED THIS MORNING!

Then some pencil-squeezer who regularly soils his trollies over four-footers for a quarter will scribble, "He doesn't have the killer instinct." Okay, so I'd have to agree with that, or he'd likely have killed me after walking off the last green at the Atlanta Athletic Club last August, after posting one of the greatest four-round totals in major championship history, and still getting the consolation prize.

He knew he was going to read more of the usual the next day, and dahling, I just know he was dying to talk to me. But to his eternal credit, he did not act at all inconsolable. In fact, in a dignified and courageous manner, he gave quite the opposite impression. It just goes to show you he can act, too.

I got through my entire career as a player by figuring out early that if I aimed low enough, both figuratively and literally, occasionally I would do something of which I was proud. I think that every Tour player is the best player either never or ever to have done something. I never won a major championship, but I remain convinced I am the best player ever to have vomited on an opponent in a Ryder Cup. You won't read that in the history of the game, because it's like

Phil's gambling and Monica's dress. That is to say, it should have been nobody else's business.

Okay, enough already. I can't take the constant pleading. It was Lanny Wadkins, Kiawah Island, Sunday night, parking lot, gray slacks, and he was begging for it. Now for God's sake, let me be. My career's in ruins already.

As for Phil, I think he's the best player ever to have won a wager.

Survivor

It's hard to say how we all got here. I mean, who knows how the ship went down? Like the wreck of the *Edmund Fitzgerald*, "we might have capsized, we might have split up, we might have broke deep and took water." But somehow, the golf crew of the *S.S. CBS* ended up together on PGA Tour island, a bunch of misfits, tossed together by the winds of fate.

We're three weeks from rescue now, with the NEC Invitational at Firestone in sight, but the experiment has taken its toll. At the weekly tribal council, Venturi, the barnacle-encrusted old sea dog who is chief of "Hybalzi," the tree-house tribe, keeps voting himself off the island, but no one will let him leave. The Reverend Clampett, our spiritual leader, put the wind up all of us the other day by brewing up a batch of what he called "homemade lemonade." He had that strange "there's nobody home" look about him, and of course there were no takers, in case it was one of those cult mass-suicide deals, like Jonestown. Hey, we're all a little paranoid.

Austin Oosterhuis, the international man of mystery, is keeping us on our toes as usual, by renting tiny cars, showing up for work early, and doing all kinds of research. "That is my bag, baby!" It's disgusting, and hopefully, it'll never catch on. Speaking of disgusting, Bill Macatee goes missing for weeks, and then shows up in Armani pants and a $500 bowling shirt like the older woman's Ricky Martin he is. All coconuts and beach rumba, but he does improve the view periodically.

Meanwhile, "Dragnadzi," the nomadic tribe of Kostis and Feherty, continue to prepare for the merge at the PGA Championship. When the tribes come together, we will be joined by Cap'n "Jules" Verne Lundquist, and Rear Admiral Sir "Moby" Dick Enberg, who recently jumped ship from an NBC dredger. Kostis is acting shirty, and I'm convinced he has a goat tied up somewhere, although he refuses to share its whereabouts with me. He vanishes from the compound in the middle of the night, and I'm pretty sure I hear bleating now and then. Everyone is trying to get into a favorable bargaining position, because up until now, Jim Nantz has been the only one able to hold his breath long enough to hunt underwater and put food on the table. He's also the one we hide behind when the weather turns bad, and while the rest of us are definitely getting out of here shortly, with football coming up, Jimmy looks like he might be marooned here forever.

But the one that I really worry about is McCord, who is losing his marbles. I know that may not sound like I'm going out on a limb here, but I think the man is trying to do too much. After he started spending lot of time on his own out on the rocks, talking to a mollusk he claimed was the reincarnation of Howard Cosell, he was given special dispensation to leave the island to play golf, and since the Masters (a week during which he was not particularly busy), he has had the same clothes in his suitcase for twenty weeks in a row. Just the other day he showed up for work topless, and it was apparent that he has been working on a tattoo of the seventeenth at St. Andrews. His left nipple is the Road Hole bunker. I wouldn't mind so much, but every time he sits down, it becomes a par-3. His eventual aim is to have the front nine on his chest, and the back nine on his back. He started to tell everyone about the Valley of Sin, but thankfully, he was shouted down. Even by his standards, this is unusual behavior.

I'm starting to feel like the most normal person on our crew, and I'm on medication. But I still think I have a great chance of winning the big prize. That is, as long as they don't find out I've been talking behind their backs. For God's sake, bring on football.

Climbing Down from the Tower

There's comfort in familiarity, someone once said, and if that's true, we at CBS are in for a period of squirming around on the sofa. After thirty-two years of continuity in the lead analyst department, it seems we will be forced into finding a replacement for Ken Venturi, who is making noises about hanging up his headset, possibly as early as the end of this season.

He's been threatening to do it since I showed up (a coincidence, I'm sure), but this year, with his commitment as captain of the U.S. Presidents Cup team consuming so much of his time, he appears to be serious.

There are a lot of people out there who would like the job, but precious few who actually qualify, and most of those are still involved in the irritating business of trying to persuade the pellet into the pot, so to speak. Like, they're playing, you know?

It's hard to persuade a man to quit playing golf at the peak of his powers, and getting harder now that the Senior Tour is making millionaires out of dunderheads like McCord. Kenny, of course, was forced into television by a serious finger injury, but these days, hardly anyone gives their playing partners the finger with anything like the passionate sincerity that he still possesses, so the chances of us getting that lucky again are remote indeed. Given the urgency of our situation, I'm all for going out there and puttin' the hurt on someone myself.

But on whom? We need to find, in my opinion, someone who has won a major, isn't afraid of giving an opinion, has the respect of the players, and isn't worried if some people think he's a jerk. Curtis Strange is the only other lead analyst who scores in all four categories, and dammit, he's working for ABC! I'd do the job myself, but I'm only one-for-four.

In my capacity as network nuisance, I have been conducting unauthorized interviews with prospective candidates for a while. I have narrowed it down to a short list of four front-runners: John Elway, Wayne Gretzky, Michael Jordan, and a small basset hound named Desmond, which has since been ruled out after it urinated on Nantz's left leg. With all the electrical equipment on the eighteenth tower, CBS cannot risk a short-circuit that would leave Nantz looking like Don King.

The problem is, Kenny is hard to replace, to say the least. In the few paragraphs that follow I am going to write something of an obituary for him, even though I'm pretty sure he's not dead yet. It's just that I'd like him to know how I and many others feel about him while he's still around. I love him. Of course, you know this means the old goat is going to survive me, don't you?

Working with Kenny is fun, but the real perks come after the show is over. You never know who is going to show up. Old cops in Chicago, old singers and actors in L.A., old stories everywhere.

I'm forty-one, and yet when I'm in Kenny's company, I frequently find myself, like some sleepy little boy, asking him to tell me a story. But instead of the Freddie the Fox and Peter Rabbit stories my dad used to tell me, these tales are in black and white, of baggy-trousered men with leather grips and jerky putting strokes, from the days when cigarettes were good for you.

I never tire of hearing about Hogan and Snead, and Mangrum and Sarazen, the drinking and the card games, and the driving across America with one pair of shoes in the trunk of a car that has its only wooden bits on the outside. With tales of gamesmanship on the course, and fair play, too, Kenny can bring you so close to the action, you can smell linseed oil and Gallaher's Blues, and hear Sinatra crackling on a bad AM radio.

If you get lucky, after a couple of Crown Royals, he might seize you by the knee, and, with sparkling blue eyes and an evil grin, tell you about a round of golf he played with friends in Phoenix back in the 1950s. Kenny has more hair now than he did then.

In a hangover fog, with a couple of swift ones to straighten them up some, they teed off: Kenny, Bob Goldwater, Phil Harris, and Bill Worthing. On the first green a dog runs between Bob's ball and the hole just before he takes the putter back. Unfazed, he rolls the ball up to the edge of the hole. His playing partners are amazed at his concentration. Kenny watches the dog scamper down the fairway, and turns to Bob and asks, "My God, didn't you see that dog?"

Bob looks at Kenny and says, "Was that a real dog?"

One of my favorite Kenny stories is of Phil Harris and his first telecast at the old Crosby. He was up in the eighteenth tower at Pebble Beach, sitting with Kenny and Pat Summerall, whom producer Frank Chirkinian had framed on camera, with Phil off camera to Kenny's right. Phil was not yet accustomed to the subtleties of working in the booth, as the viewers found out when a hand appeared in the shot, tapping on Kenny's shoulder, followed by a violently stage-whispered, "Kenny, I'll be back in a moment, I've got to take a leak."

Mind you, at least Phil had the decency to leave the tower to perform his ablutions, as at least one other announcer who used to work for us occasionally did not.

Kenny was an infantry sergeant who served in Korea, and during the Cold War on the Russian border. He is a loner who chooses his friends carefully and keeps them for life. He is fiercely loyal, and at times, disturbingly honest. It's safe to say that he does not suffer fools gladly, even though I must say he has been remarkably patient with me.

He is the longest-serving lead analyst in any sport, on any network, and when he retires, we are in deep doody. I hope we can have the old silver fox back for the Masters and the PGA Championship, both of which would be unimaginable without him. At Augusta in particular, he continually astounds me by reading every putt correctly. I played the Masters once and have been involved with three telecasts, but even I can tell you that this is harder than reading a Russian newspaper in a darkroom. I only have the fifteenth green to worry about, and I'll get that wrong every now and then...and again.

They say you don't know what you've got till it's gone. Well, the American golfing public will find out when Kenny goes. I know I will miss him dearly. Like Summerall once said when he was asked by a journalist if he would miss Sundays with Tom Brookshire, "I'll miss him even more on Saturday nights!"

Once, at the Ameritech Seniors near Chicago, Kenny was sitting in the clubhouse dining room with Tommy Bolt when Billy Casper happened by.

"Hey, Kenny, how come you're not still out here playing against us?" Casper wanted to know.

"I'm a broadcaster now," Kenny replied. He is lean and hard, strong as a whip. Casper is not.

"How do you keep yourself in shape, if you don't play?" Casper yelled back. Kenny stabbed a crooked finger at the spherical superstar, and announced, "I have a picture of you on my refrigerator," leaving Bolt laughing so hard he fell out of his chair, and leaving Venturi, as always, one up.

A Salute to Kenny

This past weekend featured the departure from the CBS airwaves of Ken the Great. This season I've attended about a dozen farewell dinners thrown in his honor and learned a bunch of things about him I never knew.

Also, I've noticed over the last few years that Kenny Venturi is tight with only a few close friends, but recently, for some reason, he has been surrounded by thousands of idiots who appear to be tight with him. Damn, but that man knows a lot of people! I did a little math in my head, and if the seven degrees of separation thing is even close to correct, then the only person on the planet that Kenny hasn't influenced is an eighty-seven-year-old one-legged midget Samoan man with bad teeth who now lives with the former Roman Catholic Bishop of Cheltenham, England, who is now a female wrestler. Kenny was never into wrestling.

Kenny is moving from Marco Island, Florida, to Palm Springs, California, or so the papers say. I think he bought the place in the desert just so he has somewhere to hang all the signed memorabilia he has received from people like Jack Nicklaus last week and Byron Nelson a couple of weeks ago. Not to mention stuff from Frank Sinatra, Dean Martin, and Joey Bishop, and every other rat in the pack.

Bishop always called Kenny "Vinny," and Kenny tells a story about the day after the 1964 U.S. Open, when he walked into one of the very dangerous Italian restaurants he used to frequent in New York City, to join "da boyz." Bishop held Kenny's face in both hands and said, "Vinny, we saw ya staggerin' off da last green yesterday after yuh had won da U.S. Open and collapsin' inta a heap and bein' helped to yah feet an' collapsin' again an' me an' da boys just wanted tuh saytayah dat it wuz da greatest act dat we evuh saw!"

You should hear Kenny tell dat one. Or the one about how he got the job thirty-five years ago. Dr. Cary Middlecoff had the seat at the time but CBS had offered the position to Kenny, who could no longer compete because of his hands. Kenny told them that he didn't want anything that belonged to someone else and that he wouldn't take the job unless the good doctor gave it to him.

He called Dr. Middlecoff in his room at the Akron Towers hotel, asked to see him, and the two men sat down over a martini. Or seven. Dr. Middlecoff apparently didn't like the way the affair had been handled, but saw instantly in Kenny someone with a sense of honor and decency, and so he shook his hand, and passed on the torch.

Funny enough a similar thing happened just a few months ago, when Lanny Wadkins was offered the seat. Lanny only took the position because Kenny wanted to go. This past weekend, Venturi leaves on his own terms, and yes, mistakes, he's made a few, but he most definitely did it his way. Joni Mitchell added that "you don't know what you've got till it's gone."

But just wait till you hear Wadkins when we get him lit up!

Next Question, Please

I've been doing a lot of speaking recently, some of which, unlike my writing, actually makes sense. You know the sort of thing. Some big corporation wants to entertain its clients on the golf course and then at a dinner afterward, so they hire the services of some big-time Tour player or announcer.

Of course, these people are expensive and hard to get, so often they end up with me instead. Call me old-fashioned, but I really enjoy myself at these affairs, probably because I like yelling at people, drinking heavily, eating too much, and getting paid for it.

Now, people are naturally curious, but they are also a little predictable, in that they frequently ask the same questions. The two most popular inquiries are: What is it like to work with Gary McCord (who was invariably their first choice for the evening anyway), and what's my favorite golf course? So for your enlightenment, I thought I'd answer both.

The first is easier so I'll start with McCord. You don't know the half of it, I can assure you. The man is a menace to society. To think that millions of law-abiding Americans put their trust in such a man and even consider for an instant that what he says might be true. We are talking about a social deviant who has been known on occasion to draw up —before a telecast, mind you —a list of six appalling words, with full intent of getting them all on air. There is no adjective too awful or verb too vile for his evil mind and, frankly, his treatment of the Queen's English is sometimes more than I can stand.

Words like "bulbous" and "putrid" are bad enough when used within context, but when he announces that he is going to try to get the words "crevice" and "crusty" into the same sentence, it's enough to drain my double-A's and make my antenna droop. But even this pales into insignificance compared to his worst word-strangling, which comes in what we call our "hole openings." (Don't laugh, that's actually what we call them.) You know, when a tower announcer, at the top of the show, describes his hole for you. (I'm sorry, but there is no way to write that without it sounding very rude.) McCord will invariably do something like this:

"Hi, I'm Gary McCord [as if we didn't recognize him], and today I'll be giving you my expert opinion on the sixteenth hole, a cantankerous dogleg left, blah blah...."

Wait a minute. I'm thinking "cantankerous" is an adjective, used to describe an animate object of some kind, not a golf hole, which just sort of sits there and waits to be played. You try telling that to Old Handlebars, though, and you'll receive a dissertation on the word's Latin origin, which, although completely fictitious, will seem at the time entirely convincing.

Even Bobby Clampett, who should know better, gets sucked in. Earlier this year, he described the fifteenth at Harbour Town as a "Long John Silver par-five." Presumably this means it's a partially blind hole with a wooden dogleg and a parrot behind the green.

At the Masters this year, the Reverend Bob was commenting on Greg Norman's poor scoring on the par-fives when he said, "Normanly, Greg abolishes the par-fives." Whoa, I thought, no wonder he's won more money than anyone else! Taking potshots at Bobby is not as much fun because, unlike McCord, he refuses to fire back.

Right. Where was I? Oh yes, McCord, the silly git. There also is the matter of his clothing. The other day, he came mincing into the TV compound wearing a pair of shoes, the likes of which I had never before seen. It is no small mystery to me that he is beaten up so seldom, for these were a pair of, how shall I say, not brothel sneakers or brothel creepers, but brothel cruisers, I believe would be the best description.

They forced the eye northward to discover the face of the lunatic that might have the courage to wear them. A smiling face that was. The sort of smile that said, "My life is perfect, how's yours, shorty?" I looked at them for about ten seconds, with a sort of a mule-staring-at-a-new-gate denial, and said, "What the hell have you got on the end of your legs?"

"Those," he answered, "are a pair of genuine, bona fide Norwegian halibut stalkers, and don't laugh, they probably cost more than your car!" I was thinking, with soles that thick, they probably get better mileage, too.

Add to this ghastly footwear some kind of ridiculous hat, along with the mirrored sunglasses, the mustache, and a Tommy Bahama shirt hung out over a pair of muy peligroso pants, very dangerous trousers indeed. He frequently looks like a demented South American dictator—Generalísimo Atrocity Garcia—pacing back and forth in his tower, gesticulating wildly as he announces himself to the threshold of pain and back down again.

Another of his favorite tricks is to ask me to read some bizarre breaking putt on the very green that he has been sitting behind for hours, but I have just reached. He always picks a putt that I haven't had a chance to look at—for fear of putting some player's nose out of joint—generally teeing me up like a Strata with, "I know you've been studying this one, Fairway Feherty, so why don't you bring our viewers up to date." Of course I'm forced into having a stab at it from fifty yards, and when I shank the call, he about wets his Depends with mirth.

They say what goes around comes around, and I have a cunning plan. Now that His Evilness is a Senior Tour player, he is at the mercy of us announcers once more, and he has made the fatal error of asking yours truly to caddie for him this month in Dallas. It could be the end of his second playing career.

The humiliation he suffered at the Ameritech Senior, which was on our CBS air in July, will seem insignificant by comparison. By the time I've finished with him, he'll be, as Rowan Atkinson (aka Mr. Bean) once said, "Like a blind man in a dark room looking for a black cat that isn't there."

If he gets anywhere near contention, which he probably will, I intend to feign heart failure and flop around like a trout on his putting line. Of course, he will chip over me, but there are any number of ways for a caddie to bring down his player, and I intend to invent a few new ones.

Okay, that about covers the first question, and now that I come to think of it, I've forgotten the second one. Oh well, maybe I'll see you at dinner sometime.

An Average Week . . . Not!

Firstly, let me say this....I am not whining about my job. However, occasionally even I, despite having the easiest job in the universe, can have a rough week. The Buick Classic was a tough task for player and broadcaster alike due to several frog-strangling downpours, a sky that spent most of the week hovering six inches off the ground, and the occasional cosmic crackle, which always makes yours truly decidedly skittish. But hey, even that was okay. The week before was really hard work. Here's my diary.

SUNDAY NIGHT: Fly to Seattle for CBS media day at Sahalee, site of the 1998 PGA Championship.

MONDAY: Played eighteen holes, felt like I was in an episode of *Land of the Giants*. Never seen bigger trees closer together. The snakes slither in single file here. Suffered through a press conference, did six stand-ups with local TV stations. Took a ferry to some island and stayed overnight with idiot friend. Drank too much.

TUESDAY: Got up this morning at sparrow's fart for ridiculously early flight to Toronto. Hung over, flight bumpy. A bad combo. Man sitting next to me asks if I have a weak stomach. I show him I can throw it farther than most. Canadian immigration official decides to interrogate me as to why I am staying only one day. I offer to stay longer if she will only let me go. In the background, I hear the snap of a latex glove.

WEDNESDAY: Wake up feeling much better. Ready for all-day affair with Andersen Consulting. Clinic in the morning goes swimmingly, then they all play golf and I hit one shot with each group. Have cocktails, dinner, etc., and then I speak for about thirty minutes. Everybody laughs at me. I think this is a good thing. Limo takes me back to airport hotel, where I set alarm for 4:45 a.m. and head downstairs for bar and hockey game.

THURSDAY: Alarm goes off at 4:45 a.m. This doesn't seem fair. I don't feel very well. Think I got a bad slice of lemon last night. Anyway, get packed and check ticket. Notice that flight to New York doesn't leave until 8:30. Why the hell am I up so early? Lie down again for a wee doze. Wake up three hours later, make panic-stricken dash for next available flight and arrive at Mt. Kisco, N.Y., just in time for charity day. Do clinic in hungover stupor. Everybody laughs at me. Not sure if this is a good thing. Sleep three hours in the afternoon, come back to speak at dinner. Everybody laughs at me and this time I don't care. Feeling better, so I have a couple of adult beverages. Order cab for five o'clock to La Guardia. Doesn't seem fair again.

FRIDAY: Shuttle to Washington Dulles, get to TPC at Avenel in time for Kemper Open rehearsal. Back on CBS schedule now. Breathe large sigh as I see that we don't go on the air until 4 p.m. tomorrow. Set alarm for 12 noon. That seems fair.

Out of My Element

Gary McCord and I had an enlightening experience at last year's Sprint International at Castle Pines. We were the only two announcers available to work the two-hour ESPN show on Thursday, which was a total rainout.

Two hours in a Colorado summer thunderstorm in a studio with McCord and Feherty. It's not what you think. We were like those two old guys on the balcony in *The Muppets Show*, except we weren't funny.

About five minutes into the show, I wanted my mommy. People kept shining hot bright lights in my face and pointing cameras at me. Worse than that, they wanted me to say Jim Nantz-like things in a comforting Jim Nantz-like way.

The whole debacle gave me a clearer understanding of why CBS pays Nantz all those coconuts—and just how easy my job is by comparison.

I have the best job in the world. The hardest part about it is convincing my employers that no one else can do it. I spend a lot of time striding importantly around the TV compound, carrying a briefcase that holds all my important stuff.

I'll go through it now and tell you what's inside. Let me see, there's several fragments of the column you are reading at this moment, a packet of Skittles (some of which have escaped into the crevices), two highlighter pens, sunscreen, a CD of Puccini's *Turandot*, and a copy of *Mad Magazine* with a picture of Scott Hoch on the cover.

Not a lot of people know this, but I asked him and he confirmed it. I think it was taken in sixth grade. And, yes, he's a lot funnier than you might think.

Anyway, I digress, as usual. The fact of the matter is, any idiot could do my job, even the idiot that edits my column, but don't dare tell him that. I don't have to research anything, as all I do is describe what I see. How do you research something that hasn't happened yet?

If you know the answer to this question, please don't tell me. The other guys have to download all kinds of information into laptops—you know, bios, facts and figures, names of players' wives, children, and dogs, etc.

What a nightmare. When people ask me if eventually I want to work in a tower (as if there is some kind of promotion involved), I say, "Hell, no." That would mean I might actually have to do some work, something I've managed to avoid for almost forty years and I can assure you, I have no intention of starting now.

Peter Kostis, the evil genius, almost had a bright promotional idea the other day. He suggested that we should run a competition at each CBS venue, the prize being a chance to be an announcer for a day. We could hold auditions by the putting green and give the lucky winner a headset and a mike. He (or she) could hold hands with me all day inside the ropes.

I pointed out that the end result might be the loss of my job to some member of the public and quickly beat him into silence with my *Sports Illustrated* (swimsuit issue, of course).

In my job, I spend most of my time on the ground with players and caddies, so it's a bit of a culture shock for me when I get ordered upstairs into a tower. It's an entirely different discipline, in that I need some. In the tower, I have to do research and learn how to pronounce everyone's name correctly.

I still can't say Hjertstedt and every time I say Lickliter I risk getting fired. But I can read the blimp card like an old pro, and I can throw it to commercial, even when someone is yelling, "You moron!!!" in my left ear.

None of this is easy.

But what really bums me out is they let everyone play with the telestrator except me. I mean, in the name of all that's right and fair, they even let McCord doodle on the damn thing occasionally and, as much as I love him, I wouldn't trust him to sit the right way 'round on a toilet seat.

I've promised not to draw a mustache and glasses on anyone and still no one trusts me. I just don't understand it, but it's chapping my cheeks so badly that I'm going to break an unwritten rule of broadcasting and shamelessly rat out my fellow announcers.

You've read what the pros know that you don't. So, here's what the announcers know that you've always suspected.

They have absolutely no idea what they are drawing when they use the telestrator to break down a player's swing. He can hit it one hundred yards to the right of the fairway with a swing that looks exactly the same as the one that propels the pellet down the middle.

It's only the body language after the shot that gives us a clue where the ball has gone. If, after a swing, a player runs off the right edge of the tee and body slams an elderly lady in the gallery in order to see his ball land, it's a fair bet he's hooked it.

If he leans to the left on his follow-through, the ball has gone right. If he puts his hand in his right pocket and lifts his left heel, he's adjusting his underwear.

Now that, unlike the swing itself, is worth telestrating.

No, I'll be happy sneaking through the shrubs for the next thirty years, just as Rossie has done, the wiley old coot. He's got it dead right even though, just like me, he gets it dead wrong on occasion.

What people tend to forget is that even current Tour players read putts wrong and hit the wrong shot a lot of the time. What makes them think that we ex-players should be any different?

In Istanbul, the Author Calls It Quits

Istanbul airport is a strange place. Having seen the movie *Midnight Express*, I swore I'd never go near Turkey; but somehow my partner and I got involved in building one of the first eighteen hole layouts in the country, on the Mediterranean coast near Antalya. It turned out to be a beautiful place, not at all like the movie, but I had never been anywhere where so little was known about golf.

A customs officer stopped me and asked what was in the big black bag. "Golf clubs," I said, to which he replied, "Yes, but what are they for?"

"Now there's a point," I thought, and I started to explain what they were and how the game is played.

"You see, you take one of the big ones," I said, pulling out the driver as his pal reached nervously toward his handgun, "and put one of these little balls up on a piece of wood stuck in the ground. Then you hit it through the air onto some short grass and go find it." He nodded approvingly, stroking his chin.

"Then you take one of these irons, and hit the ball onto an area of even shorter grass, where you try to hit it into a hole in the ground with one of these, which is called a putter!" I announced triumphantly.

"Yes, yes," he waved dismissively, "but why?"

He got me on that one. I had no alternative but to admit that it was my job. He took off his mirrored sunglasses and said something in Turkish to his colleague, who responded by shooting coffee out of his nose, almost collapsing in hysterics. The man looked at me as if to say, "You poor, unfortunate bastard," and waved me on.

Walking toward the sliding doors, I clicked my heels twice to see if I was still in Kansas.

It occurred to me that golf probably made as much sense to him

as underwater nose-billiards would to me, and I think it was probably there, in the only international airport I've ever been in where
you could still buy a live chicken, that I thought about "why" for the
first time. That question turned into a signpost at the crossroads of
my career, and I've been hurtling toward journalism or something
similar ever since.

If it's anything like golf, it'll take me twenty years to find the brake.

Tiger's Race Is the Human Race

On a recent Sunday, in our golf telecast compound tucked deep
in the woods, a telephone rang. "Why are you showing so much
of the black kid?" asked an irate viewer. "Aren't there any white
folks playing?" He was politely told that his television was equipped
with an on/off switch specifically designed for his problem, and he
was welcome to join the other three people in America who
weren't watching.

I was in a green-side tower at the time trying to announce a
formula one car in a race of go-carts, but had I taken the call, I
would like to have added that his TV was also equipped with what
I would call a bigot switch, otherwise known as the brightness
control. "It can turn Danny Glover into Mel Gibson or Madonna
into Whitney Houston, sir, depending on your personal preference,
and what the hell, if you're into MTV, use the color knob as well,
and you can even make yourself a Japanese Michael Jackson."

You see, I'm well used to dealing with bigotry and hatred. I
grew up with it in Northern Ireland, where, centuries before the
red-white problem here that we white folks solved by extinguishing
one of the most earth-conscious civilizations ever to have existed,

in order to make room for a black-white problem, the Irish were allowing ourselves to be labeled as the stupidest race on the face of the planet.

I can't put my finger on the exact date, or my thumb on the precise name, but one of these apparently worthless, incredibly stupid bog-trotters (no doubt an ancient relative of mine) accidentally stumbled upon a way to gain the respect of those who were taunting him, and in so doing, started to respect himself. They were laughing at him, so he laughed with them. (It's a mind-blower, isn't it?)

Better than that, it was funny, and eventually the funniest exponents of the most ancient joke of all, the Irish joke (okay, okay, so the Jews did it first, give me a break, I'm trying to make a point here), turned out to be the Irish themselves, in the process gaining not only the respect but the admiration of the rest of the world, no less.

Hell, I think I'm a genius!

Of course, the reason we gained the moronic reputation in the first place still manifests itself in the province I love so much. We have more than our fair share of moronic behavior. Every July 12 a group of fathers take their sons by the hand and pass on the hatred by marching with the bands through the "enemy" territory, in glorious celebration of meaningless conflict some three centuries old, in which King William (the vile Protestant) defeated King James (the vile Roman Catholic) in the Battle of the Boyne, a victory that ensured that the monarchy would remain Protestant. Whoop-de-doo.

If old Jimmy boy had prevailed, the only meaningful difference to modern-day British and Irish Society would be that the Archbishop of Canterbury (the head of the Church of England) would now wear red socks and an even sillier hat.

The Irish are a classic example of why history should not be taught in schools. Something that happened three hundred years ago or a million years ago should not dictate how you feel about someone who lives across the street from you today.

It doesn't take a genius to figure this out, but unfortunately it takes only a tiny misguided percentage to screw it up for everyone else. People of all races have the right to dignity, and I also want to be judged by the content of my character, which will hopefully, at least in part, be judged, if not by the color, then by the thickness of my skin.

I think my parents did a pretty good job of bringing me up, and I'm just as proud of them as Tiger is of his, and I can't help but think that the beautiful pale-brown skin of the Masters champion might just be a little thicker than his public relations people would have us believe.

I also think his old man, much mocked and criticized for his predictions of global greatness for his son, may be a lot wiser than many had first thought.

When Earl was asked by Oprah, "What race did you bring your son up to represent?" he replied, "The human race."

I think Tiger will be seldom wrong if he takes his dad's advice.

Of course, I could be mistaken. I mean, you know how stupid we Micks are!

Late Night Lunacy

Now that 2001 is upon us, get ready for all the Arthur C. Clarke retrospective stuff, and also for the new season of the critically disclaimed *Late Night Show*, featuring McCordless (the new digital version) and, well, me. The show, now in its third season, airs after Letterman on Thursday and Friday nights for the first five weeks of CBS golf, starting at the Sony Open in Hawaii. This year, Gary and I would really appreciate it if somebody, somewhere, actually watched.

In the last two years, very occasionally, someone has admitted to us they stayed up that late, but it always seems to be the same type of person. There's one in every village. You know the guy: overcoat in the summertime and shirtsleeves in the winter. A couple of teeth missing, a permanently constipated expression, and a small dog with some kind of a skin disease on a leash. McCord calls them "idiot savants." Yeah, and perverted insomniacs. Apparently, that's our demographic.

I know it's aired late, but to be so totally ignored is extremely discouraging for two fully grown announcers, who willingly subject themselves to the kind of idiocy and humiliation that only can be aired after midnight. For example, in one episode last season from the Warner Bros. Studios, I wore an apricot whalebone gown with matching sun hat and parasol, last worn by Barbara Stanwyck in *The Big Valley* in 1965. I thought I looked rather fetching, but who knew? McCord was ironclad in a suit of medieval armor, and needed his helmet altered so it didn't wad up his handlebars.

The whole thing just reeked of professionalism and attention to detail, as did the show from San Diego, in which, with the full cooperation of the California Highway Patrol, officers "Rock McCord" and "Dirk (Thrust) Feherty" were ultimately arrested and formally indicted on charges of "really bad acting," by none other than Cheryl Ladd of *Charlie's Angels*. We were taken downtown, thrown in the slammer, and molested by a 350-pound inmate of indeterminate gender, all in the name of a golf highlight show.

So Robert DeNiro put on forty pounds for his role in *Raging Bull*. Big friggin' deal. And while I'm on a roll, how many announcers have hijacked the MetLife blimp and thrown themselves out over Venice Beach, California, only to have been spotted later, stumbling out of the Viper Room in Los Angeles, chased by a couple of elderly women?

All right, Brookshire and Summerall, but that was a long time ago. The point is Gary and I are doing our best to carry on an old tradition. To its eternal credit, CBS has never been afraid to allow some announcers to look stupid so that others may appear intelligent. For Gary and me, this is a labor of love. In fact, greater love hath no announcer than he who lays down his career for the idiots he works with.

On the other side of the camera, we are equally blessed with production from Jim Rikhoff and Chris Svendsen, both of whom should be chained up somewhere, away from anything sharper than a bar of soap.

Of course, none of this would be possible, either, were it not for the men of the PGA Tour, and the nature of the game they play. Golfers are great people, and I think it's unlikely that these shows would get made in any other sport. At the end of last season, in the last of our highlight shows at the NEC Invitational, for the second time I hosted our CBS awards show, the Golden Ferrets. It's a golfing version of the Oscars and I think it's safe to say one of the least coveted awards in all of sport. But for the last two years, some of the best golfers in the world have taken their parts very seriously, each and every one of them, apparently willing to make themselves look almost as daft as I do.

Justin Leonard looked longingly at an over-stuffed Beanie Baby mounted on a wooden and brass plinth, and reminisced about how it felt to hold the Claret jug, and since that day, how he had longed for the moment in which he would "stroke the Ferret."

Nick Price, the owner of two PGAs and a British Open Championship, said he didn't want to go down in history as the best player never to win a Ferret, and Jose Maria Olazabal, a two-time Masters champion, told the world that as a little boy in San Sebastian, he always dreamed that one day he would hold the coveted Golden Ferret.

Ernie Els, a giant among us in more ways than one, was big enough to lovingly hug the Ferret, and say, "At last, I've won one! The Golden Ferret is mine!" Then I walked into the frame, snatched it from him, and marched off saying, "Sorry Ern, you were second!" Ernie just looked back at the camera, shaking his head. If you'd seen it, you'd love him more than you probably do now.

Then, of course, there was the winner of the Golden Ferret for the second year running: Tiger Woods. Those of you who have seen the commercials (and if you are one of those who haven't, please have the decency to fall over, because you are dead) know that he's pretty good at this sort of thing already.

McCord and I are taking full responsibility for his acting prowess, due to the fact that he frequently rehearses with us. This scene, however, he wasn't getting paid for. The presentation ceremony took place during a practice round, on the second green, with buddies Mark O'Meara and Notah Begay at hand. Tiger's acceptance speech was suitably heartfelt and movingly sincere, and as he held his trophy Ferret aloft and kissed it for the crowd, in the background Notah and Mark held their caps over their hearts.

I nearly wet myself laughing, as did everyone else except McCord, who is very old and is frequently ambushed by his bladder. He tries to avoid laughter, in case he wets somebody standing close by. If you're ever around him when anyone says something really funny, keep on your toes. Don't send me your dry cleaning bills; you have been warned.

At the end of the day, it's all about work and how much we enjoy it. Gary and I have unbelievable jobs, occupations that most people would sell their firstborn in-laws to have, and we are both aware of just how lucky we are. In truth, we would probably be unemployable in any other industry.

Often, we'll be sitting in some airport bar on a Sunday evening, making very loud small talk in the hope of being recognized, when some poor individual—who actually has to go to meetings and write reports and stuff—will turn an ear our way and realize who Gary is, at least. Sometimes he gets to sign an autograph, while I look the other way, tapping my foot and trying to appear nonchalant, as if it doesn't matter that this person doesn't know who I am.

McCord will then gloat, until the guy says, "Thanks, Mr. Fingers, you're the only one of the old Oakland A's I didn't have!" Hey, you have to have a recognizable face before somebody can mistake you for someone else. Gary's face, of course, is much more familiar than mine, and I'm glad to report considerably more punchable, although I think that has more to do with the shoes he wears than anything else. I'm fighting Kostis for custody of him as I write, and when I win, footwear is the first of his attire that will be tossed.

This is pathetic to read, I know: Two grown men pleading for recognition in the middle of the night. But I will tell you this: I am not doing this show again if nobody watches this year. Last year, I did a nude shower scene with Kostis. Normally, that's something that both he and I would try to avoid, but in the end it didn't matter. Nobody watched. Even McCord, who was in the scene, did it with his eyes closed, and insisted on wearing a full wet suit, "In case they splash me." He truly is the man who put the first four letters in the word, "analyst."

I played tonsil-hockey with a seven-hundred-pound sea lion at the San Diego Zoo, and it took me three weeks to lose the taste of rotting flounder. In between all of this, we actually did golf highlights each night, so listen up, you putterheads. We start at the Sony Open in Hawaii again this season and already I can feel a grass skirt and a pair of coconuts coming on. Gary and I will probably be the last two left on the island—the crotchety old goat, and the guy with the love handles and the hairy chest. Trust me, neither of us is making a million.

Starting Off on the Wrong Foot

Well, now that Week One of the CBS *Late Night Show* and the West Coast Swing is under our belt, it's off to Pebble Beach for McCord and me. After the best part of four months off, last week was something of a shock to the old system. Being on the air was a little nerve-wracking at first, but we soon got into the swing of things, as our merry band of idiots hit their stride.

For example, it took Clampett approximately forty seconds to kill his first word. I don't remember who he was talking about, but he described them entering what he called, "Unchartered Territory," which of course means, "Territory which has not yet been rented." This, combined with, "There's no quit in John Daly," established him as the early-season leader in the race for the coveted Wooden Microphone. He won't have it all his own way, mind you, as McCord too was in fine form, suggesting at one time that everything that sloped downhill toward Pinnacle Peak was an optical illusion.

As for me, I got the word *poop*, into my second sentence of the season. Not bad, even if it was followed by *deck*. It still counts.

Of course, we're hot on the heels of the football announcers, who are no slouches themselves when it comes to adding foot to mouth. This year, we have had a rash of Richard-related incidents, the best of which came just a couple of weeks ago at the Philly-Chicago game, when the venerable Dick Enberg threw it to sideline reporter Bonnie Bernstein, who had cornered Chicago coach Dick Jeron.

Bonnie said, "Thanks, Dick," then turned to look at the other Dick, did a double take to camera, and said, "Two Dicks, wow!"

Earlier, at the Army-Navy game, when a player trotted back onto the field after a particularly bone-crunching tackle moments before, Dan Dierdorf turned to Dick Enberg and said, "He doesn't even have a limp, Dick." All this means of course, is that the golf crew can say whatever it wants for the rest of the year. At least that's what I'm going with.

There was some golf last week, too. How about that little whippersnapper Ty Tryon? I was really hoping his first name was short for, "Tyrone," but alas, no. William Augustus is the lad's real handle, and his dad nicknamed him after Chevy Chase's character in *Caddyshack*. Tyrone Tryon would have made Clampett's head lock up completely.

Obviously, the boy didn't get off to the start he wanted, but he was pretty impressive all the same, and he's got a heck of a pit crew to keep him lubed and fueled too. I lost count of how many were in the entourage, but included were two swing coaches, an image consultant, a yoga person, the ubiquitous agent, and a physical conditioner. (There had to be an attorney in there somewhere, you just know it.) The only advice I'd offer would be to the image consultant. "Get rid of the rest of them, and then you could leave, too." At least the boy's father had the sense not to show up. I like him already.

James Joseph Waldorf had a decent week, too. On Sunday he wore his customary stay-back-my-head-might-explode ball cap, and a shirt with big pineapples, kabobs, fish, and tropical cocktails all over it. The last time I saw an article of clothing with that much food on it was after my three-year-old daughter had barfed on her pajamas in Hawaii.

Duffy's a good lad, though, even if he does get dressed by covering himself in wood glue and running headfirst into the closet. The unconfirmed rumor is that he got his nickname from his dad, because when he was really little he kept falling on his duff. Come to think of it so did I, but my dad never called me "Arsey."

I was lucky to get away with it, I suppose. Anyway, this year I am determined to take a leaf out of Billy Connolly's (my favorite comedian) new book, and if I haven't heard a decent rumor by 11 a.m., I'm going to start one. Duffy has his name sewn into his hat, and McCord has his sewn into his underwear will do for a start.

It's rumored also that big John Daly is going to have a banner year. This one I believe. In a couple of weeks he's taking McCord and me on a road trip in his new bus, which makes Frank Lickliter's Hummer look like the Barbie Jeep. He has forty-seven guitars in there, and McCord isn't allowed to play with any of them, so it'll be cool. I've always wanted to be a roadie on a West Coast Tour.

Chapter Five

A Confederacy of Idiots

Abjectively Objective

A ny professional athlete who attempts to jump from competition to commentary is liable to land gumshield-first into a number of problems, not the least of which is the ethical dilemma of what to say and how to act whenever one of his buddies appears on the screen in front of him.

It's even worse if that buddy is moonlighting from his day job, which is actually your job, too. You can see how it might get confusing. Thankfully, this doesn't happen to me very often, due to the fact that only one of my colleagues plays on a regular basis, that being McCord, and he couldn't putt his ball into a black hole. In space, that is.

That's a good thing, though, because if he could, he certainly wouldn't need to work in broadcasting, where, like me, he can suck and still get paid. Of course, there was the good Reverend Bobby Clampett at the U.S. Open at Pebble Beach a couple of years ago, but that was on NBC, and he exploded in the second round like a hot bottle of stout.

The Strange person who also scribbles around these parts played great earlier this year in Memphis, and it was interesting to see how the boys at ABC got after him. Gary Koch was NBC's whipping boy when he made the field at the U.S. Open this year, and his colleagues had some fun describing his action in the first two rounds.

But all the networks do golf differently, so what's a bewildered

CBS announcer to do? It's not possible to leave McCord alone when he's on our air. Most surely, the general public is entitled to an honest, informed, and unbiased description of the events that appear before them, but then again, a little demented entertainment wouldn't be such a bad thing, either.

My favorite athletes-turned-announcers are McCord, John McEnroe, Charles Barkley, and Dennis Miller, all of whom are more than a little sick and twisted, and rightfully proud of it. (I'm giving Miller the benefit of the athletic doubt here, and I couldn't give a rat's ass who gets upset about it. I figure he must have spent most of his formative years running away from people who wanted to beat the crap out of him, and in my mind that makes him a world class sprinter.)

Hey, these are sports, and hopefully a diversion from sometimes hellish reality. Anyone who reminds us of that is doing a good job. These are guys who will err on the side of buddy brutality rather than be accused of any kind of weenie favoritism. Which brings me to a confession.

We were broadcasting the SBC Senior Classic a few months ago, the only Senior Tour event that CBS covers, and we'd had a long layoff from being on the air. Most of us don't carry our brains around on a stick and have the sense to take a little time off before this, the final grueling six-week stretch of our television season.

But McCord, steaming plonker that he is, had chosen to spend his vacation chasing the pill on the aforementioned Grateful Nearly Dead Tour. McCord's been in so many hotel rooms this year that he has invented at least seventeen new uses for the Gideon Bible, none of which involve any actual reading. He tells me if you take one, slam it closed on the end of your nose and yank hard, it makes a dandy pair of nostril tweezers. Fortunately, most of us have no idea of the lonely road a man has to take in order to make such a discovery.

Anyway, after weeks of hitting the ball magnificently and missing every single putt he looked at, my poor, hapless friend managed to get himself tied for the lead after round one by a cruel twist of fate. As a consequence, he was featured prominently in our Saturday coverage. For the network, it seemed like a bonus, and given my relationship with McCord, I felt I should be able to turn the whole thing into a subhuman interest story, at least.

I set off from the compound with every intent to be a chigger in McCord's shorts. I knew that if the tables were turned, he would do the same, because that's what friends are for. But then, a strange thing happened to me. As I strode up behind his group, I found myself being overcome by guilt (which is a useless emotion if ever there was one, especially if you haven't done anything yet) and a curious feeling of affection for my colleague who had been up until that point the target of whizzing barbs from every corner of the TV compound.

Virtually everyone on the crew had a suggestion as to how I could either embarrass, vilify, or otherwise roast their colleague. Even the *Chicago Sun-Times* had as a headline that morning, "Loony on the Leaderboard!"

Oh, yes, I thought. He will be mine.

Covertly, I watched him play the par-5 eleventh hole at Kemper Lakes, where he dumped his second shot into the greenside pond, dropped under penalty, hit a beautiful sand wedge shot stiff, and tapped in for par. As he blundered toward the twelfth tee looking hopeless and forlorn, suddenly the bell rang and we were on the air.

With an angel on one shoulder and a trident-bearing little demon that looked remarkably like McCord on the other, I decided at that moment that I would do the whole show undercover like a stealth reporter, if you will, flying under enemy radar. As much fun as it would be to skewer him, the better part of me wanted to leave him alone in the ardent hope that he would play well and perhaps even win the tournament. Bless his elderly little cotton socks, I thought.

As it turned out, there was only one flaw in my plan. Apparently the only thing more sensitive than enemy radar is friendly radar. McCord's mustache antennae began to twitch, and by the time he had reached his tee shot, he had sniffed me out. Then, the damnedest thing happened, over which I had no control. There was I, out of the goodness of my heart, about to cut the old fart a break for a change, and the next thing I know he's in my face, torturing me.

While I'm in the middle of trying to say something sensible about Dana Quigley (who was the leader of the damn tournament), McCord is poking me in the ribs and making flatulent sounds into my microphone! He tells me he's bored and needs somebody to talk to. Now my producer is yelling at me. In fact, he yelled at McCord, too, forgetting that for once the silly bastard wasn't wearing a headset.

About half an hour went by, and I tried yelling, but it had absolutely no effect on McCord, who by this time was taking a few seconds off to hit the occasional shot, then running into the woods after me. To the three or four innocent spectators, it must have looked like a cross between a golf tournament and a scene from _Deliverance_.

This lasted about two holes, during which he tossed a shot back to par. Then he went back to being borderline suicidal/insanely happy, which on a golf course is about normal for him. But by this time I was in shock, and although I'm not usually a highly strung announcer, I don't think anyone but the greenkeeper's dog could hear anything I was saying. Fortunately, no one noticed my absence. Either that, or nobody was watching.

In the end, revenge was mine, largely because we had about fifteen minutes of fill at the end of the show in which I was able to interview him, and accuse him of wilting under the glare of the television cameras, thus extracting some satisfaction from an otherwise traumatic experience.

The following day, during a rain delay which lasted the entire show (the course, like many of the Senior players, doesn't drain quite as well as it used to), Macatee and Oosterhuis cornered him on a sofa in the locker room and interviewed him half to death.

Served the swine right.

The Late Night Show, Take Two

Well, it's T-Minus two weeks and counting until the CBS golf season starts up, and once again the evil McCord and I will be doing late night shows on Thursday and Friday evenings for our first four weeks, starting in Phoenix.

Sadly, due to my partner's newfound success on the golf course, I fear we may have to take things considerably more seriously. No fart gags or blimp hijackings this year, now that I am working with one of the elder statesmen in golf.

Of course, if you believe that, you're probably a wrestling fan and reading this by accident. No, you'll be glad to hear that during the off-season his weirdness bought a new home in Scottsdale with a huge backyard, complete with a concrete half pipe, which he has been using to get himself in shape for our grueling shooting schedule.

Each morning, after being beaten with a copy of *Golf Magazine* by his lovely wife Diane, he smothers himself in Vaseline, skateboards naked for forty minutes, and after four large wicker and oat-bran muffins and a quart of prune juice for breakfast, it's off to Peter Kostis's house to use the bathroom for an hour or so. After that it's a brainstorming session with me and our *Late Night Show* producers, Jim "Don't Shout at Me" Rikhoff and Chris "I Don't Think You Can Say That" Svendsen.

So far we've come up with "Golf in the Year 2100," featuring Tiger Woods IV versus Davis Love VII in the final of the Lunar Matchplay Championship, where the Sea of Tranquility is a lateral, and McCord is still calling the action, as he was cryogenically frozen eighty years earlier. Another frozen, hairless cat. Ha, ha.

There will be a "Who wants to be a billionaire?" feature, hopefully with Leslie Neilsen, and, "A morning in the life of a Senior Tour superstar," where, with hidden cameras, we will follow McCord from the moment he opens his eyes until he has assembled himself into the vision of loveliness that we are used to. Historic, never-before-seen bathroom mirror footage of the mustache ritual, including the famous application of the Viagra powder to the tips, is what you can expect.

Hey, it's after Letterman, so we figure we can do whatever we like, 'cos you'll all be asleep anyway.

The Retiring Type

In the last while or so (which, in Irish terms, can be anywhere from a few minutes to about five hundred years), we've had our fair share of great sportsmen retire from the schoolboy pastimes they were lucky enough to have called their work.

We will not soon forget Wayne Gretzky, his gloveless hands raised, thanking the people of Edmonton, or John Elway and his emotional farewell in Denver. Michael Jordan, of course, left Chicagoans heartbroken.

In our own sport, first there was Arnie and then Jack on the Swilcan Bridge, waving farewell to their adoring public. Hard-bitten, cynical, and verbally flatulent as I am, even I couldn't watch either of them without welling up. I was astonished by my own ability to imagine how they must have felt, for in truth, I have absolutely no points of reference in my own career that allow me to feel even the slightest empathy. I don't even remember my own retirement. I just woke up one day and I was an announcer, although I do have a faint recollection of a fateful afternoon at the World Series in Akron, Ohio.

I was sitting in the bar at the Hilton, dressed in my Naugahyde shorts and coordinating purple Formica T-shirt, blending in with the décor as always. A creature in its natural habitat. Always the professional athlete, I was sipping an Absolut and Gatorade, when I was cornered by the then executive producer of CBS Sports, Rick Gentile, and coordinating producer of golf, Lance Barrow—neither of whom I knew from a bag of French fries. I immediately tried to look as heterosexual as possible. Lance, a member of the Fort Worth Diplomatic Corps, went straight for my most vulnerable vital organ: my wallet.

"Hey, we've noticed that your game sucks worse than a nine-dollar vacuum cleaner. Here's what you could be makin' if you worked for us." He held up a check. I had no idea what either of them did for a living, but I agreed to their terms immediately, hoping against hope it didn't involve rubber gloves, Shetland wool underwear, or anyone named Nigel. People hate me because I'm lucky.

The rest is history. No tearful farewells, no emotional speeches, I just deleted myself from competitive golf, and I was the only one that noticed that something had disappeared. But, like a bad bottle of Guinness, I came back noisier, with greater force, and considerably more noticeable than before.

One of the strange side effects that comes with being an announcer is that, even though you might have the IQ of a slice of pizza with really stupid toppings—like arugula and hearts of palm (in other words, "bits of wood")—people suddenly consider you to be an authority, even if you didn't stay in a Holiday Inn Express last night. Now, I'm even a writer, too, although you've probably noticed that if you are reading this. But I digress.

The reason that I set off on this particular tack, which has only re-occurred to me in the last few seconds, is I recently spotted someone who was allegedly playing his last competitive round on the PGA Tour, and if it wasn't for me, nobody might have noticed.

At the John Deere Classic, the majestic career of the great Charlie Rymer came to a fittingly moving close. After a glorious opening seventy-six, Charlie, one of the game's best-loved congenital idiots, happened to bump into yours truly in the lobby of the delightful Isle of Capri Hotel and Casino, in Davenport, Iowa. We greeted each other in our customary style.

"Hey, fat boy," I said. "Nice playin' today…Four under, huh?"

"Yeah, up yours," came the reply. "That's it, nobody can force me to do this anymore. I'm done."

It was the news I had been waiting to hear for a while. Charlie had had one foot on the Tour and the other in TV for too long, and his two chosen professions were now so far apart that his nuts had finally hit the deck. Sometimes you have to hit rock bottom before you can bounce.

The next day, I was up in my perch behind the sixteenth hole when Charlie blundered through, one-under for the day, but missing the cut by miles. He looked up at the tower, gave me the finger, threw a ball against the Plexiglas, and staggered off to the final two holes of his PGA Tour career. There were a couple of corn-fed bystanders who looked decidedly confused when I leaned over the edge and shouted, "I love you, Charlie!" and he blew me a kiss.

To me, it was a strange quirk of fate that Charlie had chosen the same day as Kathie Lee Gifford to pull the plug. Give or take a couple of hundred pounds, some makeup, and several enormous kidney stones, the two of them have a lot in common.

For a start, they both have multiple careers, talk about their kids a lot, and I think it's fair to assume that neither of them has slept with Frank Gifford recently. Also, they both have decided that they would be better off doing something else.

In Charlie's case, I think this is a great idea for both him and golf viewers, but lest we forget, here is a brief résumé of a career that for most of us will be difficult to remember. I mean forget…No, I was right the first time.

Here is his career capsule, some of it in his own words.

Height: Six-foot-four.

Weight: At thirteen years old, Charlie was six-foot-two and 240 pounds. He is now thirty-two years old and says he's taller.

Birthdate: December 18, 1967.

Birthplace: Cleveland, but not the one in Ohio.

Residence: Formerly Greene County, Georgia, where he was a prominent citizen and instrumental in the implementation of the area's landmark safe-sex legislation, which made it compulsory to mark the animals that kicked. He has now moved his triple-wide up the highway to Athens, Georgia.

Family: Wife, Carol, known in the area as "Saint Carol"; sons, Charlie, two, and James, four. Was introduced to golf by his grandparents, "to get him out of the house because he was eating the drapes."

College: Georgia Tech (chewing tobacco scholarship, 1991).

Turned pro: 1991.

Professional summary: 1992. Made cut at Chattanooga Classic.

It was at this point that I decided that perhaps it would be better to ask Charlie for his own personal top three career highlights. We were in the production trailer at the International, and Peter Kostis had come up with the bright idea of putting a heart rate monitor on Charlie for the telecast, to see what his pulse got up to after some of the climbs in the rarified atmosphere. He sat across from me, strapping it onto his wrist. It read 105 beats a minute, just while he was sitting on the sofa.

I asked him, "Give me your three greatest moments in golf."

Quick as a flash, he pointed a finger at me and said, "I tied for thirty-seventh in the '97 Buick at Westchester...Tiger was forty-second.

"Then there was that time I beat Davis Love by ten shots in one day."

There was a pause, as Charlie looked vacantly at the ceiling and stroked his chin. He looked back at me, and for a moment, I saw a massive ten-year-old, shirtless, barefoot, in dungarees and a straw hat, sucking on a grass stalk. His head is the size of a watermelon. He is a gentle, misfit giant, who has probably listened to people make fun of him all his life. In that instant, I realize why we are all so fond of him. Then he looked at me with a crooked frown, reached into his pants to adjust his underwear, and said, "I can't think of another one."

You see, in the world of male professional sports, there is a jock mentality, a locker room protocol, in which the esteem that a man is held in is measured in inverse proportion to the amount of insult he can absorb. Simply put, if you walk through a crowded locker room, whether you are a hockey player, a football player, or a golfer, the rules are the same: If everybody calls you an asshole, you are probably a great guy; if you walk through that locker room and nobody calls you anything, you are probably an asshole.

This makes Charlie Rymer one of the greatest people in our sport. His presence evokes the most creative abuse, which is absorbed with easy grace and returned with self-effacing humor. Underneath the big Deputy Dawg disguise lies a razor-sharp wit, and this—combined with the fact that he is actually a very fine player who has shot sixty-one three times—makes him a perfect candidate for TV. All he needed to do was stop playing.

As Jack Nicklaus was making his way down the eighteenth fairway at St. Andrews this year, Tiger Woods, the man who could be king, was on the first tee. Such an occurrence happens in a hundred years or so, maybe. When Charlie Rymer was trudging down the last at the TPC at Deere Run, there was no logical successor on the first tee there or anywhere else, for that matter. An individual like Charlie will be pretty hard to replace. He said to me after his round:

"Y'know, I'm not the smartest guy in the world, but I think I just figgered it out. It's really hard to play this Tour when yer an 11-handicap."

I don't think so. I think it just took him a little while to figure out what he does best. I just hope the fat gasbag doesn't get my job.

Cavemen at Hilton Head

No doubt you heard at some stage during the course of the Masters, the phrase "a tradition unlike any other." Well, once the Masters is over, traditionally, I first have my buttocks surgically unclenched at Augusta General, and then I head to Columbia, S.C., for the Hootie and the Blowfish "Monday after the Masters" pro-am, where I traditionally play like a man with a really bad hangover. Fortunately, no one cares, as this is a two-night/one-day event in support of local charities, in which the golf is the least important element. It's kind of relaxing. All kinds of athletes and celebs show up, plus musicians such as Edwin McCain, Sister Hazel, and Creed, who play golf during the day and music with Hootie and the Blowfish at night. It is the coolest event of its kind that I have ever played in, in one of the nicest cities I have ever visited, and it's a credit to the boys in the band that they care so much for their hometown.

Then, it's on to Hilton Head, where, traditionally every year, McCord, Kostis, and I share a house just about fifty yards from the sixteenth green, and even closer to the TV compound. This of course means that nobody goes anywhere all week, especially the vegetable McCord, who occasionally does a telecast in his night-dress, and then goes straight back to bed. On the downside, the house is also used as the dining area for the entire crew, who routinely rifle through our personal stuff, shortsheet our beds, and one of them always leaves a traditional floater in the bathroom. This kind of foul play invariably leads to more childish locker room behavior throughout the week, but on Saturday night, we put away our childish things, lock out the rabble, and settle down to watch a man's game—playoff hockey.

Every year, on the Saturday night of Hilton Head, three male announcers traditionally build themselves a small campfire in the middle of the lounge, paint a couple of bison on the wall, and then slap each other until a dominant male emerges, who instantly seizes custody of the remote control. Then we park ourselves in front of the box, armed with an appalling amount of red wine and pizza, to watch Neanderthals on skates hook, slash, board, trip, punch and talk dirty to each other all night. For me, it's the sport with the icing on top, and the last of the real "guy" sports.

All of us are expressly forbidden to express our masculinity whilst watching golf, so we jump at this once a year chance. Kostis, who is a disturbing Greek person from Maine, knows all the rules and most of the players. He regularly barks out obscure technical details, and has a nasty habit of telestrating on the screen with a Sharpie, while McCord, who is an escaped mental patient from southern California, just sits there, squeezing slices of pepperoni into a miniature puck. We found out last year that he can't see the real one, as he got so close to the screen that his mustache exploded in a burst of static electricity.

And me? I am a fat Irish person from Texas who prefers just to sit by the fire, burp loudly, and clip my toenails. Then I throw the clippings into the flames, and watch them writhe as they turn Halloween orange, blacken and die....naughty toenails.

Traditionally, none of our wives has ever come to Hilton Head. I can't imagine why.

Slip of the Lip

I'm in a slump. We're getting toward the end of the season and I am carrying my brain around on a stick. Everyone on the CBS crew is experiencing difficulties at this stage, even Bobby Clampett, who can no longer distinguish between Peter Kostis and myself. I find this particularly upsetting, as Kostis is a gnarly old Greek and I am a svelte young Irishman. I love Bobby dearly, but Peter and I neither look nor sound alike.

Before I go any further, I would like to take this opportunity to congratulate Bobby (the human laundry basket) on his incredibly cunning plan to capture the U.S. Open. Not a lot of people picked up on this, but the Reverend Bob ran his golfing machine at dead slow, at a grave risk to his own personal self. In fact, he seized up completely a couple of times, and had to be loosened with a surreptitious squirt of mineral oil in his left ear. Had the tournament been a fifteen-rounder, I'm pretty sure this evil ploy would have worked and put everyone, including Tiger, into a coma.

If this sounds like sour grapes, that's because it is. Before the qualifying, I hit him in the knee with a crowbar, but wouldn't you know, it just served to make his address position look a little more natural.

Anyhoo, we were working the Memorial and Clampett asked Kostis instead of me about Tiger's second shot at eleven. And, he asked me to read Justin Leonard's putt on the fifteenth green, even though I was five hundred yards away, back on the tee with Tiger. Kostis was with Justin, and did his best to impersonate me. That confused Bobby to the extent that someone had to be sent to the fifteenth tower with a blunt object to restart his mind. Meanwhile, Tiger marched on relentlessly toward victory, unaware that the soundtrack to his movie was being butchered by two idiots and a man who looks like a clone of Harpo Marx.

It's just that time of the year. Having said that, mind you, earlier in the season we were at Colonial, the site of perhaps Clampett's greatest verbal blunder a few years back: After watching a second shot hit the green and spin back violently, he blurted, "Good heavens, look at the jism on that one!"

The remark was totally innocent, indicating something of a sheltered past for the man who, due to his deeply religious beliefs, has been known as "The Reverend Jism" ever since.

Of course, this phenomenon is nothing new. Announcers have been making verbal blunders on the air for years. Sir Henry Cotton, one of the greatest players of all time, worked on the occasional telecast with Peter Alliss, and our editor in chief, Sir George Pooper, recently reminded me of a famous broadcast blunder during one such occasion. In a ladies' event many years ago, Sir Henry and Peter were watching a helicopter flyover of a short par-four on their monitor in the eighteenth tower, all the time thinking that the viewers were watching the same image.

"A pretty little hole," said Peter to Sir Henry, who replied, "Yes, but I can assure you, it was a good deal tighter in my day." Which of course would have been perfectly innocuous, had not the folks at home been treated to the sight of Marlene Floyd bending over to pick her ball out of the hole during the exchange. Oops!

Steve Melnyk once uttered at Augusta that "the wind is rushing from the players' rear," and once, as an announcer, Floyd was describing the awkward stance of another LPGA star and said that she was in real trouble because, "She has a huge bush between her legs!"

One of my favorite golf broadcasters was the great Henry Longhurst, who for years worked for the BBC with Alliss, his budding young assistant. Renowned for having a morning snifter or twelve before he got on the air, Henry was an economist when it came to words, but every one he used somehow seemed to fit the occasion perfectly.

On the seventy-second green of the 1970 British Open at St. Andrews, Doug Sanders had just missed his famous three-footer for the championship, when, after a perfect pause, Longhurst quietly uttered, "What a pity." No analysis, no post mortem, just, "What a pity," and the feeling that Henry knew all along that Nicklaus would be the champion.

Longhurst was also an extraordinary writer who was obviously in love with golf, and in the early days of televised golf he was largely responsible for educating the great unwashed on both sides of the Atlantic in the vagaries and subtle nuances of the game. In his later years, he was prone to letting his mind wander off, back to the days of thick flagsticks, slow greens, and stories from smoky clubhouse snugs.

Often, there would be golf going on in the background as he was reminiscing, but what he had to say was always more interesting, in a decidedly Wodehousian fashion. One of my favorite tales of old Henry took place at the Sumrie Better Ball championship at Bournemouth, in the south of England, back in the 1960s. The tournament was being led by the great English duo of Neil Coles and Bernard Hunt.

After a liquid lunch, Henry needed help to climb the steps to the eighteenth tower and seemed unsteady as he sat down. Someone asked him if he was going to be able to get through the broadcast, to which the great man shot back indignantly, "I shall be fine, as long as I don't have to say Hunt and Coles too often!"

Growing up in the British Isles, I was often enthralled by Longhurst, and of course, Peter Alliss, who is now himself the silver-tongued old devil. Peter is the elder statesman of British golf, and is thankfully carrying on Henry's grand old habit of reminiscing and ruminating, because, as some of you may have noticed, the action on the screen is not always riveting.

My first foray into television was the old Johnnie Walker World Championships in Jamaica a few years ago, and naturally, I was a little nervous. The leader, Loren Roberts, hit his tee shot on the first par-three on the back nine. It landed in the water just short of the green, but miraculously bounced out just short of the putting surface.

The camera did not pick up what I had just seen, so, under orders from producer Jack Graham, I scurried over to see if I could find the explanation for this bizarre bounce. In the edge of the hazard, I found a coconut bobbing gently up and down, which upon further examination, revealed the telltale dimple pattern of Loren's ball.

Feeling like Sherlock Holmes, I gleefully hit my talkback switch to tell Jack, who told me to find a minicam by the next tee, as he was going to give me the opportunity to explain what had happened to the viewers.

As I took up my position with the coconut in front of the camera, I was enveloped by the sudden realization that this was to be my first ever live on-camera report, which caused my mangoes to shoot immediately northwards, to take up residence on either side of my Adam's apple. There was a fruit salad stuck in my throat when they threw it to me, and by that time, all I was capable of doing was to wave the coconut in front of the camera and say, "I'm down here, holding Loren Roberts's bruised nut!"

This prompted a Homer Simpson style, "D'oh!" from Jack Graham, who then suggested in the nicest possible way that perhaps I should elaborate, for the benefit of those viewers who had every right to believe that I had just escaped from the Montego Bay Institute for the terminally nervous. Remarkably, I managed to get hired again, although not by Jack.

Augusta, of course, is the place where everyone feels that I am most likely to put spike marks in my tongue, and earlier this year, I nearly did. Tiger had hit his tee shot from the fifteenth tee and obviously had spanked it, judging by the look on his face, which we had framed in a close-up on his follow-through. Due to a strong draft, no one had got near the second crosswalk all day, but I was curious to see where this one was going to end up, as out of the corner of my eye I noticed that the crosswalk was thick with people.

Then, I made the classic announcers' mistake. I took my eyes off my monitor and stared up the fairway at the ball, which was bounding down the hill toward a group of ladies who were oblivious to the incoming missile until the last moment, when, with shrieks of amusement, they jumped out of the way.

In my infinite wisdom, I assumed that we were following the ball from the flank camera, and I said, "Whoa, the ladies had to lift their skirts for that one!" This, of course, was a reference to days gone by, when a mouse might have run into the room or something and startled the fairer sex. I thought it was quite a charming comment—that is, until I turned back to my monitor, and to my horror, noticed that we were still tight on Tiger's face!

Following a small, white object as it hurtles through the sky is a tough job even during the best of times, but in England, in the autumn, when the skies are often a dreary gray, it can be impossible. I was at home watching the World Matchplay Championship from Wentworth, just outside London, and, as always, I was hypnotized by the incomparable Peter Alliss.

A ball had been launched from the seventeenth tee on the famous old Burma Road course, and the cameraman, perched high above the fairway on a fire truck platform, was giving a fair impersonation of an ack-ack gunner scanning the skies for enemy Messerschmitts. Alliss, who knew in which direction the ball was heading simply by having observed the player's body language on the follow-through, was trying to coach the hapless lensman toward the spot where the ball had come to rest, as inconspicuously as possible.

"I believe that one is probably over on the left side," he waffled in his deliciously rich, plummy tone, as the cameraman panned slowly to his left, which of course, was Alliss's right.

"No, I mean the golfer's left," said Peter a little tersely, as the cameraman pulled as wide as he could, and started to pan ever so slowly, still in exactly the opposite direction.

"Okay, to your right," said Alliss, now clearly having given up any semblance of trying to be covert in his coaching, when the camera stopped abruptly and then started to move back at an elderly snail's pace toward the ball. Some five seconds of silence passed and the ball had still not made it into the frame, when, in the background, an exasperated Alliss uttered the what-should-be-immortal line, "Dear God, by the time he gets there, Gauguin could've painted it!"

Hooray for the men and women who cover our sporting events, say I, and may we never be perfect, or pretend to be so. Just like the athletes we cover, our mistakes are often the best part of the show.

Sam's Club

Given the serious nature of recent Ryder Cup competition, it goes without saying that the job vacancy for captain of the European team needs to be filled by an upright man of solid reputation, given to neither frivolity nor mischief. As the master of the great ocean-going steamer that carried Sir Samuel Ryder and his little golden trophy across the Atlantic might have told you, a captain must never gamble, and show no tendency toward strong liquor.

Bearing all this in mind, one could be forgiven for asking, why the hell would anyone pick Sam Torrance?

Maybe it's because the competition itself has changed over the years since Sir Samuel got used to steaming back across the Atlantic, empty-handed. For so many years, the Great Britain and Ireland team was hindered by the great British and Irish tradition of losing with an almost institutionalized grace, accompanied by twelve quivering, but stiff upper lips. Thank you, sir. May I please have another?

Still, the men of those teams fell in love with the Ryder Cup, because it was about playing the game, and nothing else. The Ryder Cup is the last bastion of pure professional sport on the planet. Okay, maybe the Iditarod dogsled race is in there, but it's not exactly made for television. Actually, now that I come to think of it, the Iditarod is similar to the Ryder Cup in another way because during the event the competitors sometimes have great difficulty in locating their testicles, albeit for entirely different reasons.

In my only Ryder Cup experience, Kiawah in '91, I was so nervous that as I stumbled onto the first tee for my initiation, mine took up residence on either side of my tonsils, where they stayed until late Sunday evening. My partner for that afternoon four-ball against Lanny Wadkins and Mark O'Meara was this year's captain and my dear friend, Sam Torrance.

I was shaking so badly that on my first two swings it was a miracle I made contact with the ball, but somehow I managed to fudge it up there about twenty feet short of the hole. The ground was moving as I set up over my first test of fine motor skills, and during my putting stroke, everything moved, except my bowels. And that was close.

I kind of scuffed the putt up to about four feet short, and three feet left of the hole. O'Meara looked away, and if that little swine Wadkins had been drinking anything, it would have shot out of his nose. Sam made the half, and on the way to the next tee he put a bear-like arm around my shoulder, and squeezed me tight. It was a delightful shade of green I was, apparently. He grinned, let me go and began to roll a cigarette, as we walked to the second tee.

"Just think," he said to me, "you're on the same team as Seve, Faldo, Langer, Olazabal, Woosie, Monty, and most impressive of all, me!"

"Aye, I suppose I am," I said, feeling an irresistible smile creeping onto my face.

"This only happens tae a few people," he continued, "so you'd better be up tae enjoyin' it."

He flicked open an old brass Zippo, took an enormous hit on the Old Holborn, and blew the smoke in my face. I still love the smell of it.

"So dinnae be a prick," he grinned, "or ah'll join Wadkins an' O'Meara, an' ye can play all three of us!"

I made a ten-footer on the last green that afternoon to halve the match, and give us a vital half point, and as I write I can still feel the electricity from Sam's bear hug. The thought of it gives me goose bumps. During that week, Sam made me feel bigger, and better, and more important than I ever had. He, Bernard Gallacher, and the veterans on the team gave me and the other rookies, including David Gilford, Paul Broadhurst and Steven Richardson, a sense that we were part of a special club, a brotherhood if you like. It's a feeling that lasts a lifetime, and one upon which Sam has thrived for more than two decades.

Some of the greatest armies in history were filled with men who were willing to die for their leader, and in order to earn such devotion, those leaders spent a lot of time with their men.

Sam has not lectured his team, unless you consider a lecture to be telling dirty jokes over cold beers in smoky bars, or playing cards in a hotel room. Over cold beers. He has gambled on the golf course, and probably robbed them, but more than anything else, he has made them feel special, because now, numbered among their friends, is Sam Torrance.

Sam has given the media short shrift, at least in press conferences, because he has no time for anyone who wants to make a story out of anything but the golf. He cares little for speeches, or ceremony. Like a fighter, he just wants the bell to ring, and to get it on. It's killing him that he isn't playing, but he knows he has a great team that has a great chance.

Win, lose, or draw, you can be certain of one thing, there will be no stiff upper lip, largely because no one has seen Sam's upper lip for years. For the best part of three decades, the European golfing public has known exactly how Sam Torrance has felt. The Belfry holds special memories, tears of joy and a red V-neck, a broken toe, and bitter disappointment. For the record, he tackled a Yucca, and no, he hadn't been drinking. (If he had, he probably would have beaten the crap out of the cactus as well.)

I think Sam will be the greatest captain the Ryder Cup has ever seen, but then again, I'm a little biased. Like the rest of the European team, and many of the Americans, I love the man. I know him so well, but then, if you're a golf fan, so do you.

Handshake Agreement

When I turned pro back in 1976, I think it's fair to say that I had no need for an agent, unless he also happened to be a part-time psychiatrist accustomed to working with those suffering from delusions of grandeur. As a five-handicapper, the only way I could have commanded a fee from an equipment company was if I had promised not to play their clubs. But by a bizarre series of events, I actually got quite good after a while. I don't really know how to explain it, it's just that every time Mr. Fate felt quirky, he happened to bump into me. The stranger thing is, it's still happening.

Wouldn't you know it, I digress. In 1980, I was offered a chance to go to the United States to play the mini-tours and prepare for the PGA Tour's Qualifying Tournament, better known as Q-School. I, genius that I still am, signed a contract that guaranteed all my expenses would be paid and all my prize money would go to my newest best friend, my first agent.

This less-than-profitable arrangement lasted about two years, until I got fed up with playing poorly and not getting paid for it, so back to Europe I went, in search of an agent who could make me some money for playing like a sick chicken. Again, I was lucky enough to find one. A friend of mine, Gordon Brand Jr., introduced me to his agent, Chris Mitchell, a former English amateur who had played on the same international teams as Nick Faldo, Mark James, and Sandy Lyle.

The man was an obvious idiot, so naturally we got along famously. His partner at the time was Allan Callan, the former road manager for Led Zeppelin, and he was given the task of weaseling me out of my first contract. He did so by threatening to nail my previous agent's right foot to the floor, thus rendering him incapable of walking in anything but a circle for the rest of his life. Mission accomplished.

Chris and I shook hands, and that was the only contract we needed in the fourteen years he looked after my affairs. In an industry where agents are often despised, he was universally adored because of his immense likability and the fact that obviously he was not in the game to make a fortune.

I was always marketed as one of the boys, largely because Chris knew I didn't know how to act any other way. He made me a lot of money, all of which got spent one way or another, but holy mackerel, one way or another, it was fun. He and I would be at some swank cocktail party before a big tournament, and he would shin up the tent pole and pull the trigger on a fire extinguisher just to loosen up the proceedings.

Once, in the Old Course Hotel at St. Andrews during the Dunhill Cup, I was with the Irish team in the lobby bar celebrating the fact that we had just been beaten by Kuwait or somewhere or something. There were about sixty or seventy people with us, singing and drinking, obviously under the impression that we had won, and Mitchell had been suspiciously absent for about twenty minutes. I knew he was up to evil deeds.

Facing the area in which we were sitting, the elevator doors were opening and closing, swallowing and regurgitating hotel guests. Every time the bell rang everyone waited for the door to open and tried to coerce the occupants to join us. Suddenly the doors slid open to reveal Chris, standing stark naked but for a pair of black calf-length socks, holding a large potted plant in front of his wedding tackle. A small potted plant would have sufficed.

A hundred jaws also hung slack as he peered out from behind the foliage. "Oh, I'm sorry," he said, "I must have the wrong floor," as an elderly couple got in with him, and the doors closed.

Later that night—in fact about three in the morning—we decided it would be a brilliant idea (as one does) to play the eighteenth hole of the famous Old Course in the dark. Chris, who thankfully was almost fully clothed at this stage, shanked a 5-iron into Rusack's Marine Hotel, and then fell headfirst into the Swilken Burn. Lord, how I miss him. But strangely enough, and I think I must attract these people, I now have another bona fide born-again buffoon looking after me.

Barry Terjesen, who works for Eddie Elias Enterprises, has clients who include Peter Kostis and Gary McCord, and I know, I know, I know, enough already. I know this should have been a dead give-away. But all he wanted was a handshake, so I was sold. It might have been against the odds, but it has been one of the smartest things I have ever done.

Barry is of Norwegian decent, and for those of you who don't know, the Scandinavians tell Norwegian jokes the same way everyone else tells Irish jokes. Barry says a Norwegian extrovert will stare at *your* shoes when he is talking to you.

I rely on Barry for everything I do off the golf course, although when the two of us get into a motor vehicle together with the intention of actually moving the aforementioned mode of transport to another location, I think the best we've ever done is two U-turns. It always turns into an Irish-Norwegian Laurel and Hardy scene. You know, Olaf and Mick?

Earlier this year, he picked me up at the West Palm Beach airport to take me to the Medalist for an infomercial I was to make with Greg Norman. After about ten minutes in the car, I, sharp as a bar of soap, noticed that the Atlantic was on the left. I said, "Terjesen, you're an idiot. We're supposed to be heading in exactly the opposite direction." He looked at me and uttered the immortal phrase, "I know, but we're making great time."

He once rented a car with a global positioning satellite system, parked it, and met me at the gate as I got off a flight at DIA (Denver's Idiotic Airport). Then, naturally, he couldn't remember where he'd parked the car. At the Masters this year, he called to pick me up at the house I was sharing with Kostis and Sean McDonough to take me to a speaking engagement. There were a few cars in the driveway when we came out of the house and Barry said, "Whose is the blue one?" When I told him that I didn't know he headed back indoors to find the owner in order to have it moved so we could leave. About twenty seconds passed and he emerged looking sheepish. "Actually," he said, "that's my car." List that one under things that Mark McCormack has never done.

In a business where agents frequently speak with lizard lips, forked tongue, and shed their skins every now and then, Barry Terjesen is an anachronism. He started his career as a prosecuting attorney, valiantly taking on the task of ridding Ohio's Amish country of a highly sophisticated cartel of pig and chicken thieves, and now ironically he finds himself representing a group of thieving pigs and chickens, such as McCord and myself.

Like Chris Mitchell, the secret of Barry's success lies in the fact that he is honest, kind, hardworking, and sincere. Also, just like Chris, he should never be put in charge of a ride on a lawn mower. People really like him, and whenever I go to a corporate outing or a speech that he has set up, the person in charge will invariably tell me what a pleasure it was for them to be charged too much for my services by him. List that under things that Mark McCormack's clients have never heard.

Obviously, none of these people have ever been in an automobile with Barry, but to give him a break, I recently had the pleasure of the company of the the former Editor-in-Chief of *Golf Magazine*, His Imperial Wonderfulness, the Right Honorable Rear Admiral Sir George Peper, who picked me up in a $4-a-day rental car to take me to the ESPN Zone restaurant in Chicago, where I was to speak to a bunch of *Golf Magazine* types.

He handed me a map, and after about twenty minutes of driving around downtown Chicago in ever decreasing circles, it became apparent that if we didn't stop and ask for directions, the car was going to disappear up its own tailpipe. George simply could not understand why I couldn't find Ohio Street on the map.

In fact, all I could find was Michigan Street and a big-ass lake on the right. Of course, it turned out I was looking at a map of Milwaukee, and in my own defense, Chicago also has a Michigan Street (all right, Avenue, smart-ass) and the same big-ass lake on the right. So maybe it's not all Barry's fault.

Having said that, I did get a call from McCord the other day, just as he and Barry were making a U-turn in a wheat field in the middle of Amish country, and upon that, ladies and gentlemen of the jury, I rest my case.

Men Behaving Badly

On the European Tour, Tuesday is traveling day. Most of the players travel through London and sometimes there are forty or fifty of them on the same aircraft, many of whom will be sharing rooms at one of the official tournament hotels. It's tougher to travel over there, tougher to communicate and generally a lot more like hard work than it is on the U.S. Tour, so players tend to stick together more. It's also a recipe for "men behaving badly."

Wednesday is pro-am day, and therefore the last occasion on which one can feel dreadful and still do no real harm, so it stands to reason that Tuesday night should be a rip-snorter!

Here's the theory: Tomorrow you will spend five and a half hours with four people who in every likelihood will speak no English. Therefore it is your duty on a Tuesday night to render yourself into a similar condition.

When one of the Tuesday night terrorists of the European Tour decides to hang up the old suitcase and take a club pro's job, it's almost like a death in the family, so it was with great sadness that I heard this morning, that one of my old running mates has retired.

After twenty-five years of being very successful and very silly, Carl Mason is getting a real job. He will be sadly missed. Although many on this side of the ditch will be unfamiliar with the name, he is still a fine player who has won a great deal of money playing golf. He is a true journeyman pro, who is survived by names like Torrance, Cooper, Riley and Boxall to name but a few, who will carry on the great Tuesday night tradition. They will see on occasions, who can pee the furthest off the hotel roof. (I believe I still hold the record for that one, albeit wind assisted.) They will lock each other out of their hotel rooms preferably naked and in the middle of the night, and they will actually wet themselves while trying to play snooker. They will occasionally throw up on the golf course on a Wednesday morning. I miss them all, and as for Carl Mason, I have no doubt he will be back for the occasional guest appearance.

With Friends Like Sam...

It's a little early to start talking about the next Ryder Cup, so I won't. It's not as if you won't be hearing enough about it when the media starts their inevitable biennial diatribe about how the matches should be an American rout, by virtue of the fact that people here have actually heard of some of the U.S. team members. But there I go, digressing again.

No, this month I'm going to perform a background check, presidential style, upon my very bestest friend in the world—Mr. Samuel Torrance, the captain of the 2001 European Ryder Cup team and undisputed world light-heavyweight champion of the noble art of falling-over-your-own-luggage-at-the-airport. To give you even a small idea as to how close we are, my wife Anita and I named our infant daughter Erin Torrance Feherty.

Actually, I'm delighted to be able to say that next year, once again, both captains are two of my favorite people. (No, wait a minute, that would mean that each of them is two persons. Never mind. If you're smart enough to have passed fifth grade math, you're probably not reading this anyway.) The thing is, Sam and U.S. captain Curtis Strange also have been friends for years, and if any two (or four) people are capable of getting the Ryder Cup genie back into the lamp, it is they.

Okay, so I lied. I've done nothing but talk about the Ryder Cup, so here's the background. In customary political style, much of what is written here will be either false, intentionally misleading, or even downright untrue. The rest will be heavily biased toward my candidate. There will be prizes for anyone who can spot the wee true pieces. (That was one of the false bits.)

Samuel Robert Torrance was born in Largs, Scotland, a little way west of Glasgow. In order to get to know my friend Sam, you must understand where he came from. He is the only son of the greatest golf teacher that Europe has ever seen, Robert Torrance, and his wife, June.

Bob taught me for many years and, in my opinion, knows what Hogan was trying to do better than Hogan did. Like the great man, Bob is fairly economical with his words, which are spoken in a kind of Glaswegian Swahili that only those close to him can understand.

Once, on the practice tee at the British Open at Muirfield, I was walking with him and Sam, listening intently to Bob, when a well-known player (in the world's top five at the time) shouted over, "Hey, Bob, how about a tip?"

Bob stopped abruptly in mid-sentence and looked around. Seeing who it was, he winked, told us to hold on, marched over, whispered something conspiratorial in the player's ear, and stood back to watch him hit. Almost instantly, the ball began to fly straight and true. As Bob walked back to join us, the player shouted his thanks.

I asked him what kind of tip he had offered and he replied, "Ah telt him never tae wipe his arse w'ya broken bottle," as we walked on. "Never tie yer shoelaces inna revolvin' door" was another of his favorites, but he only used it on people who were having trouble with their short game.

Needless to say, Bob is a column all his own. Or possibly a book.

Sam was the pro shop kid at Routenburn, where his dad was both pro and greenkeeper, and he grew up with the game, turning pro at age three and a half. His mom once told me that when he was born, he had fine dark hair all over him. I don't think he ever lost it. He is the hairiest person I have ever seen and rather than shave, he sets fire to himself regularly by dropping hot ashes from his roll-yer-own ciggies. He often has been photographed with a cigarette behind one ear and a pencil behind the other. A beautifully balanced character.

Since 1971, when he joined the European Tour, Sam has played about 650 events, more than anyone in the Tour's history. He has also made it look like more fun than anyone in history. I was fortunate enough to travel to about 250 of those events with him, to places like Madrid, Stockholm, Hamburg, Paris, Dubai, Rome, Milan, and Amsterdam, to name a few.

As captain of the European Four Tours' world championship team in 1991, he issued a no-practice decree to us, and, as we watched the other teams suffer in the 110-degree Adelaide heat, we sipped cold beers in the clubhouse. Naturally, we won.

He was my partner and mentor at the 1991 Ryder Cup, and through the ups and downs in my career and personal life, he and his wife Suzanne were always there, ready to celebrate or support. It's a strange thing to say, but one of the highlights of my career was his win at the '95 Irish Open. My most cherished photograph is of him, after holing a putt on the second playoff hole, hoisting me into the air in a giant bear hug, with a grin that lights up my office.

Sam and I spent ten years together, traveling the European Tour and around the world. If I finished my round before him, I would regularly check the scoreboard to see how he was playing, always hoping he would tie me, so we might play together the next day. In all those years, it only happened twice, and both times the bastard beat me.

I must have played one thousand practice rounds with him

and he was always my partner. I have never met a better gambler. Playing with Sam was like a license to extract cash from your opponents, who were always affectionately referred to as "mullets." Once, at Wentworth, we were playing against a couple of mullets and were one-up through eleven holes when Sam called me over to the edge of the twelfth tee where he had trapped a little snake under the head of his 5-iron.

Snakes are an uncommon sight in the British Isles and there is only one poisonous species. I decided that I'd do a Marty Stouffer and identify the little fella. I grasped Sam's 5 iron and ran my right hand down the shaft to about a foot from the clubhead, under which the little serpent squirmed furiously.

"That, Samuel," I announced pompously, "is an adder, the only poisonous snake in Britain," and I attempted to flick the scaly little bugger away. The problem was, I flicked him just a little fat, you see, and he wrapped himself around the shaft and popped up just enough to sink one of his little gnashers into the tip of my right index finger.

"Oh, dearie me," said the hairy one, in a bladder-endangering fit of laughter. "You've been bitten by the only poisonous snake in Britain."

"Maybe I'd better go in," I said. Sam thought for a while—about a millisecond. We were about two hundred smackers in front at this stage. "Nah," he said. "It's just like a bee sting. Don't be such a big fairy."

So on we went. Within a minute or so, my fingertip was totally anesthetized. You could have whacked it with a mallet and I wouldn't have noticed. By the time we had gotten to the fifteenth tee, the finger was swollen, ramrod straight, we were only one-up, and Sam mentioned that it was unfortunate that the snake hadn't bit me on the willie. By the eighteenth green, my right hand was twice the size of my left.

We won the match and an hour later I was in a hospital bed being pumped full of cortisone and painkillers. The doctor said that the centrifugal force generated by swinging the golf club checked the progress of the venom and might have saved my life.

Sam said he knew that. Outside the hospital, reporters waited for him to come out. "How is he?" one of them shouted. "He's got blood poisoning and they doubt very much if he'll make it," Sam said, as he walked toward his car. He opened the door and turned to face them, enjoying their shocked expressions. "Oh, you mean David," he said. "He'll be fine. I thought you were asking about the snake." I had to read that the following day.

Sam has won twenty times in Europe, and he's not done yet. He is undoubtedly the best-loved player, by peers and the public alike, ever to have played the European Tour. He will be the greatest captain ever, whether the team wins or loses.

My only concern is that, after his initial pep talk before the opening ceremony, the entire European team may be seized by an irresistible urge to rip off their underwear, don kilts, and paint half their faces blue to face the Americans. That would get things off to a rip-roaring start, wouldn't it?

Especially if the wind blows.

Chapter Six
Pet Peeves

Travels with Davey

I often think of how lucky I've been over the years to have visited so many wonderful places, all in the name of golf. But lately, I have to admit that traveling is starting to get a little old.

Don't get me wrong, I still enjoy myself once I arrive, but the journey there and back is wearing a little thin. While air travel in the United States is infinitely easier and more convenient than anywhere else in the world, flying to and fro is still pretty tedious.

Take security, for instance. Nowadays, between the ticket counter and the airplane there is an outstanding chance that you will be groped, probed, or in some other way fondled, either before or after the compulsory MRI.

Then, once on the plane, it's a crapshoot for whom you sit next to. Just last week, I found a man, some of whom was sitting in my seat. Most of him was in his own seat, I just got the overflow.

It turned out he weighed 650 pounds, or slightly less than the starboard engine, and to think that I was charged excess baggage for a particularly heavy piece of luggage. I wonder how much his ticket cost. But to give him credit, he was a good sport. When I asked him, as is my wont, how the hell he got to be that size, he told me it was on account of how much he ate.

When I told him that on an aircraft I'd never felt so close to someone, he let out a belly laugh that created an intestinal tsunami that almost bludgeoned me into the aisle. I told him he should consider a job as an NHL goaltender, as it would be completely impossible to score against him.

However, while he and I were conversing politely, the gentleman sitting directly behind my large friend started to crank up the volume. Those of you who are frequent flyers have no doubt experienced the Foghorn Leghorn Syndrome. We were at 30,000 feet, but you could have heard this guy on the ground.

Every passenger on the aircraft was made aware of the fact that he had kidney stones and, believe me, we felt his pain. He finally quieted down when the man sitting behind him offered to remove the stones manually.

His silence didn't last long and he started bellowing again during the meal. Eating and talking that obnoxiously don't mix, so I turned around to look at him and in the loudest voice possible asked the flight attendant for an umbrella. That did the trick.

On the way to the baggage retrieval, nature called and I encountered one of the great redeeming factors about many airports: The rest rooms have no doors. (Of course, the stalls do!)

And, there are generally real paper towels available. You see, I believe the hot-air hand dryer is the single most counterproductive innovation in personal hygiene. I admit to a hand-washing fetish and my mummy thinks there is something wrong with me, but bear with me here.

The hot-air dryer is time consuming and frustrating. Therefore, when it's the only choice available, fewer people will wash their hands. When you place a hot-air hand dryer in a rest room that has a door with a handle or knob, those of us who are decent enough to wash our hands must grasp the handle that the other filthy swine have contaminated!

This obviously defeats the purpose, but yet again, I have the solution. If no paper towels are available after washing your hands, go into one of the stalls and unravel a couple of yards of toilet paper (we call it "bumf"; don't ask me why). Using the crumpled bumf, grasp the door handle to the rest room, open the door, and wedge your foot in it.

Now, look for the trash can, which is usually over by the basins, and attempt your best fall-away jumper while backing out the door. Don't worry if you miss; it serves them right for having a handle on the door.

Down at the baggage retrieval, one of the worst aspects of human nature is revealed: selfishness. A line is painted on the floor some four or five feet away from the carousel, behind which we are all supposed to stand, in order to leave enough room for everyone to retrieve their bags, right? In reality, everyone jams against the carousel along with their Smarte Cartes, forming a six-foot-thick wall of tubular steel and humanity that would deny Jerome Bettis his athletic bag.

While I'm on the subject, would the man who invented the Smarte Carte please stand up? Okay, so the joke is on us. It is without question the most inappropriate and dangerous piece of baggage-carrying equipment ever invented.

If you push it, it has a mind of its own and if you pull it, unless you have the gait of a Japanese tea girl, it will sever your Achilles tendon. The only way around it is to pull it behind you either well right or well left of your body, which will, of course, lead to a nasty back spasm.

And, if you're unfortunate enough to be traveling with golf clubs, well, that's a whole new set of problems. If you set the clubs sideways on the Smarte Carte, you instantly disqualify yourself from making an entrance into an elevator and greatly increase the risk of having that same Achilles tendon rear-ended by the Smarte Carte driven by the person behind you.

These accidents happen because anytime you approach the automatic sliding doors (which are always infuriatingly slow) you are forced, due to the nature of your wide load, to abruptly slow down. Of course, you can set your clubs long ways at a slant and hold on to them with one hand while pushing with the other.

But then, once you've negotiated the sliding doors, the ramp from the curb down onto the street will pitch your clubs forward into the path of the nearest cab, no doubt piloted by a Latvian man who up until three weeks previous was a goatherd.

I have a solution for all of these problems and his name is Sky Cap! Even though he charges me three or four times as much as the Smarte Carte, I almost never feel like tying him to the fender of my rental car and dragging him to my hotel.

Ah, yes, my hotel. "I'm sorry, Mr. Feherty, but your room isn't ready yet. Would you mind having a seat in the lobby?"

"Oh, yes, I'd love to."

Eventually I get into my nonsmoking room that smells like Denis Leary's index and middle fingers. I crack open the mini-bar and pull out an approximately armpit-temperature beer. I take my libation into the bathroom to turn on the shower and wait for the pathetic hot-air hair dryer that takes five minutes to warm up.

The towels are cleverly rolled up and cunningly stacked above the toilet so that when you pull one down, the one beneath it falls into the water.

I pull back the sheets on the bed only to find something short, black, and curly in the shape of a question mark just below my pillow. The question is: I wonder who that used to belong to?

The one redeeming factor about this kind of traveling is that now I wait until Sunday to go home, as opposed to the end of my playing days when I was beginning to be a regular on the Friday-night flights.

The upside of my day job now is that even when I do it badly, I still get paid. And, the Sunday-night flights have become my favorites because when I get home, I know and love the one who asks the questions.

Chewing the Fat

Captain's Online Log, Stardate July 22, 2002. Planet Earth:

I must admit to being a little bemused about this latest episode in the history of air travel. I think Southwest Airlines is to be commended on the stance it has taken over the issue of airborne fat people. I hope I can still say the word *Fat*, without fear of being sat on by some lard-crazed activist of bovine dimensions.

Maybe "circumferentially challenged" would be the politically correct way to put it these days, but if you find yourself playing elbow hockey in the middle of three seats against a couple of salad-swerving dirigibles, and the only position left is center-forward, I think you have a right to be a little miffed. They're fat, you're thin, and you're probably getting thinner.

Now don't get me wrong, I like people in general, even the gigantic ones, as long as they have a good attitude. But it's not my fault if some people choose to freebase cheesecakes by the dozen, and I think it unarguable that I am entitled to sit by my personal self, in the space for which I have paid with my own money. I understand perfectly that an unfortunate few are extremely overweight due to glandular problems or for other medical reasons. But hey, I'm claustrophobic, so we're even.

Another thing: Where the hell are these massive new malls-with-wings I've been reading about for a while now? Not that I'm overeager to get on a plane that holds a thousand people. There's even talk of having a chapel in the back of some of them. I can't think of a single damn thing that would be more out of place on an airplane. Most people are skittish enough when they fly these days, and it's a rock-solid certainty that the first time a pilot announces over the PA that the plane is experiencing technical difficulties, the faithful will stampede to the nearest place of worship for a bit of last-minute shameless begging, upending the damn thing in the process. (Actually it would work for me, as long as the chapel was outside.)

But it's not like none of us ever thinks of death in an aircraft. I always do, especially during the pointless safety lecture at the beginning where we're all told about the vital seat-cushion flotation device which to the best of my knowledge has never, ever, in the history of commercial air travel, saved anyone's life after a jet airliner of any size has crash-landed over water. A large aircraft doesn't land on water, period. It crashes, period again. And you my friend, just like me, are done in, pure and simple.

I have already taken the precaution of informing my wife and children that in the event of my untimely demise in an aviation accident, it will be unnecessary for any of them to imagine what I might have been doing in the final seconds. They can rest assured that I will be in the galley, smoking, drinking, and having sex with myself (no, wait a minute, I don't smoke), and if anyone listens to the cockpit voice recorder, in the background they might hear me yelling at the pilots that they're idiots.

Of course, there might actually be an unlikely upside to being embedded in the cheesy folds of an enormous person. In the event of a crash, maybe they would act as some kind of an airbag, but I doubt it. No, I think the answer to the whole thing is to charge people by the pound, including their luggage, and be done with it. There would be a lot less luggage, and a lot less people flying too, which is a win-win for the seriously selfish, and cynical, traveler like me.

No doubt, fat people would try to get around it by giving themselves a helium enema, and having a friend take them on a string to check in, but I can't think of a better solution, outside of a really, really big CEO starting his own airline for fat people only.

How about, "Celluflite," with the slogan, "If we can't get your ass off the ground, we'll taxi you there!"

I probably shouldn't admit it, but I couldn't have written this without the diet pills.

Expletive Unchained

I have to say I'm a little worried about the latest spate of criticism directed at PGA Tour players over their allegedly disgraceful language and behavior. Apparently some are worried about the example we're setting for our children. In comparison to other professional athletes, most golfers already behave in a positively monastic manner, and I for one hope we're not heading for the vow of silence as a prerequisite to membership of the PGA Tour.

No, what I'd like to see here from most of these guys is a little more emotion, rather than less. And at least in golf we usually have the audio to go with the lip movements that can be so hard to read on the sidelines of other sporting arenas, such as the baseball or football field.

I imagine one of the few advantages of being a lip reader would be the ability to understand every single word that the likes of Jon Gruden and Don Zimmer are saying when they start to foam at the mouth. Not long ago during the NFL playoffs, Gruden (whom I don't know at all, but I think is insanely brilliant) had occasion to disagree with one of the officials on the field.

No, honest, he did. At least he was either disagreeing with the nice man in the striped shirt or trying to bring down upon him some kind of biblical catastrophe, like a plague of frogs, or maybe Jerry Falwell. I did my best to read his lips, and I think he said, "You vapid rockchucker, you ever hear of Lasik? My Dog! Ray Charles could've seen that with the lights off. Lou can glow me, you ashpole!"

Well, it went something like that.

If great men like these have the decency to go completely bananas on national television, in the process stripping bare their souls, I think the networks have a moral obligation to those of us who are soft of hearing to let us in on what's being said, even if they have to run subtitles. I mean, why should the deaf have all the fun?

In most things there is a balance between good and evil, dark and light, and a truly delightful, yet evil game like golf is a good example. No other game I've played can be more infuriating one moment, or uplifting the next, so how is a mere mortal supposed to keep his emotions on an even keel when he plays? Personally, I never did, and I'm proud to say I never said anything like, "Aw, shoot!"

Hey, there, your rectitudinousness, I know which word "shoot" is replacing, and the real question is whether it's more offensive, or even damaging, than "shit."

Call me old-fashioned, but I'd rather be shit on than shot at.

Not that I have anything against anyone who wants to say stuff like that, but I don't want to hear any complaints from them, either, if I choose to yell at the top of my voice what they really wanted to say and then beat the crap out of my golf bag or some other guilty-looking inanimate object. It had it comin', okay?

And this is golf, not chess. Just stay out of my way when I'm embarrassing myself and you might even do yourself a favor by accident. Watching a fully grown adult male toss all the toys out of the crib and then spit out his pacifier is funny. You could laugh at me instead of getting all huffy and superior up there on the moral high ground. The essential difference between the people who lose control of themselves while playing golf and the antics of other athletes is that with golfers, the anger, bitterness, resentment, and vitriol is directed at their very own personal selves. I'm pissed off at me, pal, not you!

If a guy does serious damage to a golf course, then charge him for it. That's fine. But if he's whacking himself in the nuts, calling himself names, or blaming the Almighty, I say turn up the volume and enjoy yourself. It's the Almighty's fault, anyway, for giving us free will. When he did, I guarantee you ten seconds later he stamped his foot, slapped his forehead, and said, "Shit! I knew I shouldn't have done that!"

The bottom line is, this issue isn't about what some people say, it's about what some people hear, and their narrow-minded reactions to it. Some of these people want to abdicate their responsibility as parents, and would rather have someone else deal with, or intercept, difficult questions from their children: "Daddy, why did that man say a bad word?"

"Because he's evil, son, and he doesn't think like us. Unlike us good folk, he's doomed."

If my dad had told me that, I would have thought, "Oh shit, I'm doomed."

I know we should hold ourselves to a higher standard, but I think we already do, and there's no need for anyone to get his or her panties in a wad at the moment. Professional golfers have always given a good account of themselves, and they probably swear less often now than they used to. It's the digital sound and these bastard microphones that are dropping everyone in the shit. Oops!

And, consider this: That foul-mouthed, evil-tempered, heathen scumbag just might give a fortune every year to underprivileged children, or spend time at St. Jude's in Memphis putting a smile on the face of a five-year-old girl who doesn't have hair anymore.

He might give the homeless wino at the red light with the scabby dog and the sign that reads, "Need money for beer," twenty bucks every now and then. Also, he might be really pissed off at himself if his public display of self-loathing has upset anyone, but he doesn't need you to hate him, or criticize him, because that's precisely what he was doing to himself at the time.

And, there is another way for Daddy to answer the awkward question from junior: "He shouted, 'Gonads!' at the top of his voice, son, because he's mad at himself. He's being a little hard on himself, too. It doesn't make him a bad person, but if I ever hear you say that word in front of your mom, I'll kick your ass."

"Why, Dad?"

"Because I'm your father. Now shut the hell up."

For me, tennis died when John McEnroe quit. I didn't approve of all his behavior, but I loved to watch it. It was great television, and it was the way I would have felt, too, if the myopic, sleeping sonofabitch in the deck chair on stilts had called that one out on me. McEnroe strengthened us and oxygenated our blood when we watched him, because we felt that just like us, he was weak, yet he could do these amazing things.

A couple of months ago, Pat Perez went berserk on the eighteenth hole at Pebble Beach, and it also was a lovely thing to see. A lot of flair, a hot temper, and a beautiful flaw, otherwise known as the impetuosity of youth.

You could tell that he cared so much it was almost killing him, and you knew he'd be back. Tiger is mellowing out a bit, but I'm thankful he's still capable of the occasional blast of nostril steam and blasphemous burst from the lips.

I can handle explaining it to my kids, no problem. In fact, it can be quite useful at times, when you're trying to explain that a word is never evil, unless there is an evil intent behind it, and sometimes you should just get over it and play ball.

Like Tiger does. Like virtually everyone else on the PGA Tour, he's a good role model for our kids.

A Message from the "Meridian Mail Lady"

After four weeks on the road I'm fit to be tied up and thrashed with a packet of Skittles. I'm also ready to seek out and strangle the sadistic jerk who designed the "Meridian Mail" voice messaging system, which for some ungodly reason is installed in virtually every hotel that I stay in these days. Anyone who travels will be familiar with the following scenario.

Only one thing is more irritating than a long voice mail, and that's a long message that exists solely for the purpose of telling you that you have a long voice mail. If I had anything to do with it, I'd devise a system that would deliver a painful electric shock to the ear of anyone who can't say what they need to in ten seconds or less.

And an extra jolt for anyone that says "Good-bye" to a tape recorder. When you get out of bed tomorrow morning and stumble into your kitchen, try saying hello to your toaster. It's the same principle.

"Hey, it's Bilgewad. Call me back at 555-2341, and I'll tell you what I was going to say to the recorder."

How bloody simple is that? Instead, most of the messages I get are pointless, rambling, anecdotal diatribes that could be edited to these six words. CALL ME BACK, YOU MORON. Now that, I can do. What I can't do without yelling at an inanimate object, is listen to this kind of asinine, time-wasting verbal diarrhea:

Meridian Mail Lady: "Hello" (like we're supposed to answer back), "You have accessed the hotel's voice messaging system," pause...forever...

I KNEW THAT. IT'S THE VERY REASON I HIT THE BUTTON MARKED "MESSAGES."

Meridian Mail Lady: "The Meridian Mail messaging system can

be accessed from any hotel telephone, or any touch-tone telephone in our solar system."

By this time, I'm holding the handset in front of my face, and I am answering back. "For the love of Pete, what's the message?"

Meridian Mail Lady: "You have one new message, and a text message at the front desk, which you probably picked up two days ago, but hey, we love screwing with your head. In a moment, I'm going to give you your messages, but first, here are your personal, in-room, Meridian Mail options. To record a personal greeting..."

SWEET JESUS, TAKE ME NOW.

Meridian Mail Lady: "...press 2. To transfer to an operator at any time, press 0. To listen to your messages, press 1. (To end your agony, check into a decent hotel.)

Now I'm irritated enough to stab angrily at the 1 key, and I accidentally hit 2 at the same time. Well, almost. Naturally, I hit the 2 key .000000894 of a second before the 1, and end up having to leave a greeting after the beep. The greeting is the sound of the handset being repeatedly beaten against my forehead.

Meridian Mail Lady: "If you are satisfied with your greeting, press 1."

YEAH, YEAH, YEAH, IT'S FINE, YOU EVIL BITCH. 111111111111111111111111111111—BITE ME!

Now I'm calm again. I'm okay. Just give me the message, that's all.

Meridian Mail Lady: "Message one, delivered at 9:03 p.m., Thursday, February 14, from a hotel room..." (In the background, a couple of muffled thumps, followed by McCord's voice: "Hello...hello?" Then two or three bleeps, as McCord hits zero several times, then he says, "Operator at any time, my ass! Screw this voicemail system, and the turds who dreamed it up!" Several muffled thuds, and the sound of a chocolate pillow mint being smashed up with the TV remote, which accidentally disarms the mute button, followed by exaggerated screaming from a Spectravision movie.)

Meridian Mail Lady: "To replay the message, press 3. To save the message and move on, press 5. For message cleanup, press 7."

HMMM. I should save that one, but okay, I press 7.

Meridian Mail Lady: "You have chosen message cleanup."

OH, OH, OH, I BLOODY WELL KNOW THAT, YOU VICIOUS, HEARTLESS BITCH.

"To delete all the messages you have heard, press 1 now."

ALL RIGHT... 1, FREAKING 1, FREAKING 1, FREAKING 1.

Meridian Mail Lady: "You have chosen to delete all the messages you have heard... (Eight-second pause) To confirm the deletion, press 1 again."

AAAAAAAAAARGH! I AM NOT PRESSING ANYTHING, ANYMORE! (Deep breath.) IN FACT, I'M GOING TO FIND OUT WHERE YOU LIVE, AND SHOVE THIS TELEPHONE RIGHT DOWN YOUR BIG, HAIRY, THROAT. THEN I'M GOING TO...

You get the picture, I'm sure. Four weeks on the road with a wife and five kids at home, and the term "stir crazy" starts to make sense. Everybody complains about cell phones these days, but at times such as these, I'm glad to have one. My three-and-a-half-year-old daughter leaves two-second messages.

"Night-night Daddy, I love you."

I save those, so I can call myself up and listen to her before I go to bed. Then, even the indestructible, inextinguishable flashing red light on the bedside phone doesn't bother me.

Thanks, I feel better now.

House Guests

Sad to say, Carnoustie is the only course on the British Open rotation I haven't played in the dozen or so Open Championships (that's what we call it) that help checker my career. I did play the Scottish Open there a couple of times, so I know the course and I'm really going to miss being there this year.

However, one aspect of the Open I won't miss at all—the accommodations. Because of the influx of fans, places to stay for the week can be difficult to find and expensive as well, because hoteliers know they have the market cornered.

For this reason, players often rent houses, the occupants of which presumably go on an all-expense paid vacation, thus avoiding all the unwashed louts that invade their towns. If you don't mind the thought of some strangers sitting on your toilet and going through your stuff, it's not a bad way to make a few bucks.

Houses at the Masters, for instance, go from $7,000 or $8,000 to upward of $30,000 for the week. For this kind of cash, as a renter, you want to be sure the owner doesn't check on you every day to see if you are rifling through her knickknack drawer or goose-stepping around the kitchen in her underwear whistling the "Star-Spangled Banner" with the toilet plunger on your head.

I have stayed at the Zimmerman house in Augusta for the last three years and I have never once laid eyes on Mrs. Zimmerman, who, I'm sure, is a very nice woman. For the record and her peace of mind, I have never done any such thing in her kitchen. For a start, I can never find the toilet plunger.

But I digress, as usual. The houses that come up for rent at the British Open are generally of a slightly different standard and the occupants can have a very different attitude than that of the Zimmermans, who pretty much leave their house as they live in it.

Once at Royal St. George's, two other players and I rented a small house for the week for the ridiculous sum of £3,000. The owner had all but stripped the place bare of anything of any comfort, leaving us cracked coffee mugs, a few ancient bone-handled knives and forks, slippery toilet tissue (particularly upsetting), and threadbare towels.

The bathroom consisted of a dusty pink basin and can set, which went beautifully with the grimy avocado tub with the separate hot and cold faucets. In order to take a shower, you had to plug two rubber thingies onto the taps and hook the hand-held shower onto a bracket on the mildewed wall. Then you had to hope like hell you could regulate the temperature in time before the eight-quart hot water tank ran out. There were only two temperature settings in the shower: shrink or scald.

Also, the bed linen was nylon and there was a padlock on the linen closet. The first night, I snagged a toenail getting into bed and threw a complete wobbly fit. I ran down the stairs, found a screwdriver, and took the door off the linen closet. Inside was all the linen, cutlery, china, and toilet tissue we would need.

We were all right until we noticed that every time one of us stood at the kitchen sink, an elderly lady was sitting in the kitchen of the neighbors' house across the back wall, some fifteen feet away. She was obviously watching us.

We tried a couple of cheery waves, but she just sat there glaring with a cigarette hanging from the corner of her mouth. After a couple of days, this began to really irritate me, so the next morning I washed the dishes wearing nothing but a Speedo and a pair of fake breasts. (Don't ask; I used to travel with a rubber chicken in my hand luggage just to freak out the security people at the airport.)

Anyway, that afternoon I came back to the house early after a practice round. My two housemates were out on the golf course, so when I heard a bump upstairs, I knew something was up.

I got my sand wedge, went to the foot of the stairs, and called up, "Who's there?" No answer. Now, like in most elderly British houses, the floorboards creaked. I thought I heard just such a noise coming from my room as I crept slowly up the stairs, hoping for once I had picked the right club.

I pushed open the door to my room, which appeared to be empty until someone simultaneously sneezed and banged their head, which moved the dust ruffle around the bed. I hooked the wedge under it and lifted it up to reveal the intruder—the old bat from next door.

She was desperately trying to reinsert her false teeth. She sneezed violently again, hitting her head on the box springs and sending the teeth skating across the hardwood floor.

"Can I help you?" I asked and offered my hand. She took it and I pulled her out so she could stand. The front of her housedress was thick with lint and dust and a dead moth hung from the arm of her spectacles.

I reached around the bed, picked up her false teeth, and handed them to her. "You might want to rinse these, they're a little dusty," I said. She marched, tight-lipped, into the bathroom across the hallway, and returned moments later, looking defiant and a little fuller around the mouth.

"I'm sorry, young man," she said, "but I'm the owner of this house and last night I heard a terrible crash. So, I thought I'd check to see if anything had been broken."

I looked at her thoughtfully. "Presumably, then, you thought we'd broken the floor under this bed."

She looked at me malevolently and said, "I wasn't expecting you back this early. Aren't you supposed to be practicing?"

"No," I replied. "I perfected the game at lunchtime." I told her that the crash she heard was probably me falling over a rip in the carpet by the back door while I was carrying a brown paper sack full of empty gin bottles we had found in the larder.

I pointed out that we had paid to rent the house and its contents for the week and the only thing the house contained at the moment that we didn't need was her. Now in full battle-ax mode, she replied that, taking into consideration the damage to the linen closet, her entrance was justified and she intended to keep the £200 security deposit.

I told her that would be fine and ushered her to the door, assuring her we could find a way to do much more damage than that.

Players from this side of the Atlantic have often avoided the Open Championship for this very reason. Housing is incredibly expensive, considering what you get, or rather what you don't get. Also, if by some twist of fate, the weather is good and the temperature climbs above seventy degrees, every ice machine within a thirty-mile radius will break.

Anyone reading this who has been there will know this is true. Barmen still take ice out of the bucket with tongs, one lump at a time, as if they were dropping diamonds into your glass. Then, as if they knew the cruelty of the gesture, will pour room temperature liquid over the two cubes, melting both in the process, thereby nullifying the whole point of the exercise.

If you're planning to go to the British Open—which, despite all of the above, I still think is a very good idea—there is no way you can avoid crappy accommodations, but there is a way to pay less for them.

It's very simple: Don't book anything in advance. Just show up. Then look for a parasite who has been hoping to suck the green out of someone's wallet, but as yet has been unsuccessful.

The local real estate parasites will have lists of them. A lot of these people will have booked their vacations in advance and will be wetting themselves at the thought of having to pony up for the trip themselves. This puts you in the driver's seat.

Just stride into the local realtor's office and say something like, "My good man, I'd like to rent a house for the week. Say, something like three small bedrooms, one bathroom with a shower I have to run around in to get wet, and a black-and-white television with one of those turny knobs to change the channels."

I guarantee he will have a dozen or so similar properties and you should offer about a third of what they are asking to leave room to make it seem you're willing to be generous.

So, in other words, if you have no plans for Carnoustie this year, you're already ahead of the game —and in much better shape than you might have thought!

I Say!

Hey! I might seem thick-skinned and cynical to some of you, but the truth is, underneath all the blowhard rhetoric I'm a sensitive soul, and easily wounded. So zip it, you morons, or if you have to whine, at least try to do so in a literate fashion. I mean really, some of the e-mails that are gloatingly forwarded to me by the idiot editors of this rag are so contemptuous, and unworthy of publication, I sometimes feel compelled to complain about myself, just so I can read some decent criticism. Then, out of the blue, comes a letter from my kind of critic, and I find myself in a position where someone else has written my column for me! I love this country!

Of course, everyone who has ever written to me has always said that they will never read the magazine again, so the chances are, this will fall on deaf ears, or blind eyes, or swollen whatevers. But for the record, just in case some of you are lying swine, this is the sort of thing you should be writing, you poor misguided fools!

Dear Mr. Feherty:

What on earth were the editors thinking, when they hired you, you drivel-scribbling bog-trotter? I have been a subscriber to *Golf Magazine* for more than thirty-seven years, and never in that span did I feel the urge to put pen to paper for the purpose of verbal castigation, until the day that some cretin allowed you to weasel your way between these formerly pristine sheets. Now, I find myself writing a letter of complaint every month, and wasting time I could be spending upon something useful, such as sharpening every knife in the house, or lancing boils down at my practice. Today, when I turned to the back page, I found an epistle so vile, it almost made my

bile boil. For fear of accidental propagation, I steadfastly refuse to quote your ghastly prose, but this I will say:

I have been a fan of golf, the written word, yachting, and naturism for many years, so imagine my horror as I read your offering from last month in which you butcher three of these four categories. Indeed, if stupidity is an art form, then you sir would appear to be the Michelangelo of our time. For your enlightenment, quality individuals such as I do not need to be kept abreast of the history of your digestive tract. Furthermore, I think to print derogatory statements about anyone who elects to spend their free time alone on a yacht, in the middle of the Caribbean, is entirely superfluous to the requirements of any reputable periodical, even if that person has been tied to the mast, with his trousers around his ankles. Also, I would like to know how you knew about that (and any other hobbies you may have).

I have spent many months at sea in quiet contemplation, with one of my greatest rewards being the tears of joy upon my wife's face when I have returned to dry land. (Thank heaven for her sturdy friend Muffin, who always seems to be there for her when I am away.) You, on the other hand, mock the life of the solo mariner, as if you have some knowledge of how it feels to sit with your legs dangling over the edge of the deck, playing Wagner on the soprano tuba to the migrating squirrelfish that dance around your brightly painted toenails. I think, sir, that you have not.

Perhaps, Mr. Feherty, you would be well served to spend a little time in such solitary confinement, not at sea, but in an institution specifically designed for rehabilitation of heathen orators such as yourself. You most certainly should be separated from your offspring, and allowed no further influence, lest one or more of the poor children should later in life find themselves scrabbling frantically at the same greased flagpole to which you now cling. It is clear that you rise barely above the scum-encrusted cesspool of your own demented imagination. I feel sorry for Willard, your dog.

I canceled my subscription to your publication some months ago, but to my dismay, some imbecile renewed it, and sent it to me as a kind of twisted gift. I was hoping against hope my letters might make a difference in the quality of your work, but sadly, all I see is a slow deterioration in standards, and a callous disregard for journalistic integrity that is all too common in our society today. In order to figure out your moral standards, all one has to do is read any of your mindless commentary about that Tiger Woods chap, who is another blot on the formerly fair landscape of this great game. Your sycophantic, groveling support of such a foul-mouthed upstart makes me queasier than I've ever been in a thirty-foot swell, after a supper of tripe and anchovies. Nobody likes a showoff, and if that is the way the game is headed, then I'm taking up the Peruvian nose flute, changing my name to "Smedley," and spending more time afloat.

While I'm up and running so to speak, here's another thing that throws the cut of my jib off kilter. Is it just me, or do both you and that horrible McCord chap lose about seventy-five points off your respective intelligence quotients every time you are in close proximity to one another? I live right next door to two elderly ladies, and I swear, when you two morons are on the air, it's like listening to one of their damned bridge parties through the letterbox. If you asked me to, I would wear nothing but a schoolboy's cap, and give you both a damned good thrashing with a jockey's whip, but what are the chances of not being arrested for that, in this namby-pamby day and age? When I think back to the good old days, when I used to get naked and play the cello in front of the television, it brings back memories of Henry Longhurst, and Brent Musburger, Jack Whitaker, and Judy Garland, who is thankfully still at ABC. It almost makes me want to weep. Sadly, I am now incapable of tears, due to the constant lashing of salt water in my face, but that doesn't mean I don't lament for the kind of quality in golf broadcasting we had back then. An occasional period of silence was not a sin, and no one felt it necessary to bastardize the English language. I honestly believe that if Mr. McCord could breathe through his ears, he might never stop mangling the Queen's English. This alone is a crime against humanity, and I'm sure to be as hyper as he appears, he has to be on smack caffeine or something similar.

Mr. Feherty, I doubt if any of this advice will reach its intended target, as nothing I have written in the past has ever elicited a response, but let me close by saying this: I intend to write to the chairman of every company that advertises in your magazine. I will warn them of the peril in which they place themselves, every time their corporation appears to be associated with the likes of you. Then, I am going to contact the Chief Wizard (I mean the head of our lodge), and also every religious leader in the country. (Except the Baptist and Jewish ones, whom I do not trust.) I am going to ask them to join with me in a gesture of solidarity against the kind of trash journalism displayed inside your back cover. From now on, we are not paying any attention to this magazine, and instead reading, *Naturism, Golf and Yachting!* which is a splendid new publication,

filled with wholesome articles, and advertisements for all kinds of
terrific outdoor stuff, including a full range of rubberware, and a
matching spatula and grease-proof thong set of my own design,
for barbecuing on those choppy days up on deck.

Yours Sincerely,
Dr. Norman Hackett-Daly
Obsequechobie, Fla.

Of course, I'd have to reply.

Dear Dr. Daly,

Thank you so much for your letter, which is the finest I have
ever received. I have an admission to make. It was I who renewed
your subscription. You're welcome.

Sincerely,
David Feherty
cc: Gary McCord

Pro-Am Purgatory

Much has been written about the attitude of Tour pros to the
ubiquitous Wednesday pro-am. The difficulties of concentrating
on the day before the tournament while playing with nervous
amateurs are many.

However, no one seems to offer these quivering victims any
advice. Well, here are my "Seven Steps to Pro-am Heaven"—for
pro and amateur alike. A few dos and don'ts of playing with the

pro—a road map through the purgatory of the pro-am.

I always try to imagine what it would be like for me if I were plucked out of my comfort zone and thrust into the spotlight, say, onstage with Bruce Springsteen or into the boardroom with Bill Gates, and told not to make an idiot of myself. The truth is that neither Bruce nor Bill would expect me to be any good at all. I, on the other hand, would still like to give a decent account of myself, or at least limit the damage.

The first thing to remember is that your pro requires one thing from you—that you enjoy yourself. The reason we play for so much money these days is that you do enjoy the game, you do buy the equipment that you don't need, and you do love to watch us on television. So, don't be overawed: Chances are you do something for a living that we would be completely useless at. A good pro will always do his or her best to put you at ease on the first tee, so when you make your first swing that makes contact with the planet nine inches behind the ball and measures 4.8 on the Richter scale, you can at least have a laugh at it, too.

Some of the best fun I've had on a golf course has been with complete hackers who have had enough confidence in what they do in other walks of life to laugh it off without self-consciousness, while enjoying the walk and the banter.

So, here are a few guidelines that will help both you and your pro enjoy the day:

1. GET A CADDIE. It's the only way to play the game. You can walk free of hindrance and have the club handed to you clean and

dry. If possible, get one of the Tour caddies whose man isn't in the pro-am. For fifty dollars, you can have someone who is used to being screamed at, blamed for the weather, the rate of inflation, and some of those hard-to-explain skin rashes. Mind you, he won't be able to club you because you don't know which part of the club the ball is about to bounce off of. However, he will be able to regale you with stories on and off the course most people are never privy to.

2. BE READY TO HIT. Even if it isn't your turn. Discuss with your partners the concept of "ready golf" before you tee off. This means forgetting whose honor it is—if you're ready, just go. Pro-am play is hideously slow at the best of times and your pro will really appreciate it if you make the effort to keep it going.

There is nothing sadder than watching a finely tuned athlete walking slowly into the woods to whack his forehead on a Scotch pine just to relieve the pain of watching a 23-handicap account executive from Sheboygan agonize over whether to miss the green by seventy yards with a heavily disguised 11-wood or a very fat 4-iron. It makes me droop just thinking about it.

3. NO CELLULAR PHONES. At the very least turn them off. The surgical removal of a cellular phone from certain regions of the anatomy is painful and, to the best of my knowledge, is not covered under most company health insurance plans.

4. GET A YARDAGE BOOK. And ask a Tour caddie how to use it. This will make the pro very happy. Contribute to your pro's mental well-being by being the first "ammy" in the history of his pro-am

career not to ask the question: "How far have I got from here?"

There are only a certain number of times in your career you can be asked this question before your spleen bursts. Mine burst six years ago.

5. OUT OF THE HOLE? Pick it up. And, be sure to tell your pro when you have done so. Not only will you contribute to the pace of play, but you will avoid the awkward situation of having the pro wait, expecting you to hit, while you are rummaging around in your bag looking for that three-year-old stick of gum that's making everything sticky. In this category, there is only one thing worse than waiting around for no apparent reason, and that is waiting around for a very bad apparent reason; i.e., holing out for a 9, net 8.

6. FORGET ABOUT SCORE. And, don't be upset if your pro doesn't know how your team stands. Remember, it's a Wednesday. He probably doesn't even know his own score.

7. WATCH YOUR FEET. Be very, very mindful of the line of your pro's putt. Look at television coverage of a golf tournament and watch how respectful the pros are of each others' lines. Quite often a player walks sixty or seventy feet around another player's marker just to avoid stepping over it.

There's no need to take it to these extremes, but ask your pro where his line is and he or she will show you where to step over. Remember, this is our office. How would you feel if you were in the process of finishing a very carefully written letter to your boss and I came in wearing a pair of golf shoes and did a Highland fling all over it? I thought so.

Finally, if any of you are still interested in playing this game with anybody ever again, try not to give the pro any advice on how to play the course, even if it is your home course and you've been a member for seventy-five years. Trust me, he knows more about it than you do just by looking at the yardage book.

It's a question of knowing what to look for. Even giving the occasional line off the tee can be dangerous because you don't normally play two club-lengths from the back edge of the back tee. I don't know how many times I've heard, "Oops, I could have sworn you could have carried that bunker!"

If you follow those rules, you should have a great day. Remember, there is no other sport where you can play alongside the pros in such close proximity without being injured.

Despite what you've read, we can have fun on a Wednesday, too. And, as I said, thanks for the prize money!

Alphabet Soup at the Grocery Store

I was at the grocery store the other day, stumbling around the food for fat people and fitness-in-a-bottle section, searching for something that would curb my appetite without raising my heart rate to 790. Of course, such a product does not exist. There was this guy there, a brown-faced, brown-legged, brown-armed type with two white feet and a white right hand who was shooting sheepish glances in my direction. Call me Sherlock, but I figured he was a left-handed golfy type. I braced myself for the chase, and trundled my shopping cart around the corner and into the next aisle. A few moments later, golfguy slithered into view, and when I made eye contact he turned quickly and grabbed the first thing he could find off the shelf, and began to peruse it seriously. Seizing the moment, I set off toward him, and as I passed I whispered, "Actually, I prefer the ones with wings," and made the turn into the next aisle chortling to myself. This was fun.

Later on, I'm in the ten, items-or-less lane behind a woman who is attempting to pay for a toothbrush with a check, but she can't find her driver's license. There is a woman at the next cashier, in the one-thousand-items-or-more wide lane, who is going to have run carpool and made dinner before I get out of here. Then, golfguy sidles up behind me. "You're the guy who works for ABC, right?" he grins. I give him my best, "Someone else is using your brain cell" look. "I can't even spell ABC," I say. "I'm a mobile microphone holder for CBS." "Oh right," he says undaunted. "Sorry about that, Feherty, that's right. I should know, I did your tax return last year. I work for the IRS, can you spell that?"

Instantly I regretted not having had the foresight to have picked up a bottle of Pepto-Bismol, in the, "You're about to soil yourself section." There followed a transfer of sheepishness.

Funny enough, it turned out that golfguy is actually a truly wonderful human being, who now owns an autographed picture of me. Also, I said I'd get him one of Curtis.

Chapter Seven
A Tour of the Tour

Playing Partners

A few months ago, I wrote a piece on equipment, which, due to the amount of income *Golf Magazine* derives from manufacturers who advertise within our pages, is a sensitive subject to say the least. Upon initial reading of the column, our esteemed editor immediately soiled himself and set about deleting anything he felt might cost us money.

Writers tend to get a little miffed when this happens, generally because it tends to mean more work for the writer, but I am a pig with a different snout, as my grandfather used to say. Why he used to say that remains a mystery to me, but as usual, I digress.

This month I'm going to tackle a subject that probably should be shot with a tranquilizer dart before it is touched with a cattle prod, provided it is safely behind titanium bars at the time. As always, I rely upon my editor to delete anything that might eventually cause pain or physical harm to my own personal self, so don't be surprised if the only things that appear after this paragraph are two apostrophes and a question mark. I give you marriage on the PGA Tour.

'?'

Just kidding.

Golf marriages are under more pressure than most due to the amount of time that couples must spend apart. There is no worse feeling than when you realize that your spouse has been playing with someone else's equipment. It often takes people longer to get over a betrayal than a death, for at least dead people aren't around anymore.

Then, of course, when you do get over it, there's the mulligan! How do you find the courage to tee it up again?

In order to make a living as a Tour professional golfer—or even as a semi-Tour semi-professional golf broadcaster—one must have a high opinion of one's self and the ability to make work your number-one priority, at least for a while. This means that your wife (and I will assume the male role for the rest of this article) will have to be content to play second fiddle to a self-important pillock. At least, that's what my wife tells me.

First, there is the question of, "To follow or not to follow?" If she follows her man while he plays, she risks suffering the opinions of the gallery, who have no idea who she is. And there will always be a few who are so expert, that they feel it necessary to slander her hubby. More than one unsuspecting critic has tripped over a surreptitious spousal shoe, sending the scoundrel headfirst into a pine tree.

Some pros like their wives to follow and some do not. However, the ones that do not are seldom dumb enough to share this feeling with their wives. It goes kind of like this: "Honey, do you want me to walk with you today?" Which actually means, "Should I come with you today, or just hang around the room here at the Stumble Inn and maybe try to get the chewing gum out of the carpet?"

Make no mistake about it, there are more fulfilling things for a woman to do than trudge around a golf course, surrounded by idiots, just so she can hand her husband a granola bar as he walks from the twelfth green to the thirteenth tee pausing only to whack his putter on the ball washer. Sometimes it's harder to watch golf than it is to actually play it.

On the other side of the coin, the man is out there suffering, too. You've just hit a fat 9-iron from a soggy lie, and as you're picking the divot out of your nose, you notice the tubby balding guy with the ponytail and the cigar who has been walking two paces behind your wife all day so he can get a good look at her ass. Of course you can't go over there and rescue her from this leering idiot, as this would display juvenile insecurity, and anyway, you're supposed to be thinking of getting up and down for par, you moron.

Sometimes the intuitive wife will sense that her husband really doesn't need her to be around and so she will slip off quietly and leave him to go about his business. The husband, who of course believes that his wife couldn't make it around the golf course if he didn't make eye contact with her at least once every couple of holes, notices her absence after a while and even though he didn't want her there in the first place, he's now really pissed off that she left.

The bottom line is, it's just not easy for anyone, and this is what it's like sometimes when golf couples travel together. When they're apart, it can be just as difficult. Scheduling and time changes make it hard to call at the right time, and frequently one party appears to not want to talk to the other, which will invariably put the caller's nose out of joint. All your wife needs is a baby on one arm, two boiling pots, third-grade math, and a dumbfounded eight-year-old, with the Cartoon Channel blaring in the background, and when the phone rings it's zero-to-bitch before you can say hello.

You, on the other hand, are in Memphis, where it's two hours later. Because of this, your digestive system is just enough out of whack to have caused you to visit the dreaded Porta Potti at 9:40 that morning after you had played only two holes.

You've walked like John Wayne all day, shot seventy-eight, and are now in bad, bad need of a cold beer and a decent meal with your friends, who are waiting for you in the lobby, when the phone rings. It's your wife and you immediately realize that this is going to be a listening, not a talking experience, so you tell her that the boys are waiting downstairs, and you'll call her back after dinner. She's just eaten macaroni and cheese with the kids, and you're going to the Palm. This does not make her feel any better, but of course she'll do her best not to make you feel guilty. Not very.

By the time you get back it's too late to call, so you wait until morning, by which time she's convinced you've spent half the night at a strip club, and on the way to the golf course you realize that the two pounds of cow and the acre of French fries you consumed last night have done nothing but guarantee you another near-childbirth experience before you make the turn. Also, you'll need twenty-six on the back nine to make the cut.

Welcome dear readers, to a slice of married life on the PGA Tour. Golf marriages are under more pressure than most and all too often are subject to the sad schism or remorseful rift. My own divorce was a public and humiliating affair that effectively ended my playing career and at one stage cost me my two kids, fifty pounds of my body weight and virtually everything I owned.

I met my new wife Anita when I was at rock bottom, and it is a testament to the kind of woman she is that I now have my boys back plus two more and finally my dream come true, a sixteen-month-old baby girl, who, like her mother, is impossibly beautiful and must be obeyed at all times. Also, I now have a new career and I've managed to put sixty of those fifty pounds back on, and dammit, I've enjoyed every ounce.

Mind you, I've just been left in charge of our baby girl and three of our boys for the last five days and I'll tell you what. If my wife doesn't come back by tomorrow night, I think I'm either going to die of exhaustion or check myself into a mental institution.

If I'm going to give you an example—and I believe I am—I might as well go straight to the top. Barbara Nicklaus has always looked great, managed to raise great kids, keeps beautiful homes, and has had the love and courage to go the distance with a man who reached the dizziest heights in sport—and she still had time to help keep his feet on the ground.

I think (after the last five days) this is the equivalent of winning about five hundred major championships. Just ask Jack who had the easier job.

Remembering a Friend

I went to a memorial service the other day, along with a bunch of friends and colleagues. I traveled to Orlando on a little Lear jet which is owned in part by Dave Pelz, and it was a very pleasant and uneventful flight in the company of good friends. It was the same flight, in the opposite direction, that Payne Stewart and his friends embarked upon just a few days before.

The scale of the memorial service, and the turnout, were enormous. It would have been a surprise to Payne, who was blissfully unaware of how much respect he commanded among his peers. It was not always this way. He had changed somehow, over the last few years, but not a whole lot, it seems to me. He was always generous, and to me at least, he had always been kind. On the surface, he was the same friend I had known for fifteen years. He was a great winner and an even better loser. His Ryder Cup match concession to Colin Montgomerie typified the character into which he had evolved, largely because of the inner peace he had achieved through his newfound faith.

Now, I am not a Christian, but something strange happened to me during the service. Everyone who attended was given a "WWJD" (What would Jesus do?) wristband, like the one that Payne wore, and just like everyone else, I tried to slip it on. It occurred to me that the first thing Jesus would do, would be to help me put the darned thing on, and I suppose he did, with the help of David Toms, who was sitting to my left. I figure that Jesus, in order to make it through his extraordinary life, must have had a sense of humor.

It was kind of nice to see some of the players wearing plus fours (I can't stand the word "knickers") on Sunday at the Tour Championship, as a tribute to Payne, but it was also a graphic example of why no one should ever be allowed to wear them again. They should be retired, like the jersey of a player who cannot be replaced. Payne was the only player in the modern era who could ever carry them off. Anyone else that wears them looks like they are trying to guarantee that they never get laid again. Now, before anyone gets upset about that last line, trust me, Payne would have loved it. I just want to remember that silhouette as being his, and his only.

I've been wearing my wristband for a few days now, and I have no intention of taking it off anytime soon. I'm a pretty happy guy for the most part, but I've got to admit, Payne Stewart left us feeling a lot happier for a reason I do not yet understand. In his honor, I'll wear it until it falls off, and then, maybe, I'll get another.

In closing, I'd like to thank Tracey, Chelsea and Aaron Stewart, whose amazing courage last Friday went a long way toward healing those of us who loved Payne.

Arnold, King of Sport

A few months back I wrote about my favorite golf course, which is Cypress Point. If I were allowed to play only one more round of golf, it would probably be there, but lately I've been thinking...with whom would I play? I've never been one to let a little thing like death bother me, so I decided it wouldn't matter if my partner has already been planted.

A lot of people sprang quickly to my mind, occupied all the available space, and then a fight broke out between the late Sir John Gielgud and the New Zealand soprano Dame Kiri Te Kanawa. As we know, girls fight dirty, and I had to stop thinking about it when Sir John let out the most fearsome coloratura squeal and fell backward into a drum kit belonging to Led Zeppelin drummer John Bonham, who, of course, died of rock-star enthusiasm back in the 1970s.

Boy, was he something. The only person I never knew who made my calves sore from listening to music. Bonham didn't play the drums; he tried to kill them. Try listening to the live "Whole Lotta Love" medley from the BBC Sessions CD, and then go hit a tee shot. If you're not fifty yards longer and stone, motherless deaf, I'll send you a sleeve of Stratas. I dunno, maybe there's something about dead drummers that appeals to me; Keith Moon was another guy I'd like to have seen trying to hit a golf ball.

Now that I come to think of it, it's a fairly eclectic group of people from which I must choose. George Carlin is in there, even though he hates golf. Anyone whose mind works in a way that allows him to discover how we can tell when a moth has farted (it suddenly flies in a straight line) is in my starting lineup.

Willie Nelson, too, and he does play golf. I think Willie Nelson's face should be on Mt. Rushmore. In fact, much of the uncarved piece of Mt. Rushmore pretty much looks like Willie's face already, so there wouldn't be much work involved. Willie just makes me want to be an American. He looks half cowboy, half Indian, half up yours, and half I love you. I know, that makes him two people, but I don't care. Peace, man, and leave Willie and me alone, we're goin' golfin'.

This is so hard. Every time I think of a favorite, another pops up. I mean, who wouldn't want to play with Sean Connery? I'd love to hear him say, "You're a shight for shore eyes, Pushy." Or, more realistically, "Shut up and hit the shtupid ball, you fat Irish git." Yeah, I'd pay to be insulted by Sean Connery.

Then there's another of my favorite actors, Jack Nicholson, except he supposedly doesn't suffer fools particularly gladly, and I doubt very much if I'd make him want to be a better man. Not that I'd want to, as I kind of like the image I have of him. I imagine the risky part of actually playing with any of these people is that I might run the risk of exploding one of my myths, or accidentally setting fire to a legend.

McCord runs into this problem all the time. I don't know how many times I've heard him say to an adoring fan, "Look pal, I'm not an announcer...I just play one on TV, okay?"

There are a number of people with whom I wouldn't necessarily need to play, but of whom I'd like to ask one question. Like the first guy to have had Lasik eye surgery for a start. "Let me get this straight...A doctor comes to you with a new idea that went something like this: 'Hey, you with the Coke-bottle glasses, come here! No, over here! Thanks. How about you let me point this little red-hot laser into your eyeball, and burn off a piece of your cornea? Whaddaya say?'"

Somebody said, "Okay!" and it wasn't Tom Kite. I would like to meet the kind of idiot that would agree to such a proposal, that's all. It would tend to suggest that while we know that love is blind, it might just have stupidity as a bedfellow.

Playing golf with any of the aforementioned would be a thrill for me, but in truth, I'd probably rather have the chance to just hang out with them or maybe have dinner. You know, observe the creature in its own environment.

Which brings me to Arnold, King of Sport. If I had one round left to play, I would rather play it with him, for more reasons than I have space to write. In my career I only played with him twice, first in the third round of the 1980 Canadian PGA Championship, and then twenty years later with that beautiful thing Joey Sindelar, in a nine-hole skins game for a children's charity in Rochester, New York.

In Canada, he marked my card, which is one of my most treasured possessions, and is now framed in my study. In Rochester, Joey and I got our comparatively youthful asses kicked, as Arnold won all nine skins, then signed about eight thousand autographs, jumped into his jet, and buzzed the golf course on his way back to Orlando. I had never seen anyone try so hard to win anything and be so kind at the same time.

But the incident that cemented my already firm conviction that Arnold is one of the greatest humans that ever lived happened at the Presidents Cup in Manassas, Virginia, where he was the U.S. team captain. It was one of the first events I worked for CBS, and I was standing on the practice putting green, decked out in full broadcast regalia, chatting with Mark O'Meara, when Arnold, who was mingling with his players, sauntered over and put his index finger and thumb around Mark's neck, and gave him the kind of playful squeeze that usually costs about a hundred bucks at the chiropractor's.

Then he shook hands with me, and wished me luck in my new career. I don't really recall how our conversation led to the point where I was telling Arnold a story, but I will never forget the feeling he gave me by simply being interested. I was having a conversation with Arnold Palmer, in front of hundreds of people who were obviously under the impression that he and I were buddies! Talk about a thrill—I had goose bumps on my hair.

Then, it happened. I lost him. One minute he was listening attentively, and the next he was staring over my right shoulder, obviously riveted by someone or something other than me. I shifted nervously a little to the right, but Arnold shifted with me. Then, suddenly, he looked back at me and said apologetically, "Oh, sorry, David...over your right shoulder. Whoa!"

I turned around to see what had distracted him so badly, and indeed, he was right. A drop-dead gorgeous, chestnut-haired little vixen was directly behind me on the other side of the putting green, about thirty yards away. I turned back to face the great man, who was grinning broadly at her. "You're right Arnold," I said. "That's my wife!"

He looked at me, grinned over my shoulder, and, never breaking stride, said, "Nice job!"

I turned again, and gave a cheery, "Hey, look at me, I'm talking to Arnold Palmer" kind of wave. Anita smiled and self-consciously waved back. Then I looked at Arnold, who was waving, too!

Arnold had always been my hero, but this was the point where I retired his number, commissioned the bronze, and named the new wing on my mental hospital. God, how I loved this man! Later that day, I introduced him to Anita and, wouldn't you know it, she fell in love with him, too. Everyone does, you see, because Arnold has an extraordinary ability to make everyone he meets feel special. Yeah, that's it: Arnold doesn't make you feel privileged, as do many famous people; he just makes you feel special.

Now before you dismiss this as a shameful piece of brown-nosing, there is one other reason I want to play with Arnold. The old fart beat me like a big bass drum the last time out, and he enjoyed it way too much. We need to make this the best of three.

Touched by an Angel

It seems to be happening less and less these days, but occasionally good things still happen to good people. During this past year, the courage and dignity that Stuart Appleby has shown us has made him something of a folk hero wherever he plays. What most people forget, however, is that he was well on his way to becoming one of the game's most admired men anyway, even before his tragic loss. It seems kind of sad to me that he had to achieve our admiration in this way.

It doesn't happen very often either in sports or in business (just ask Mark McCormack), but occasionally nice guys do make it to the top. In golf, names like Steve Elkington, Fred Couples and Nick Price spring to mind, and I believe that Stuart is in the same category. For most of us, the loss of a loved one is usually followed by a period of private grieving, but for Stuart it was a self-inflicted public ordeal which melted the hearts of even the most cynical sports fan. It was obvious to us all that it would have been easier for him to withdraw from the spotlight, but instead he chose the hardest, narrowest path possible. On Sunday it seemed that his path widened, as the others fell by the wayside and perhaps a piece of his life fell back into place when he holed out on the seventy-second hole en route to winning the Shell Houston Open.

I didn't know Renay Appleby very well, but you didn't have to know her to know that she was special. She would have wanted her husband to be famous for the great player that he is, and not for the player who lost the love of his life. We have a show on CBS, which I hardly ever get to watch, but this was one episode of *Touched by an Angel* that I did get to witness. I hope it's time for we in the media to let Renay rest, and let Stuart go on.

I Hate to Say It, but I Told You So

It was inevitable, I suppose. After Tiger's win at the Masters, the golf rags were full of predictable nonsense, which is my euphemism for wildebeest droppings, horse hockey, bovine loaves, or whatever you want to call it.

Frankly, it's crap. What we're dealing with here is a case of blanket denial. I hate to say I-told-you-so, but for the last few years during the course of my work, I've been doing my best to explain that Tiger Woods is in a different category, a parallel dimension, another world. In fact, he might even be of a different species, but apparently there are still some who remain convinced that part of the reason Tiger has been so astonishingly successful is that everyone else has been sucking.

Like, he has no competition, man, not like Hogan and Nelson and Snead had. Nicklaus and Palmer and Player and Casper and Trevino all had each other to battle. Watson and Ballesteros and Norman and Price wrestled with Feherty and Faldo, and don't get us started because back then the ball was made of soap, and the hole was smaller, and the wind blew harder. And they had to play in the rain as well, with those heavy old umbrellas that didn't bust those gusts. Hardly anybody wore sunscreen, they told us that cigarettes had vitamins in them, nobody got enough fiber in their diet, and in a bunker you had to watch out for the invective-laced land mines that Tom Weiskopf (with-a-lower-case "f") would occasionally leave behind him.

But now? Well, Ernie Els is a big ol' doofus, Vijay Singh couldn't play the radio, Sergio Garcia is only eleven years old, and Mickelson is left-handed, so how good could he be? When Tiger's name appears anywhere near the top of the leaderboard, these overpaid, flaccid, cocktail weenies instantly soil themselves, scream for their mommies, and start making double bogeys. They play for far too much money, they're spoiled rotten, then they go to the Senior Tour and start all over again.

Okay, I feel better now. I just hope I haven't been responsible in some way for having led anyone to believe that any of the men against whom Tiger competes are less talented than those who teed off with Hogan, Palmer, or Nicklaus. This next line is probably going to piss a few people off, but hey, I'm an announcer, and it's what I do.

I have the greatest respect for all the men who paved the way for the great players of today, but none of them ever competed against anyone like Tiger Woods. If Jack Nicklaus had been as superior back in the 1960s as Tiger is right now, the pencil-squeezers of the day might have labeled Arnold Palmer and Gary Player as gutless wonders.

When I think back about the countless times I've watched Tiger at close quarters, hitting a previously inconceivable shot with an unfeasible club from an indescribable stance out of an unplayable lie to within a few feet of an unattainable flag, it strikes me that I may not have done a good enough job of describing the scene.

At times I've been standing right next to one of those second-echelon players as such a feat is performed, and I always wish I were allowed to hand over the microphone, abdicate my responsibility, and let a more qualified person describe it. In fact, last year at Firestone, with a beautiful economy of words, Ernie Els did just that. He turned to me and said, "F*#@ me! Did you see that?" If I had drooled on for twenty minutes trying to describe it, I would have conveyed less information.

For the record, today's second-tier players—which is to say everyone except Tiger—do not suck. There is no suckage in the pack of players who follow Tiger in what is a completely suck-free zone. Retief Goosen's nine-under-par total at Augusta was a fantastic score on an extremely difficult golf course. What we have here is a case of blanket denial. Yes, I know that no one is meant to be that much better than the rest, but Tiger is, and his seventy-one on Masters Sunday was the best round of golf I have ever seen him play. That might seem a strange thing to say, but consider this: Six of the world's best seven golfers were in the final three pairings, which was unusual to say the least. It seemed to me that it might have been the first time in the history of major championship golf that if any one of five of the six leading players had played well in the final round, the only people capable of beating him would have been one of the other six.

I know it's confusing, but the point is, if the odd man out played well, short of somebody doing a Tonya Harding, no one else could win. It was like watching Paula Jones compete in a two-inch foot race before she had her nose job. It was over before it began. In fact, I felt it was over after Tiger hit his second shot to the fifteenth in the first round.

He had hit his tee shot way too far left, and was badly blocked behind the pines on the left side. In the first round of the Masters, an ordinary mortal superstar lays up, a notion that never even crossed Tiger's mind. Instead, he hit a sweeping fifty-yard hook from about 220 yards out to within fifteen feet of the hole, which was a clear declaration of intent. It said, "I will win this tournament no matter what anyone else does." I believed him.

Teeing off in the final round, Tiger was tied; three holes later, he was three blows in front. All year, and perhaps all of his life, had been preparation for the start to that round. He had fifteen holes left to play, but for the three and a half hours it took, he had only one shot left to hit—the next one.

I heard some people say they thought the last round was boring.

I must have been watching something else. For me, it was like watching the perfect combination of animal and machine in an electrifying, lithe, sinuous stalk. But contrary to popular belief, Tiger didn't terrify his competition into timorous, quivering wrecks, or destroy their scorecards by some kind of subconscious emotional bullying. The golf course took care of that. Maybe I didn't do a good enough job of explaining how difficult the golf course was on Sunday. It was played at full length, with the holes cut in brutal positions, and at Augusta that means the tiniest error at any time, on any shot, equals big numbers.

With unbreakable focus, relentless resolve, and equal parts artistic impression and technical merit, "the man" quietly put himself in a place where, if "the others" wanted to catch him, they would have had to gamble on every shot they hit. Anyone who gambles on every shot at Augusta National loses, even if they're Tiger Woods, and Tiger Woods knew that.

I'll probably be accused of writing this piece out of a sycophantic need to be Tiger's friend. Well, that would be nice, but he and I are just acquaintances, and we have a professional relationship. We don't exchange e-mail, send each other flowers, and I don't have his cell number. Sometimes he's an asshole to the media, and sometimes I'm a media asshole.

He does his job and I do mine, part of which is to give an opinion of the way things are in golf. I'm smart enough to know what opinions are like, and that everyone has one, and I think Tiger plays a game with which no one else has ever been familiar. He doesn't just surprise people like Ernie Els; I think he even surprises himself.

So with that in mind, maybe it's time we gave ourselves a break for being surprised, and one for the boys who finish behind him, too. Those who try and fail when Tiger wins are superb players, every bit as talented and dedicated as the men who challenged Nicklaus in his day and Hogan in his. To suggest otherwise is asinine.

All of Tiger's rivals give it their best shot, and none of them does anything of which they should be ashamed. If any of them had gotten away with their gambling at Augusta, Tiger would have squeezed on his throttle until the competition was once again framed in his rearview mirror a comfortable distance behind.

Everybody sit cross-legged in a circle now, link hands, gaze at the mother crystal, and say after me: "Nobody sucks. He is that good." (Repeat until everyone but you lapses into a coma, and then phone your bookmaker.)

Lehman's Class, the Ryder Cup, and Caddies

As I write, I sit in the sharp end of a Northwestern jet, headed for Dallas-Fort Worth Airport on the Sunday evening that saw Tom Lehman melt down at the Buick Open, leaving Tom Pernice with the trophy. I had the unenviable task of interviewing Lehman after his round, and as a former player, I knew how he felt. But as always, he was gracious and accommodating, due in no small part to the fact that he was surrounded by his beautiful wife and children.

In contrast to my awkward and fumbling questions, his answers were concise and forthright and as I headed for Detroit Metro Airport in my rental car, traveling way too quick in an effort to make a flight that would allow me to spend about thirty-six hours with my own beautiful wife and kids, I was struck by what I really should have asked him.

With a jet-set lifestyle and a social circle that includes captains of industry, rock stars, actors, and politicians, Tom Lehman is an anachronism in the world of professional golf. Perhaps it has something to do with his Minnesota roots, or his quietly understated faith, but it seems to me that he is a modern-day Byron Nelson, at least in his attitude toward the game, and his respect for those who play it. In a era where the game becomes increasingly popular to the MTV generation with its short attention span and penchant for one-day, made-for-TV events, he remains steadfastly behind, rooted in the Nicklaus-Palmer tradition that reeks of the fact that you can be square but still be way cool.

He wants to be on the Ryder Cup side; in fact, he'd pay to be on it. He is exactly the kind of man who should be on it. He also pulls no punches about how much he values the help he gets from his caddie, Andy Martinez. I've heard a lot recently from less enlightened players about it being possible to do just as well with a girlfriend or a buddy on the bag. That may be so, but here's a cold, hard fact. No one, and I mean absolutely no one, has ever had a great career with a buddy or a girlfriend packing their sack. No one. Period. Scott Hoch can call Greg Rita just a caddie, but Greg Rita can count up his wins from way back in the '70s. Payne Stewart has relied on Hicksy for years, and Vijay Singh would surely miss Dave Renwick. Jeff Maggert will probably win a major, but I doubt it will be with his girlfriend toting.

Just as Jim Nantz threw it down to me on Sunday, Tom's little son jumped into his arms, and the corners of his mouth turned upward. I wish I'd had the foresight, as Tom ran his hand through his daughter's hair, to ask him if he felt lucky. He had just screwed up horribly, and this might have seemed at first to be a strange question, but his wife Melissa and his kids were gazing at him with such obvious pride how could he have felt anything else?

Creatures Great and Small

Since a tiger came crashing out of the undergrowth, cutting a deep swoosh into the hindquarters of an unsuspecting PGA Tour, the rest of the wildlife has been understandably skittish. Would the Tour's animal kingdom be this jumpy if everyone went around calling him Eldrick? Heavens, no.

So, while a name isn't everything, this one certainly fits young Mr. Woods. Tiger is a predator with gleaming white incisors and an air of superiority. But Tiger is not the first, nor the only one with the well-suited nickname from the four corners of the zoo.

The Great White Shark is a name that Greg Norman wears as well as his designer clothing. Doesn't Craig Stadler look alarmingly like a Walrus? Besides being large, he's surprisingly nimble in his own environment and is an expert fisherman.

And, of course, there's the Golden Bear. In this particular forest, all the other animals pay their respects to the Bear, even the Tiger.

But I had a weird thought the other day, at least weirder than all the rest. Those aren't the only creatures in the wild. I'll bet, if my mind's eye serves me correctly, I could conjure up a few more denizens of the deep rough. At the risk of losing what few friends I have out there, simply remember: This exercise is in the name of science and animal husbandry.

Let's start with the obvious. Ernie the Lion King, ruler of the African bush. This laid-back monarch spends most of the daylight hours lounging in the shade. His backswing is a luxurious stretch, his downswing a regal yawn. He occasionally appears to doze off during the follow-through, but at the end of the day, he is usually around for the kill.

I have often wondered if it would be possible to breed an Els with a lesser spotted Couples. That would be one hip cat with a very low pulse rate.

That was simple enough. Now for the more exotic creatures. How about the Duckbilled Swedipus? Having trouble picturing this animal? Oh, try harder. Duckbilled? Jesper Parnevik?

Now you're catching on. However, don't be fooled. Beneath that wacky exterior lies the heart of an expert nest robber, getting better all the time.

I'll give you an easy one this time. The Octopus. Yes, of course. The first time I ever saw Jim Furyk's swing, for some reason it reminded me of an octopus falling out of a tree.

But the real question is: Which is more defective? My head or his swing? Furyk is winning millions and I'm off the Tour. What does that tell you? Don't you love this game?

Moving along to the next stop on the zoo tour is the Armadillo el Fiori, otherwise known as grumpicus extraordinaricus, with emphasis on the "cuss." One of evolution's great triumphs, this species has remained unchanged for millions of years.

When it is attacked, which is frequently, the Armadillo el Fiori has the ability to make himself almost spherical, which for Ed requires only a minor adjustment. He then shoots out a vile stream of verbal abuse, making even the most voracious carnivore slink off in defeat. Just ask Tiger.

The next animal doesn't need a cage, simply because we couldn't find one small enough. The Chicken Hawk, aka Fred Funk, is one of the dwindling number of smaller creatures who are talented and tenacious enough to be successful in today's world of heavy hitters.

Why the Chicken Hawk? For those of you who spent most of a wasted youth watching cartoons, or for those whose children are now doing the same, the Chicken Hawk is the tiny, dreaded nemesis of that loud-mouthed cartoon rooster Foghorn Leghorn.

It's kind of nice to see the look of surprise on old Foghorn's face, just before he falls to the ground, isn't it? "It's a joke, I say, it's a joke, son," as the Funky Chickenhawk drags off the prize.

Now that you have an idea of how my mind works, I have a quiz for you. See if you can guess the identity of the next animal. One clue: He is one of the world's great players who has yet to win a major championship.

When in a bad mood, this animal's hearing becomes so acute that he can, on occasion, hear a bee sneezing from two hundred yards. A large mammal, native to the western coast of Scotland, he looks as if he might have accidentally swallowed a large piece of furniture.

Prone to sudden mood swings, he has a violent aversion to British journalists and because I now qualify as an Irish journalist, he might never speak to me again. Fortunately, he has a pretty good sense of humor, a prerequisite on the European Tour where the rest of the herd are more likely to contract hoof-in-mouth disease.

Unfortunately, the only creature I can think of with all these attributes is called a Colin Montgomerie already, which on the face of it seems like a bizarre coincidence. But there you have it.

Now, for the final creature. It is the Chameleon, which is what

I'm about to impersonate. Blending into the background for a couple of weeks seems to be a good idea for this slithery reptile.

And I'm going to have to be careful because, remember, it's a jungle out there.

Another Side of John Daly

It's nice every now and then to read something positive about someone who has crashed and burned, and I know you all are familiar with the stories of John Daly's boozing and gambling, so today I thought I'd tell you one about him that you haven't heard.

The first time I met John was on the first tee at Rand Park golf club in Johannesburg. I don't remember the exact year, but it was in the late 1980s and John had just turned pro. I was leading by a shot after three rounds at eighteen under par from this blond American kid, who at first I found mildly irritating. I went to the turn in thirty that day and was still only one in front of the blond American kid, who by this stage I was finding extremely irritating.

To cut a short story even shorter, we were tied playing the last hole, an uphill par-5. I hit the fairway and Tarzan visited the jungle on the left, forcing him to chip out up the fairway. Seizing my chance, I hit a glorious 4-wood on the green about forty feet from the hole. Little did I know, I had him right where he wanted me. Cave-boy bludgeoned a wedge to twenty feet, I twitched mine five feet past, he drained, and I waned. By this stage he had become so damned irritating, I just had to make friends with him.

We're still friends today and I'm glad that people still see the goodness in him, and that Ely Callaway is willing to back him in his time of need. He drove his rental car across Humewood golf course that year, not in a drunken stupor, but to save the life of his caddie who was being chased by a gang armed with sharpened bicycle spokes and other instruments of death. John had made the mistake of paying him in public, and the mob was intent on making a withdrawal. J.D. cut them off, and whisked him to safety, undoubtedly risking his own life in the process.

People with small hearts don't do this sort of thing, and neither do they win two major championships. John Daly is my friend, and I wish him happiness and success, and the strength to hold on to them this time. I've heard enough negative things about him and I thought it would be nice for you to hear another side of his story.

Talking (Club)heads

I've had my butt welded to the La-Z-Boy for a couple of months now—you know, watching football, drinking beer, dozing off, watching more football, going to the bathroom, etc. Half man, half mattress. A piece of furniture for me has to be soft, comfortable, and thoroughly absorbent.

I don't play golf so much anymore, but on the rare occasions I do, I've noticed that my little Strata is visiting parts of the clubface that it never used to lay a dimple on. If clubs could speak, mine would say, "Ouch!" quite a lot.

That, however, is not the language that is emitted from the faces of the clubs belonging to the best players in the world. I know because I interviewed them. That's right, I talked to the clubs instead of the players. Hey, they have heads, faces, heels, toes, and necks, so why shouldn't they have mouths?

Go ahead, admit it. You talk to your clubs. You call them vile names, I'm certain, when your slice is headed straight for the upstairs bedroom window of that last condo on the right.

Call me daft—you wouldn't be the first—but I decided to have a word or two with what's in the Tour players' bags. You know, get it straight from the source. They speak, I listen. Don't laugh—all right, go ahead and laugh—but you know from reading this column that stranger things have happened.

It's dusk outside the bag room and all the spectators have gone home. A couple of players search for a stroke on the putting green in the gathering gloom, while the rest are back at their hotels, or at least on the way. My Softspikes squirm on the AstroTurf floor as I walk between the rows of bags. I stop and poke the microphone into David Duval's bag. "Hey, guys, how was your day?" I ask.

"Oh, you know," replies the 8-iron, "we bumped into each other a lot, banged heads as usual, and the putter has the flu. Last night somebody left us right under the air conditioner. The man wonders why he couldn't make a thing today. The poor putter's shaft is stiff and sore and its head is aching. As for those sunglasses, we all wish the boss would take them off when it's cloudy. He can't see a thing. One of these days he's going to hit the umbrella instead of the sand wedge, mark my words."

Over in the corner, a voice calls out: "Hey, microphone boy, over here!" It's Bruce Lietzke's bag, and the driver is not happy. "I'd just like to clear something up. It's a well-known fact that the big guy doesn't play a whole lot, okay? But the fruit under the headcover thing is getting a little old.

"Last fall, some idiot stuck a banana up my headcover, and it was February before I saw daylight. I had enough penicillin stuck to me to cure a clap epidemic. Nobody ever does anything to that absurd UHF antenna sticking out of the top of our bag; they always pick on me."

Lietzke's long putter immediately took offense. "Look here, you whiner—short shaft, short memory. You obviously don't remember that melting left wrist he had before I showed up. If it weren't for me, you wouldn't have a home at all. I might not look like the rest of you, but I get the job done. We pay the bills because of me and don't you forget it!"

The driver continued, "Don't pay attention to him. He thinks size matters and he's always trying to justify his existence. We've tried therapy and drugs, but nothing works. Anyway, we all got our hopes up at Christmas, when the Mrs. bought a practice net for the garage. The boss puts it up, hits three wedges, disappears for two weeks, comes back, and turns it into a hammock. Typical."

I cross the way and notice a particularly neat Hogan bag with the clubs all in descending numerical order in their compartments. The fur headcovers have side hair partings. These are obviously Justin Leonard's clubs. I poke my microphone in. "Okay, boys, where's the putter?"

"In bed with the boss," replies the 2-iron sniffishly. "Haven't been able to pry them apart since the Ryder Cup. It's pretty disturbing to the rest of us, I can tell you. It has a real attitude, you know, talking about how it has the power to move the masses and attract good-looking women. We'd put a headcover on it, but we can't find one big enough."

"Pssst, Pssst," goes a noise behind me. It's Phil Mickelson's 60-degree wedge.

"How about a word from a minority group? It's a cruel world out there when you always have to look the other way. It's like we're different or something, but the other clubs seem to be afraid of us. If it wasn't for Mike Weir and Steve Flesch we'd have no one to talk to at all.

"But the one I really feel sorry for is Notah Begay's putter. The poor thing goes both ways, and that's just not done out here, like most people are in total denial about it. His clubs are in the closet over there; sometimes you can hear them knocking at night. It's just not right."

I hear a faint rattling behind me, and I turn to face Jim Furyk's bag. The clubs are revolving slowly. "What's up with you guys?" I ask.

"Oh, don't mind us," they say. "We're just fine. It's just that it takes us a little while to get rid of the dizziness after a round, you know? Most clubs have to make only one change of direction in a swing, but we have about eight. Not that we're complaining. The trip away from and back to the ball is way more interesting for us, and we love it. We get to see a lot more than the rest of the guys, and we get hit sweeter than most of them, too."

"No sweeter than us," says Steve Elkington's 3-wood. "The only time we disturb the air is when the boss sneezes on the downswing. Mind you, that happens quite a lot. My only problem is that he doesn't use headcovers. I've rubbed faces so often with the driver that the short irons are starting to talk about us, like we're in love or something."

From the darkest corner of the bag room I hear a faint, but regular snoring sound from a bag with a "Do Not Disturb" sign obscuring the name. I tiptoe across and ever so gently lift up the sign, just enough to reveal the name: "Couples." The 4-iron wakes with a start.

"Whoa, pal, can't you read? It's mid-season, and we're trying to get a few weeks of sleep here."

"Sorry," I whisper, and head for the door, but on the way I notice a bag that sits higher than the others, bathed in a halo of light. These are the surgical instruments of Tiger Woods.

I kneel down in front of the bag, and look into the one remaining eye of the battered and faded little striped Tiger headcover. It looks like the comfort toy of some long since grown-up toddler, worn out but irreplaceable.

"So what's it like to be the best?" I ask. The little guy blinks, and rubs the spot where his left eye used to be.

"Well, it's not all glitz and glamour, I can assure you," it says. "For a start, compared to the rest of the clubs in this room, my guys are pretty weak. Everyone else is at least a couple of degrees stronger than we are, sometimes more, yet we get hit a lot harder than they do. That doesn't seem fair. Worse than that, we get hit in the same place every time, too.

"One of the few things we've got going for us is that we get hit less often than the rest, but having said that, we never know when, either. Your average golf club gets a little warning before impact, you know? Like an address position, followed by a waggle or two, but these guys never know when to brace themselves.

"One minute you have a ball bouncing up and down on your face, which is kind of fun, and then, without warning, you go from zero to 140 mph and collect one right in the kisser. We have the only 8-iron in the history of golf that has to wear a diaper. The poor thing is a nervous wreck. And as for the 3-wood, he's a paranoid schizophrenic. He doesn't know where the hell he's going to be used from next—either from three hundred yards or just off the edge of the green. We're thinking seriously about having him institutionalized."

One thing is certain, however. It doesn't matter which implements the owner of the Tiger headcover uses. He could take any bag in the room and still find a way to win. He reminds me of a story that's often told in football circles. Since I live in Texas now, I can call it my own.

Former Houston Oilers coach Bum Phillips used to say of Miami Dolphins coach Don Shula, "He can take his'n and beat your'n, or he could take your'n and beat his'n."

Who says you can't make clubs sit up and talk?

A Hero for the Ordinary Joe

The last couple of weeks on the PGA Tour pretty much summed up a lot of things that are going right at the moment. The finish at The International squashed the rumor that in order for a tournament to be interesting, Tiger has to be in the field, and the Buick Open dealt nicely with any suggestion that when the Great One is playing badly, someone else has a chance. Apparently, he has to be playing very, very, badly for that to be the case.

But how about that finish at Castle Pines? If Granddad fell asleep in the armchair during the last hour of that one, you can go ahead and unplug him as far as I'm concerned. We've become kind of used to seeing suck-it-up and get-stoically-on-with-it behavior when less experienced leaders are caught from behind, but with Rich Beem, we got treated to how a real person feels when they have a PGA Tour event sewn up, and then not, and then sewn up again, and then not, and then...well, you saw him, he looked like someone was pushing and pulling a Christmas tree in and out of his shorts. What a freaking nightmare, and what great television! I remember Rich's last win, back at the '99 Kemper, as I was on the ground with him during the last round there, too. In fact I had been with him the day before during the third round, when, on the twelfth green as he settled over a birdie putt, I suffered an embarrassing moment.

The day started off normally enough. I ate lunch, and was getting wired up in the Broadcast Sports Technology RF truck, when I was struck by an unusually painful intestinal gurgle. No matter, I strapped on the waist pack known as "Talent Pack One," slid a CBS ballcap over the brain container, and finished off the ensemble by snapping on my custom-made one-can headset over the top. Terry and Gunny, the two asshole technicians who refer to me as an "MMH" (mobile mike holder), clipped the cable to the collar of my shirt, tested the signals by almost shattering my right eardrum with feedback, and sent me out to find the leaders. Sadly, by the time I'd gone a few holes with Beem's group, it became apparent that the giant cholesterol-infested greaseburger I had consumed for lunch was looking for an exit, and an epic intestinal battle was taking place. I have a feeling I've described this one somewhere in cyberspace before, and it was pretty revolting the first time, so in the interests of journalistic decency, this time I'll try to put it into a science-fiction context for y'all:

Outwardly the scene was normal, as Talent Pack One cruised the sector 12 landing area, but within the confines of the humanoid's thoraxial cavity, suspended in a huge ball of gas, the alien creature was making itself ready for another run at the southern portal.

Outside, in the atmosphere, the humanoid they called "Beemer" was preparing to transport the white dwarf toward the event horizon, when the commander of the telecast received a distress call from Talent Pack One.

"Do not, repeat, do not call in Talent Pack One," came the plaintive cry. "I am under attack from within, by an unknown weapon, presumed biological. Southern Portal is weakening! Talent Pack One, heading for Cosmic Relief Station at warp factor 9000, Code Blue! Repeat, Code Blue! Incoming! All spectator drones in line for Cosmic Relief Station Abort, Abort, Abort! Get the hell out of my way, you assholes!"

Meanwhile back on Earth, I'm running headlong for the portalets, across the twelfth green, right behind Beemer, as he putts.

He putts, he misses!

Strangely, he is not pissed off, or at least not as pissed off as I, for despite my gallant effort to reach safe harbor on the other side of the twelfth green, as I pass him my hitherto heroic sphincter sadly surrenders to the attack of the cholesterol-bomb, resulting in a catastrophic failure of the trouser variety, or if you like, a supernova of the shorts.

Now, you all might well be asking yourselves why the hell I would share this with you, but the following day, when I joined Beemer's group for the final round, the first thing he did when he saw me was reach into his golf bag, and toss me a bottle of Pepto-Bismol.

Laughing, he said, "Take a swig of that, and maybe we can get around without hurting each other!"

So I did, and tossed it back to him.

Fast-forward to this year's final round of the International, and a conversation I had with Beemer during a rain delay. He told me that he has a swig of Pepto before every round he plays, just to make sure "nothing happens down there!" Hey, what a recommendation!

I don't know about you, but I thought Beemer's performance was one of the greatest displays of intestinal fortitude I've ever seen on a golf course, and it was made even more special by the transparent nature of the man. Here is a hero for the ordinary Joe. Steve Lowery is a great guy, but I felt that every single person who watched that telecast, from the pros in the locker room, to the folks at home, lived and died every minute of it with the Beemer.

You love a guy like that, because you know him—he's you. If the makers of Pepto-Bismol want a spokesman, they should think about paying Beem a fortune to carry a big, dusty pink bag next season.

When he was a *@#$% Golfer

Hey, I need to tug on your coat about something here. Does anyone remember when Tiger Woods was a golfer? I do, barely, and the way I look at recent events is like this: Anyone that wants him to act like a politician, should at least have the decency to pay him a bribe. Isn't that the way it's supposed to work? I don't want to hear what other people think he should be thinking, I want to hear what he's thinking, and I don't want him to have to think about it for too long either, or for that matter, have to consult with his spin witch-doctors first. I liked him better when just like the rest of us, he was allowed to be wrong every now and then.

The last time I checked, no cow ever gave Michael Jordan a hard time because she wasn't allowed to be a member of the Bulls, but for some reason our wonder-child seems to be getting more job offers to be the spokesperson for the less-than-content minority in a group of otherwise pretty damned intelligent people, than the leader of the free world. I was going through Tiger's trash the other day, and this was one of the best I found. I think I've heard from this guy before.

Dear Mr. Woods:

I write to you, as a member of the National Society for the Prevention of Cruelty to Vegetables, the honorary chairperson of Save the Algae, and a concerned citizen of the world. I may live on the other side of the ditch so to speak, but I feel it is my bounden duty to enlighten my American brethren to the brutal, mass herbicide which is taking place daily on golf courses throughout your country, and indeed, the world. You sir, are clearly one of the architects of this evil practice, and while you may have succeeded in attracting the fawning interest of the corporate nazis who attempt to propagate the vile fungus of capitalism throughout the world (not that there is anything inherently wrong with a fungus), you must be forewarned that the NSPCV is a movement whose admittedly not particularly big membership will be fobbed off at your peril.

Don't even think about it Nike. You ignore us, and we'll be up the fossil fuel burning tailpipe of your Citation 10 quicker than it takes Al Sharpton to show up with a camcorder at an NYPD crack party. Don't play dumb either. Safe to say, we have plenty of televised evidence of your all-out attack on Mother Earth and the horrifying dismemberment of the tender green shoots that are her only defense against the insidious, poisonous encroachment of man(and of course woman) kind. Can't forget the girls here, that wouldn't be cricket.

But moving right along and getting right to the heart of the matter, you, and your man and woman-made natural-fiber wearing, supremely white associates need to stop taking divots out of our planet. Okay, so you're not white, but you're supposed to be part Indian like that other big dark chap from Java that also hacks lumps out of the worldflesh. In fact, he might do more damage than you, now that I come to think of it. What sort of an Indian tears holes in the earth, ripping tiny blades of grass from the soil, without a care for the tiny shrieks of agony that only dogs and certain types of Spanish moss can hear? Answer me that. I mean, you don't even show any concern for the exposed nerve-endings of the earth's mightiest creatures, the trees! For your info, pal, the roots of a tree are like the loins of a great, defenseless giant, spearing its way into the moist, dark, poontang of the motherdung. All right, that last bit might be a little out-to-lunch, but how would you like it if someone dug a chunk out of your trouser-trout with a metal implement, traveling at the speed of greed?

Oh yes, I have no doubt you can find something in your mixed cultural lineage to justify such behavior. I've heard that groveling twat Feherty on the box, going on about the Eastern philosophical influence, the Zen calmness etc, blah, blah, blah. Dear god, I'd rather fill my backside with fireworks, and squat over a propane stove than listen to that moron talking about you. If it wasn't for that overpaid Kiwi skycap who always compromises the crime scene when he covers up your mass graves with his smelly Nikes, every time you stopped walking, Feherty's microphone would disappear up your bottom/dungfunnel. Thailand, Schmailand, whatever. These are people who have no problem genetically mutating bay grass with embryonic lemons, grinding up the fetuses and then serving them in soup! They're murderous bastards, all of them! Sorry about that, but the whole issue of genetically altered crops has me in such a tizzy. I haven't been the same since I almost strangled on the hemp thong my mother (who was a welder) insisted on wearing during my delivery.

But enough about me. Fuck you. You are hereby served with notice, that unless you support our campaign to have all sporting arenas currently abusing grass, changed to astroturf I, and the other four members of the NSPCV will protest your behavior by picketing naked outside the highly guarded entrance to the Orlando housing project in which you live. We will sing our battle hymn, which goes as follows:

Fill our veins with chlorophyll, and fertilize our sprouts.
Make it go from bad to worse for those who laugh and doubt.
Though only five, while we're alive, they will not call it sport
If plants are dying, and trees are crying,
they will have to eat our shorts.

Chorus:
They will eat our shorts, the bastards,
they will eat our shorts, the cowards,
They will gag on man-made fiber, and victory will be ours!

Every blade will be remembered, every splinter, every shoot,
Each sprout and leaf and sapling, every tuber, every root.
We will build a giant obelisk, and stain it with pitch canker
And we'll write the names of all of you, you dirty, rotten wankers.

There are 172 verses so far, and we have no problem repeating it, so it would seem we have the upper hand here, no? Uh-huh, that's what I thought, and just to prove we at the NSPCV are not entirely against sports, here's a little friendly advice for you Mr. Woods. If I say so myself, I'm a bit of a dab hand off the old mat down at the driving range, and I've noticed a flaw in your swing that old Butchie, and the moron Feherty have missed. Not that that's much of a surprise, I wouldn't trust either of those dildos to train a rosebush.

You're way too steep on the downswing. If you put a little more weight on your right foot at address, and lift your left foot off the ground at impact, you shouldn't make contact with the ground at all, which would, in one fell swoop, solve both your problem, and mine.

No thanks are necessary, but if you wouldn't mind signing with the gold pen, the enclosed humanely harvested-because-it-was-already-dead aubergine, and returning it to me in the stamped, addressed bubble-pack, I'd appreciate it. Next month marks the six-week anniversary of the foundation of the Forest of Ugby Tribe for the Introduction of Lichens to Everyone, or FUTILE, as this dedicated group of tree-dwelling oxygenaians prefers to be called. If I don't get something from you within the next week or so for their auction, you can be expecting a letter from their leader, Dr. Berry Stamens, who is a damn sight more militant than I.

Good luck with the swing change,
Regards,
Sir Norman Hackett-Daly,
Snipe Manor
Spore-on-the Mold,
Rutland, England (just left of France)

Chapter Eight

A Hallowed and Formidable Tradition of Idiocy

Here Endeth the Lesson

I was nine, finally old enough to pull my father's trolley (that's a pull cart to you Americans). He would allow me to take the occasional ungainly swipe with one of his great big golf clubs and one particularly violent toe-snipe almost neutered my Uncle Weston.

Dad always believed that after any stinging blow, a vigorous rub would do the trick to relieve the pain. In this case, he told Uncle Weston, "Don't rub them, count them."

Dad decided, in the interest of safety, it was time I had a couple of weapons cut down to my own size.

In the corner of the pro shop sat a barrel of old clubs that Ernie Jones, the club pro, referred to as the "sheep beaters." He hacked off about five inches from the shaft of a medieval 2-wood, did the same to a 5-iron from the Cretaceous period, and I was off and duffing.

With my father as a role model, I soon developed a decidedly agricultural action. I instantly fell in golf's great trap—I did what came naturally or, in other words, what felt comfortable.

I held the club in my left hand with a five-knuckle grip and stood with a knock-kneed, wide open stance. Man, it felt good. Results were another matter. I could skelp the ball up the left wing and watch it finish forty yards right of the fairway.

After ten minutes of trying to follow the flight of my ball, Dad needed a chiropractor. He worked it out that the ball was going about 120 yards with the 2-wood, but unfortunately, only seventy of them were forward.

I was the proud owner of a majestic snap-slice so severe that into the breeze the ball would frequently end its odyssey heading back in my direction.

Sensing that I might never complete a dogleg left, my father had a sudden and uncharacteristic attack of common sense. He sent me to Ernie for a course of lessons.

Ernie had his hands full, and I'm certain that his first pint of the evening, after an afternoon with me, was downed in two swallows so he could begin the process of erasing the memory of what he witnessed on the practice ground.

You try teaching an uncoordinated nine-year-old with the IQ of a toilet seat. At that age, I was like a computer. You had to punch information into me and needless to say, I was not a model pupil.

Now, listen, my mummy could teach Tiger Woods. That's easy—no offense meant to Butch Harmon. She'd say, "All right dear, I'd like you to stand with your legs straight and your feet together. Grip the club so I can see four knuckles on your left hand and none on your right. Thank you.

"Now, keep your left arm bent, your head up, and away we go!"

Tiger could do exactly as Mum directed and what's more, he'd find a way to win with it.

I, on the other hand, couldn't do as Ernie instructed simply because I didn't want to. He changed my grip, a move I vehemently opposed. Why change what is comfortable and familiar for something that feels awful? You wouldn't either, would you?

After much argument and the occasional rabbit punch, he convinced me, and when I learned how to lose a ball in the left rough, I considered myself a complete player who no longer needed tuition.

In the ensuing years, Ernie taught me a great deal more, including what now seems obvious. The day after you find the answer, someone will change the question. But it was not until I found myself at the peak of one of my many slumps that I was to learn my most valuable lesson.

In 1983, the game of golf had a firm grip on the waist of my boxers and was administering the death wedgie. I had a dose of the atomic yips and after missing ten of eleven cuts by a single shot, I was ready to quit and apply for a job as a wringer-outer for a one-armed window cleaner.

I sat glumly in a clubhouse in the north of England, looking for someone to torture with my tale of woe. (I had not yet learned that 90 percent of people don't care what you shot and the other 10 percent wish it was higher.)

The unlucky stiff turned out to be Gary Cullen, a Kenyan friend of mine. Gary sat beside me and, before I could open my mouth, suggested that I go see a friend of his, a sports pyschologist named Alan Fine.

I told Gary that I needed a shrink like I needed a worse putting stroke, thank you very much. Secretly, I had vowed to seek the man out, a kind of pilgrimage, if you like. I conjured up an image of a swami figure sitting in a lotus position, humming quietly.

I was dead right, except that he had a much bigger nose than I had ever dreamed possible. (And, I'm not nasally challenged myself.)

I explained to him that I could not get it into the hole from eighteen inches and I needed him to tell me in fifty words or less (he charged by the hour) how to overcome this problem. He asked me for the two simplest outcomes for any given putt that I might face.

I told him that I could either make the putt or miss it. Duh!! Then he asked, "What if those two possibilities were equally acceptable to you?"

At that point I realized that if my brain was made of dynamite it probably wouldn't be big enough to blow the wax out of my ears. Then he said, "The players who play the best are those who have the courage to play as if it doesn't matter." The bit that irked me most was the fact that he had just uttered the two simplest, most profound statements I had ever heard and he was still eleven words under the limit!

Then, to make matters worse, this man, who had never played golf in his life, gave me a putting lesson. Within minutes I was holing nearly everything from nearly everywhere and even enjoying the few I missed!

I learned that day what great players like Woods and Jack Nicklaus have known all along. The ability to turn one's attention inward and merely observe what is going on is the trademark of a champion.

Now, you are saying, "Your most valuable lesson hasn't done you a helluva lot of good, has it? You don't even play anymore."

True enough, but it is a lesson that was taught to me by my favorite coach, a man who I believe should be at the top of every top-100 list and not just for alphabetical reasons.

That man is Mike Abbott—formerly of the Sports Club of Dallas and now at Rancho San Marcos in Santa Barbara, California—and he was the man who would finally point my career in the right direction. He tells people that he coached me off two tours and into the commentary box.

Sometimes the best a coach can do is to tell you when to quit and play a different game. That's a real friend.

Holiday Time at the Fehertys

This has nothing to do with golf. Hey, it's the off-season, and I'm taking it off. Instead, I thought I'd share a little Feherty family history with you.

This year, my mom and dad are in Germany visiting my sister Helen and her family during the holiday season. Whenever members of my family get together for any length of time, some kind of war usually breaks out. So given this year's venue, I've been nervous. I'm pretty sure my father will try to invade Poland or something.

You see, we Fehertys have a long history of pissing each other off in this, the season of goodwill. My earliest memories of this are of my grandmother on my dad's side and his Auntie Rose, who detested each other, and who met only once a year, on Christmas Day, around the dinner table at our house. My mom always seated them as far apart as possible, lest the daggers they stared at each other would turn into real cutlery.

Gran was a teetotal, Free Presbyterian, tambourine-bashing Salvation Army widow, full of righteous indignation. Auntie Rose was an octogenarian spinster with a chin like an albino hedgehog. If you kissed her, chances were you'd need stitches afterward. She was also fairly deaf, so when Gran raised her voice, we always knew that a reference to Auntie Rose's husbandlessness was coming. I loved it!

We—that is, my two sisters and I—were warned every year that we were not to laugh at either of these two old boilers. Every year, I failed miserably. Flatulence—which, as you've no doubt noticed, is a recurring theme in these pieces of mine—was one of the things that Auntie Rose was prone to, and because she couldn't hear it, she assumed no one else could either. On one occasion she was in the process of pulling her chair a little closer to the table when she accidentally (presumably) cut loose with an ear-splitting bloomer-blast. There followed about two seconds of absolute silence around the table, and then I burst out laughing so hard that some of the mouthful of food I had shot out through my nose.

"David!" my father yelled, grim-faced, at me. I laughed even harder. He got up, grabbed his evil ten-year-old by the scruff of the neck and marched me out of the dining room, down the hallway, and into the lounge. I thought I was in for it, but instead of walloping me, dad collapsed onto the sofa in tears of mirth. We laughed until our stomachs were sore, and it was only after several failed attempts to get serious that we were able to go back to the table.

Later that night, Gran took her yearly shot at Auntie Rose, who had me cornered under the sprig of mistletoe in the doorway. "Give us a kiss under the mistletoe, darling," she said. The dreaded moment had come. I braced myself. Then Gran, who had up until then appeared to be engrossed at the TV, bellowed: "You couldn't get a man to kiss you if he was under anesthesia, never mind mistletoe!" All hell broke loose once more.

This year, I was kind of looking forward to having a quiet Christmas, with just Anita and me, our baby Erin and our two sons, Shey, ten, and Rory, six, both of whom have a tendency to laugh at inappropriate moments. But, to be honest with you, it was a little too quiet. Next year, we have plans to go to Ireland for the holidays, and for the first time in over twenty years, sit around the same table with the whole family. All too often, as our parents get older, we forget how tolerant they were of us when we were small. I hope I've inherited my old man's memory, specifically the one of what it's like to be a little boy. I've got a feeling I'm going to need it.

Creatures Great and Small (Again)

I remember playing winter golf when I was a kid. By the end of October, Bangor Golf Club in County Down, Northern Ireland, was usually pretty sodden, and come Christmas it was either a quagmire or frozen solid. It didn't matter to us, though; we played anyway. Or maybe we plowed—there wasn't much difference.

We had eighteen temporary greens, which were just crude circles mown in the fairway short of the real greens, and due to the roughness of the putting surfaces, the holes were doubled in size. A ten-footer would have been a tap-in if it hadn't been for the worm casts and the gouged evidence of wedges past.

In the British Isles, you see, it takes more than a little mud to dull the enthusiasm of the average golfer, who is a good deal hardier (and possibly dafter) than his American counterpart.

"I'm off to the club for nine holes, dear!" my father would shout as he collared Daly, the German shepherd, and me on his way out the door. A few minutes later, I'd be carving foot-long divots out of the practice ground while he and the dog watched from the snug.

My dad has always had the constitution of a yak and would play in his shirtsleeves even in December, but he was at least equally inclined to toss down a few Famous Grouse instead. You know, somebody has to drink the stuff.

The thing that was so different about back then and there was that Christmas would be upon you before you knew it. Here and now, Christmas, or at least the ghastly commercial part of it, is being forced down our necks while we're still burping back Thanksgiving. I'm not sure about any of you, but I don't want to hear "Rudolph the Red-Nosed Reindeer" every day for five weeks straight, especially not in the locker room. When is deer season, anyway?

(For the purpose of this article, I'm assuming that it's early December, your halls are already decked with boughs of holly, you have a beard rash from being relentlessly cornered under the mistletoe by your maiden aunt, and there is at least one indelible clot of pine sap attached to a piece of your furniture. It's probably the sofa upon which nobody ever sits; you know the one, in the front room where your greasy Frito hands are never allowed to set except on Christmas Day, when you force that queasy smile and open those packages of socks and the too-short haddock necktie. "Oooh, look! It's another nostril trimmer from the Sharper Image!"—which is really just Radio Shack at twice the price.)

It's still weeks until Christmas, but I'm guessing your bells, like mine, are well and truly jingled by now. It lasts so long, or is it just me? Already my children are like packs of gremlins, hunting me down and shoving grubby little wish lists up my nose as I sleep.

I grew up in Ireland, where there was always a sense of anticipation as the days of December slipped toward the 25th, but the whole thing was so minimal by comparison to the evilly coordinated Madison Avenue assault that parents have to endure these days.

Christmas used to be a simple, family affair with a nice church service and an exchange of gifts. Now it's a thirty-day fat boy, reindeer, and elf-fest, with death by caroling everywhere you go. More than a week of caroling will make your mid-winter seem bleak, all right, and the frosty wind isn't all that'll be moaning if you're hanging around me. Another few days of "Joy to the World," and I'm liable to drag one of those joyful, tin mug-waving cretins into the Disney Store and give him a good wassailing, whatever the hell that means.

I remember (dear God, I'm starting to sound like my dad) many wonderful Christmas moments from my childhood, in the days before it was a circus. Christmas, that is—my childhood was always a circus. I was the head chorister in the church choir (I was, too, you cynical swine), and occasionally we used to visit other churches around Christmastime to see if we could yell to the music louder than they could.

I was one nasty little treble, and there was a definite air of competition when my team played an away game. Every year, there was this one church that went the whole hog—or donkey, rather—with their nativity scene, which they set up at the top of the chancel steps. Everyone was very proud of it. It had the straw in the crib, a couple of tranquilized sheep, a beagle for some reason, and a tiny, rather bloated-looking, brown-and-white donkey.

There was a cardboard shepherd and everything, and it was all right there, just a few feet in front of my choirboys and me as we finished the processional hymn. We took our seats. There were no wise men, I noticed, and not a virgin in sight. Then again, we were in Ireland, so what were the odds?

There was the usual kerfuffle, clearing of throats, and blowing of noses as the congregation settled itself down in the pews for the first words of the elderly rector, who hobbled his way painfully up into the pulpit and raised his palms toward the heavens.

"We lift up our voices to the Lord," he said, and smiled benevolently down at his flock. Smiling benevolently back, the people opened their mouths to lift up their voices when the wee donkey suddenly let rip with a thunderous, cannon-like fart of such velocity that the poor animal had to skitter and clip-clop around on the tiles for a moment in order to keep its balance.

Dear Lord, the mouths of the people were open, but not a sinner amongst them did speak. Verily, it was as if the ass had struck them dumb.

For a few seconds, the unholy silence was ruptured only by the ghostly remains of the blast as it echoed around the ancient vaulted ceiling, but, alas, there was worse to come. To my eternal credit or damnation or whatever, I managed not to burst out laughing immediately, but then the donkey dropped a whopper onto the mosaic in front of us, where it landed with a loud "SPLOT."

It was the look on the rector's face that did me in. St. Paul probably got less of a shock on the road to Damascus, and if I remember correctly, his donkey got struck by lightning. I flat-out split my peas. Maybe the devil made me do it, but I laughed so hard I nearly asphyxiated myself, and one of the younger boys vomited on his cassock.

There were more tears shed that day than that church had seen in a year of funerals, and I believe ours were considerably more genuine than those of the average mourner. The rector had to wipe his glasses off twice, and his first attempt at speaking resulted in an uncontrollable snorting fit as he slapped the pulpit with the flat of his hand.

Lordy, Lordy, but someone up there has a sense of humor, and definitely works in mysterious ways. That day, the collection was a new parish record, and there were a number of requests for a matinee. They took photographs of the donkey (which was deemed to be far too dangerous for children's parties) and made a stained-glass window of the scene. It was very stained, by all accounts.

Well, anyway, I would unreservedly apologize if the preceding account has offended a single soul (although it would be a first for this column if it hasn't), and it is with tearful supplication that I beg forgiveness for the fact that, as usual, this piece has had nothing to do with golf. I have no idea why it went where it did, but I hope it gave you a chuckle. Think of it as an early Christmas present, if you like, from me to you. Yeah, I know, it's too early. How hypocritical is that?

And thank you for your mail, even from those of you who think I'm a moron. You're wrong, but, like I tell my kids, at least you're reading. Have a happy, safe, and peaceful Christmas, Chanukah, Kwanzaa, or whatever you like to call it, and if you have one, may your God go with you—and his wee donkey, too.

Fond of a Joke and a Jar

Well, I'm back from my six-day jaunt to Ireland, none the worse for wear......well, okay then, maybe slightly the worse for wear. Every time I go home, I am reminded not only of how much I miss the place and the people, but also of why I love the U.S. For a start, here in the States the words "cold" and "beer" have a meaningful relationship. Almost the first thing I did when I got off the airplane at DFW was find a chilly one and drain it...a sure sign that Texas has become my home.

But while it may be easier to get a cold one here, it's in Ireland that I get most of my material for after-dinner speaking. My father is, as they say, "fond of a joke and a jar" and surrounds himself with those who are out of their like minds. Last week, for instance, he had occasion to play with one of these idiots at the golf club where I grew up.

During the course of their round the subject of sleep came up. It turned out that Dad's pal was having a little difficulty in nodding off at night. My father, in his infinite wisdom, suggested that rather than count sheep, he should play a round of golf in his head while it lay on the pillow. "I guarantee you, you'll be asleep before the turn!"

A couple of days later in the men's bar, Dad asked his friend if his fail-safe method had worked. This was the reply. "Well you know, Billy, it did and it didn't. I played the first very well and then I bogeyed the second, but on the third I sliced my tee shot into that spinney of trees over on the right and lost the ball. I stayed up half the night looking for it!"

Where I come from, this kind of conversation is considered normal. I'm sure it's how the great Irish joke tradition got started, or in other words, most Irish jokes aren't jokes at all, they're perfectly serious.

Burned on the Dark Continent

Back in June 1976, I was a terminally optimistic, zit-ridden, seventeen-year-old five-handicapper. Naturally, I turned pro.

I thought, after a few months' practice, I would stroll through qualifying school and straight onto the European Tour. After a few months' practice and with the European Tour school behind me, I was a suicidal, eighteen-year-old assistant professional with nowhere to play.

On the bright side, my skin had cleared up.

Spending a winter in Northern Ireland and working on your game is a good way to get your handicap from five to about eleven, so it was obvious I needed to get out of there.

In those days, there was really only one place a talentless teenager without any qualifications could play, and that was the Safari Tour—a series of tournaments in what was then Rhodesia, Zambia, Kenya, Botswana, and Nigeria. I had been to Dublin once.

My dad and a couple of his pals scraped together enough money for my airfare. I wrote my name on my secondhand, white Naugahyde golf bag, my mom sewed my name into the waistbands of my underwear, and I was off to the dark continent.

I took a puddle jumper to London, followed by a DC-10 that bounced in three different countries, and finally boarded a crop-sprayer to Victoria Falls, Rhodesia. It seemed like it took about two days, mainly because it did. I stumbled onto the molten asphalt, blinking like a newborn rat. The first thing I noticed about Africa was that the sun was out.

The Elephant Hills Classic was my first African golf experience and the beginning of a continental love affair that has lasted more than twenty years. There is something about Africa: perhaps a primeval heartbeat or the intoxicating smell of the red dirt after the rains that lures the white man back again and again. Also, the beer is very cold.

Believe me, I was a very white man. In terms of sunbathing, the closest thing I had ever experienced was lying on the seaweed-strewn beach of Ballyholme Bay in Northern Ireland, where no one ever ventured into the water over knee depth. If you did, a wee icy wave might come along and lick the underside of your swimming trunks, which would induce an involuntary yodeling fit that would make a fat Austrian man in tight leather shorts jealous. But I digress.

Exhausted from the journey, I decided after checking into the Victoria Falls Hotel to take a short nap in the shade underneath a beautiful jacaranda tree in the gardens. The hypnotic sound of the Zambezi, thundering over the edge of the escarpment less than five hundred yards away, and the warm sun soon lulled me to sleep.

When I awoke, I was no longer in the shade, and my back and legs were no longer white. I decided to nip back to the room for a quick shower. In the bathroom's full-length mirror, I discovered I was decidedly two-tone. I pressed my finger into the middle of my back, and it left a curious white spot for a few seconds. Hmmm, I thought, that's a new experience.

However, it didn't hurt so I decided to take that shower. Now that hurt. The Vic Falls Hotel had a kind of faded Colonial elegance and jaded Colonial plumbing. But even one drop at a time, the touch of the water was agony.

A couple of hours later my upper back and shoulders and the backs of my legs were covered in water blisters the size of Top-Flites, and it was with a feeling of impending humiliation that I stumbled into the hotel lobby to ask for advice.

Nathan, the bellhop, did me the service of lifting my shirt. "Mister David," he said, "I have a friend in the village who will help you." At this stage I couldn't have cared less if he had an enemy in the village who would kill me, just as long as he did it painlessly.

Much to Nathan's amusement and the driver's confusion, I spent ten minutes on my knees facing backward in the front seat of a cab.

We pulled up in the middle of a cluster of mud huts with thatched roofs and Nathan told me to wait in the car, as he jumped out of the backseat, yelling something in Matabele to the driver, who turned slowly to face me and shook his head slowly, with a boy-are-you-in-for-a-surprise smile.

Some moments later Nathan reappeared, smiling like a basket of French fries, and motioning me to enter the nearest hut. Walking like a crippled wildebeest, I followed him inside. This was not your average doctor's waiting room. A small hurricane lamp provided the only light and a small shriveled black man with enormous white nocturnal eyes was apparently my only hope.

Leaving the hotel, I was expecting to visit a man wearing a white coat and stethoscope. This man was wearing nothing but a pair of disintegrating denim shorts, what appeared to be a five-thousand-year-old Mets ballcap, and a maniacal grin. "Show him your back," said Nathan.

"You show him," I reminded him, motioning pathetically behind me and trying to hide my growing panic. Nathan gently lifted up my shirt. The little man, who by now even I had figured out was a doctor of the witch variety, collapsed into some kind of hysterical trance, with his lips drawn back over his teeth, and shook uncontrollably.

After about thirty seconds of this, he jabbered something at Nathan, and then went into another convulsion. "What the hell is wrong with him?" I asked.

"Nothing," said Nathan. "He just said he never met a man so clever on one side and stupid on the other!"

The old man held one finger up in front of me, in the international sign for, "Wait here, dummy," and scurried out the door like a demented warthog. Some moments later he returned, holding a wooden bowl full of a dubious looking green paste, and what appeared to be a porcupine quill. My heart rate shot up to about 940 bps.

He proceeded to prick every blister on my body, and then smear me all over with the green paste. Strangely enough, none of this hurt, and after paying him five dollars, I was back in the cab facing backward looking at Nathan, who was doing his best to convince me that tomorrow I would be fine. By this stage of the evening, I was deadly suspicious that our next stop would be a large cooking pot, suspended over an open fire, as I felt I had just been marinated and tenderized.

The next morning, I awoke facedown in the bed. Gingerly I slid over to the edge, and managed to get myself upright enough to go into the bathroom, where I looked at myself in the mirror. It looked like I had been smothered in guacamole, which had hardened overnight.

I reached over my shoulder and tried to pick a small piece off. About a square foot of the stuff fell to the tiled floor, and shattered. To my amazement, underneath lay perfectly smooth, if a little pink, skin, which was vaguely tender to the touch. I carefully removed the rest of the stuff, took a cool shower, got dressed, and was able to play the pro-am! I promise you, they couldn't have done this at the Mayo Clinic.

The golf course was another shock to the system. Almost eight thousand yards long, the Elephant Hills Country Club was carved through the thick bush that bordered the Zambezi River. Elephant grass rough, so called not because elephants eat it, but because you can't see an elephant behind it, lined every fairway.

No one, but no one, ever went to look for a golf ball, and for safety's sake everywhere other than the fairway was deemed a water hazard. In the pond to the right of the eighth green lived a crocodile named Charlie who eventually had to be removed, because any human on the eighth green was rapidly becoming an endangered species.

The resident beasties were scary enough, but at this particular stage in African history, the Zambians and the Rhodesians weren't exactly getting along. And, the white government of Ian Smith was about to lose power to Robert Mugabe, who had promised everyone everything, just so long as they voted for him. Every now and then anti-government troops, safe on the other side of the river, would send a few rounds in our direction. The day after we left for the Rhodesian Dunlop in Salisbury, they let fly at a tourist plane with a heat-seeker, which missed but got the next hottest thing, that being the kitchen in the clubhouse. Anyone who ordered the Rhinoburger that day got it well done.

Fathers and Sons

It's Monday and I'm sitting downstairs, engaged in a futile attempt to read *USA Day Before Yesterday*, almost the only source for any sort of news outside Ireland, which is where I happen to be at the moment.

Upstairs, my two boys are apparently trying to demolish the house. Not theirs, of course. They do a remarkable job on the house we own in Dallas. The silence is punctuated by the intermittent crashing of a giant Lego tower into an antique sideboard. It could be a scene from a condom commercial. "Here's what happens," the announcer might say, "if you're not careful."

No, the house this miniature wrecking crew is taking down brick by brick belongs to my parents. We've come home for a visit.

The parents of golfers have had their fair share of air time lately, so I thought it would be fun to divulge some details of the dysfunctional duo who were responsible for providing me with safe passage through childhood.

If nothing else, sitting down to write may help me resist the urge to attach Shey, nine, and Rory, five, to the wall with duct tape. I knew the stuff was bound to have some good use.

I was brought up in Bangor, a town of 46,000 a few miles up the A1 from Belfast, on the east coast of Northern Ireland. I lived with my two sisters—Helen, the elder, and Deborah, the younger—in a middle-class environment directed by W. T. (Billy) and Vi Feherty, who have now been married for forty-four years. If this marriage is a match, neither has ever been more than one-up.

When I was little, Dad worked for a container freight company based in the Belfast docklands. Every chance I had, I went with him to work and spent many happy hours in the dockside warehouses climbing great mountains of grain sacks, chasing rats, and frightening pigeons.

The dockers were gnarly men with almost unintelligible Belfast accents and there always seemed to be one of them to catch me when I fell, which was often.

Mum served dinner every evening at six and more than occasionally we were a man short when W.T. found himself plugged under the lip of the men's bar at Bangor Golf Club. He had a keen interest in the Irish national pastimes of drinking and storytelling, occasionally finding time for a little golf in between.

At one time, he was as low as a five handicap, a miracle considering his grip resembled two land crabs in mating season. At the top of his backswing, he looked like a man trying to kill a snake in a phone booth.

On one occasion, W. T., after about eleven too many with his derelict pals at the club, dundered in about an hour late for dinner. All three of us sprouts were fed, scrubbed, and ready for bed. Mum was less than amused.

Dad, however, was in an unbearably good mood and hungry enough to eat the wings off a low-flying duck. "Sorry I'm a little late, darling. Is my dinner still warm?"

Without missing a beat, my mom replied, "It should be. It's in the dog!" This is my earliest recollection of the evil Feherty wit.

I suppose it would be inevitable that I would become interested in golf. I used to caddie for my dad and he had a couple of clubs cut down for me so I would get to take a shot amongst his four-ball every now and then.

Some years later, I would reach the pinnacle of my not-even-remotely famous amateur career, when I was chosen for the Bangor grammar school golf team. I also played on the rugby team, but the other players kept bumping into me and taking my ball. So, I stuck to golf.

Dad, then as now, was my biggest fan. There was one minor problem: Every time I spotted him, I dropped a shot. His presence used to drive me berserk and eventually I had to banish him from the vicinity.

He wasn't about to go quietly; he'd watch from afar. He'd use binoculars and, occasionally, wear camouflage. But I'd still know he was there. Such was the sensitivity of my Dad-O-Meter Early Warning System, I could hear him clear his throat from eight hundred yards.

Thankfully, I grew out of this paterphobia in time to turn pro at seventeen, playing off a stellar handicap of five. I was in John Smith's geography class, fascinated by the average annual rainfall of Western Samoa, when through the open window the scent of freshly mown grass shot through my left nostril. Transfixed, I excused myself from class and dropped out.

Later that afternoon, I told my parents that I had quit school and was going to be a professional golfer. They obviously saw something in their son that no one else could because they were the only ones who didn't laugh hysterically.

A few days later, I flew to London to take up an assistant pro's job at the princely wage of £10 per week. It astounds me now when I think of how much they believed in me.

It was the first time I had lived away from home and there were many tearful collect calls in those first few weeks. Three months later, I was home. Being a professional golfer was tougher than I thought, especially with no mommy. So, I took a job closer to home—for less money.

I struggled the first few years, but my parents' undying faith and the occasional few pounds here and there kept me solvent enough until I actually became a pretty good golfer.

Now, when I pick my way through the Lego wreckage in my sons' room late at night to steal a last kiss from their tousled little boy heads, I smell that little boy smell and wonder if they will ever know how much I love them.

They already have the scars and ugly memories of a divorce. I was never so unfortunate. I was never frightened or alone; my parents made certain of that. By writing this piece, I am saying things to my mom and dad that I can't say any other way. Tears would prevent these words from ever emerging from a mouth that is more inclined to half-witticisms than heartfelt emotion.

A lot of people say these kinds of things at funerals. I don't want to wait that long. Dad says he's not sure whether he wants to be pickled or cremated. I tell him he's already pickled and a cremation would cause an explosion liable to kill all the mourners.

Every time I clear my throat, I hear him. I am turning into my father and there is no one I would rather be.

Teaching the Tykes

I was brought up around the time that the notion, "Children should be seen and not heard," was waning in popularity. At least, it was around our house. My parents will probably tell you that I was heard rather a lot, as were my two sisters.

So these days, I normally try to arm myself with the same tolerance, as my gang of bread-snatchers runs rampant around the house looking for something to do. As they grow older and stronger, I find that duct tape is less effective in holding them to the hardwood floors. I think I'm feeding them too much.

More serious than that, She Who Must Be Obeyed has cottoned to the idea that they might be getting big enough to hit the links. "Nay, nay, and thrice nay, say I," which is Shakespearish for, "Say it ain't so."

I spend a lot of time away from home, and recently, when I've been back, I've noticed that I have a lot of children. I think I'm a pretty regular parent. We do the usual things, you know: movies, grocery shopping, swimming, feeding the ducks, they change my diaper, etc. So I'm driving down the road the other day, with a partial load of sprouts in the truck, coming back from a school concert. A hundred rhythmless white kids singing out of tune, but somehow, because my little Rory was up there, it was achingly sweet.

Shey, my eldest boy, is complaining that I am the cruelest dad in all the world because I won't buy him an Audi TT roadster for his first car. (He's twelve.) Rory, my youngest son, is asking me to turn up 'N Sync on the stereo, and in the rearview mirror I spy Erin, my baby girl (and undisputed ruler of the universe), with her finger so far up her nose that it looks like she has discovered a way to change her mind manually. Willard the Wonder Dog is seated on the arm rest between the front seats, looking like an indoor hood ornament. Everything is normal.

I'm sick of listening to ghastly, spotty teenagers warble the same five chords over and over again on the sound system, so I shut it off and initiate a good old-fashioned game of who-can-burp-the-loudest. We've just had a greaseburger session at McDonald's, and the boys are armed with Cokes, so I know I might have a run for my money. But, as yet, no one has beaten Dad, so, with the honor, I let the big dog burp.

Shey immediately disqualifies himself by burping a French fry projectile against the windshield, and Rory laughs too hard to generate any kind of gaseousness. Erin grins and claps her hands. Time- out is called. Then, out of the blue, comes the request: "Dad, can we go to the golf club tomorrow?"

"What, to swim?" I reply cheerily.

"No, to play golf."

I give a slight swerve and Willard the Wonder Dog puts a paw on my forearm and gives me his would-you-like-me-to-drive? look. I'm a little ashamed to admit this, but since I quit competing, golf has felt like work to me, and I hardly ever feel like doing it in my spare time.

The thought of my kids taking up the game is kind of scary. What if they like it? She Who Must Be Obeyed would be packing me off to the country club on a regular basis, with a pack of squealing weasels in tow.

I know I'm a bit of a cynic even during the best of times, but Tiger has a lot to answer for. Crawling out of the Woods's work comes every kind of grub, it seems, each one younger than the next. We have tantrum-throwing, golf-club-swinging toddlers on talk shows and diaper-wearing duffers in magazines. What's next? I can see the strongest sperm in the shoal, grabbing one of the tiddlers by the tail, and using him like an oversized driver to whack an unfertilized egg around the ovary. I don't know about you, but I find that image somewhat disgusting.

The fruit of my own loins are impressed with me, at least by the fact that Tiger knows who I am. Come to think of it, I kind of like that too, but it's all leading me toward the rather disturbing realization that one of these days (like today), they might want me to teach them how to play golf.

I'm not sure that I even remember how to play golf. Sure, I do an on-air tip for most of our CBS shows, but that's different. No one answers me back, and I hardly ever feel like slapping a viewer upside the head. Up until now I've been blessed, in that none of my kids have expressed a desire to follow in their dad's footsteps, with the exception of the who-can-burp-the-loudest thing, at which I am glad to say I am still the man. Hey, every kid needs a dream.

The raising of children is one of the very few things at which I do not consider myself a world-renowned authority, but then again, this could be one of the very few things I am wrong about. The only things I really try to force them to do are listen to music and read.

Harry Potter has really captured my boys' imaginations with his broomstick and wizardry, and I enjoy reading these books, too. I resent the fact that the same people who are prepared to believe that a guy turned water into wine, fed five thousand people with three kippers and a bagel, and skated on unfrozen water, want to take these books away.

I think both Harry Potter and Jesus are good for kids, and so is Tiger Woods. As far as I am concerned, his occasional profane outburst is perfectly acceptable, and I have told my kids this: If they ever find themselves in a situation similar to that which caused Tiger to explode at the U.S. Open, their father would be disappointed if they did not curse like a fishwife. Boys, if you're leading a major championship by a dozen or so after three rounds, and you rip the ears off one dead left into the Pacific, go right ahead. Otherwise, zip it, you little ratbags.

Now that's parenting. But as for teaching them how to play, my jury's still out. I feel pretty confident about my ability to improve a nonrelative's chances of getting it airborne and straightish, but the couple of lessons I have given my boys have done little to help their swings or my mental health. I'm sure it has something to do with their opinion that I am their father, obviously a moron, and, naturally, that they should do the exact opposite of what I say.

Hang on a minute there, Ethel. I think I've been laboring under a misapprehension! Why, I'm a member of Royal Oaks here in Dallas, which has one of the finest junior programs in the country. The director of golf is Randy Smith, Justin Leonard's coach, and by God, if he can steer that boy (who is not right in the head) to a British Open victory, then he must be perfectly capable of baby-sitting for me.

Sorry, I'm thinking out loud here. That's it! Well, knock me down with a pair of boxers if I'm not a foolish, carefree, and hideously wealthy young announcer who can let someone else do his chores.

God, how I love this country!

Well, Excuse Me

It's that time of the year again when, for me, golf fades into the background, and I get to be more of a stay-at-home guy. I'm still doing the occasional corporate outing and after-dinner speech, but the trips are less frequent, and not as long, leaving me more time at home to do the kinds of things that Anita, my long-suffering wife, normally has to cope with in my absence. Like looking after the little nest of vipers that is my family.

It would appear that I get a lot of mail, some of which is from people who want money. Anita tells me these are called "bills." Well, I'm all for correspondence, and communication, but these have to be some of the least entertaining letters I have ever read. Thank goodness She Who Must Be Obeyed looks after the task of replying to these idiots, otherwise I would have no time at all to write for *Golf Magazine*. Each one of them gets a personally signed note (a little oblong green one), torn from a booklet that my wife keeps locked up somewhere. I have never written one. My wife is brilliant. She looks after all this stuff, and leaves me to get on with what I do best, or most, or something.

But the other day, I found out that even she cannot protect me from everything. This was something of a bombshell to me, and I'm sure that all of you will be shocked to hear it also. Apparently, there are people out there who think that I am an idiot. Really!

The editors of this glorious rag are always telling me how absolutely marvelous I am, how clever and articulate, and how someday, if I keep up the good work, they might even start paying me. Then the other day they forwarded me three e-mails from people who seem to think I should be locked up somewhere. Well, I had no idea. The thought that some people might actually disagree with me had never really crossed my mind. The thought had tried to cross my mind on a number of occasions, but had always turned back after the first few, featureless, barren miles.

It all started after the release of the October issue and my Side-spin column, entitled "Teaching the Tikes," in which I mentioned the following in the same paragraph: Jesus, Tiger Woods, Harry Potter, and my anguish at the thought of having to teach my boys to play golf. All of these letters were in the same vein. They claimed that I am obviously anti-Christian, and I should not be allowed to bring up my own children. Well, I would like to take this opportunity to politely reply to those that I have offended, and apologize to those who felt so guiltless that they felt it necessary to hurl e-rocks in my general direction. Hey, nice try, you missed.

Hey, hey, hey there reverend, stop thumping the book, and listen up. I am most definitely not anti-Christian, and I fought for two years to get custody of my two boys. You're probably right, I'm a bad father, but I'm doing my best. I think it's quite difficult. My wife is a Christian, and I love her all the more because she knows who I am, and still loves me back. Some of my dearest friends, such as Bobby Clampett, are devoted Christians. I know I could call Bobby in the middle of the night, and there is nothing he would not do for me, a sinner. In fact, I think I'll call him tonight, just to wake him up. My travel agent, Barb Hegel, is a real Christian, who always gets me into first class, and says she will drag me, kicking and screaming into heaven if she has to. If I see you there, I'm going to drag her kicking and screaming, back out.

My children go to Sunday school, and church retreats, where they learn about Jesus, and I am happy about it. I am also teaching them that there are other religions and philosophies, and other people such as Jews, Hindus, Moslems and Buddhists, to name but a few, all of whom deserve exactly the same respect and tolerance to which we are all lucky enough to be entitled in this great country. Damn, I should be running for President! I am not teaching my kids that there is only one way, and I am not teaching them golf. I think they are old enough to know that their father is a happy unbeliever, who thinks that "after life" is the same as "before birth," and both are blissful states. I don't think that this is the correct place to express these opinions, but hey, the devil made me do it, and I think it must have been a real bummer for the recovering alcoholic, who asked for a glass of water at that wedding feast. I would bet my life that Jesus had a hell of a sense of humor.

Again, I am not anti-Christian, but I am decidedly anti-idiot.

For the gentleman who threatened to inform every TV evangelist for whom he has respect of my evilness and blasphemy, I noticed that every one on your respectable list has at least one thing in common. If each week they put aside the money they spend on hairspray, it would be enough to feed the homeless of Atlanta for two weeks, or at least to buy enough hairspray to stick them all into one neighborhood, so they wouldn't be such a bother to extremely wealthy TV evangelists.

I could go on, but I have a life. I hear my daughter waking upstairs—you know, one of those children I should not be allowed to raise. I have about four hours of joy with her before she has to go to bed again tonight. The last thing we will do tonight—Erin, Mommy, and Daddy—will be to say together:

Now I lay me down to sleep,

I pray the Lord my soul to keep.

Guide me safely through the night,

And wake me in the morning light.

Amen.

Oh, and one other thing. Every time I get letters like those that inspired this rant, there is usually some reference to Tiger that tends to give me the feeling that the writer might perhaps be judging him by something other than the content of his character.

Finally, for the record, for every piece of hate mail I receive, I get a hundred filled with love. Peace be with you my friends, thank you, and may your God go with you.

Uncle Dickie's Ryder Cup Analysis

My dear nephew,

Sorry it's taken me so long to write, but I got dreadfully blotto with Lord Derby after the Ryder Cup, and the old gout has been giving me terrible gip. Also, I've been at a bit of a loss for words. The world is full of morons, is it not? If you believe the Yankee rags, it's fairly obvious that the whole damned game of soldiers was your friend Curtis Strange's fault, you know, the fact that the European team played better than his, and all that.

I'd be grateful if you would forward this little epistle to him, to let him know that at least in the minds of those who understand why the game is played, he is held in the highest esteem. It's true, though; I did hear him encourage the Europeans. In his address at the opening ceremony he wished them the best, and very eloquently expressed his desire that the better team might win.

Personally, I'm somewhat neutral here, in that I've never been a fan of the European Union, but for the sake of the cup, I'm delighted that Sammy's team won, and yet I'm saddened by the reaction of many of the word-manglers on the other side of the ditch. What a shower of arseholes, if you'll pardon my French. Unlike the Captain, they showed no class whatsoever, not giving credit where it was due, and laying blame where it didn't belong. Cretins.

I'm told that many of them feel that Curtis incorrectly filled out his singles order form, and that they have been holding a flame to his bum ever since. The rotters are just looking for an inexpensive place to place the blame, and it's living proof that good news still doesn't sell newspapers.

But don't you worry my boy. Tell Curtis, and his wife Sarah (who, incidentally, I thought looked absolutely ravishing all week) that Gussett of the Wood thinks of him and his team with pride and joy. Why, his comments at the closing ceremony were dead on the old diddy for all of us here at Scrought's Wood.

His demeanor and grace throughout the contest accurately reflected the spirit of Sir Samuel (who was a wonderful old codger) and is the very reason he started the blasted thing in the first place. Lose with grace, win with humility, and you will find friends wherever you go. Personally, I find the theory put by the sports hacks to the American public tenuous, at best. I believe that if all twenty-four names had been loaded into my old elephant gun and fired at that chap with the iron bladder on the first tee, the result would have been exactly the same. When one side plays better than the other, it usually wins. I grant you that's a hard cup to drink from at times, but nevertheless, it's one that holds water.

I watched the whole thing on the telly in the bar at the club. Someone put that chap Montgomerie in a good mood I'll tell you, for he was bloody invincible. An absolute hero he was, and for what it's worth, you might want to think about apologizing to him. As I recall, you've been a little cynical in his direction. No doubt about the fire in his belly when it comes down to leading the troops from the front!

As for Langer, I haven't seen a jerry in control like that since Kaiser Bill annexed the Sudetanland in 1914. What an admirable man he is. From my angle it was clear that the American team was farting into old hurricane Samuel from the get-go, and Captain Strange had bugger-all to do with it once the bell rang on Sunday.

Not that the Yanks didn't love their leader. That young Toms fellow is quite the silent assassin, and the other two greenhorns, Cink and Verplank, looked like the Ryder bug bit them in the itchy spot too. All three will be back, and better for the experience. All in all, I think it might have been the most perfect of the thirty-four meetings to date, certainly from a golfing quality standpoint.

Bloody Norah, when we watch a major championship, we might be lucky to see a great shot every ten minutes. In this one, there was one every ten seconds. It was a privilege to see the two teams do battle, and I want you to impress upon Captain Strange how much the boys at the club and I enjoyed the show. Bravo, and a pox upon anyone who would cast an aspersion in the direction of any of those lucky enough to be involved. That young Woods is starting to get it, too. The Ryder Cup is not the fifth major, it's the first, and before he's done, he'll have one of the great records in it. Mark my words, you heard it here. I can't wait for the next one. Bloody good show!

Always with love,
Uncle Dickie

Family Chain

I've decided that far too many of my family have my email address and telephone number. Because I'm on the road so much, I have a fairly cynical attitude toward the whole concept of visitors at home, whether they arrive in person, or slide under the door in a letter. I have enough trouble dealing with and denying responsibility for my own immediate family, and could do without hearing from neighbors, or worse still, any of the inbred idiots who claim to dangle from the outer branches of my family tree. Sorry, but until they have opposable thumbs I'm not talking to them. The other day, one of them tried to make contact in the form of one of those ghastly blanket "family news" letters, designed to keep friends and family up to date with the mundane goings-on in their supposedly perfect lives. Whether or not these are a once-a-year occurrence, it's always a mistake to reply to them. You know the sort, little printer flowers around the border, and every paragraph a different color. I have no idea what the multicolored thing is about—maybe it's because the words are always so damned gray. *Nigella has just finished ballet, little Johnny is fourteen now, and remains a treasure to us all.* Yeah, Nigella finished ballet all right. She weighed about eighty pounds when she was three. She probably fell into the orchestra pit and took out the entire wind section. And the last time I saw little Johnny he was eight, and as I recall, a right little fucker. I want to know how he turned into a treasure.

For the people who write these letters, the thought that someone, somewhere might not be aware of their Utopian existence seems to be more than they can bear. Frankly, I smell denial. I have a fourteen-year-old too, and like most kids of his age, some of the time he's a monumental pain in the ass, but I certainly don't feel like burdening everyone I know with the details of his dysfunction. Too young to drive a car—just old enough to drive his parents berserk. If I woke up one morning and suddenly he was a treasure, I'd call the doctor, or the producers of the *X-Files* or something, but I wouldn't write a letter, gloating about him to people I hardly even know. People who do that should be locked up somewhere for a while, preferably with my children.

But if someone feels it absolutely necessary to write a letter like this (and it never is), they should at least have the decency to tell the truth. This would make them much more entertaining, and lead to greater understanding within the family unit, decreasing the chances that any of the fuckers would want to come and visit you. (Come to think of it, maybe it is a good idea). Okay, I'll take a crack at it. It's not like any of my family actually read this rag anyway, so this'll stay between us. Here goes........

Dearest family,

It hardly seems a year since my last epistle to y'all, and I'm glad to report that life for the Fehertys here in Dallas remains at its usual high level of deep and blissful joy. What a time to be alive, and surrounded by our playful, inquisitive children! Just the other day, Rory, who is now ten (I know, it's hard to believe he hasn't yet been run over in the street), asked me, "Dad, are we still bombing the brown people in the long skirts?" Such honest naïveté demands (at least on our side of the family) a straightforward answer, so naturally I replied in the negative, adding that, "the ones with the big mustaches will likely be getting it next." What a little scamp he is. He's off SpongeBob, into Court TV, and his latest career plan is to eat twenty quarter-pounders a day until he's sixteen, sue Ronald McDonald for turning him into a tub of lard, and then have his stomach stapled, "like that girl who used to be Brian Wilson's daughter." Not a bad idea, but occasionally I have to remind him of some of his less than cunning plans. For example, at Halloween he invented his own "Mutant Ninja Cheesehead Nurse" costume, and insisted on making "undercover" trick or treat calls to the back doors of everyone in the neighborhood. He managed to get bitten by three different dogs before we noticed the blood was real. He has more than a bit of his grandpa Billy in him, but we're hoping he'll grow out of it. Speaking of Dad, he gave Mum a little scare the other day when he had a spell of about fifteen minutes during which he remembered who he was. It was dodgy apparently, but with a little help from a bottle of Famous Grouse she got through it. Apparently she drank it, smashed it over his head, and bingo, now he's back to believing he's a sequestered jury member in whichever episode of *Matlock* he's seen most recently. They rescued "Winifred," a seven-year-old beagle from the shelter a few months ago, and getting acclimatized to having three mouths in the house again has been something of a challenge. She runs away at every opportunity she gets, leaving the dog with Dad, who is clearly unqualified to be a canine caregiver.

Shey is out of the school for the "Learning Different," now, and is back into the mainstream, where he is ranked 394th in a class of fifteen thousand. We're very proud of him, although he has developed a slightly worrisome habit of locking himself in his room, where he spends his afternoons repeatedly head-butting a life-size inflatable Dr. Phil doll. He made it himself, and it's really rather good. We've been trying to get him in to see a child psychologist, but can't get an appointment anywhere. It's a sign of the times I suppose, I mean all of our children have their little foibles, don't they? You have to laugh. On the bright side, I've taken several orders for inflatable Dr. Phils from members of my anger management class (which I don't need to go to anymore, you bloodsucking, parasitical bastards), and I now have him working on a life-size dirigible of Oprah, which isn't bad either if you blow it up hard enough to take out the wrinkles. He's in that defiant period at the moment, and yesterday he came home from school with a nose ring. I was having none of it, and made him whip it out before dinner. Then of course he sneezes, and even though he got his nostrils bunged with a Kleenex in time, Rory, who was seated to his right, ended up being the unsuspecting victim of a drive-by snotting of the worst kind from the new blowhole. The ring went back in, at least for the remainder of the meal. Some you win, some you lose.

And of course there's Erin, the light of her Daddy's life. Four years old now, and through her first cosmetic surgery. Nothing radical of course, just calf implants and an eyebrow lift, but the bandages come off in a few days and we're hoping she'll be pleased. The suit she filed against me is still pending, and is a tremendous worry. If only I'd let the doctor cut the cord, she would have had an inny instead of an outy, and a much happier dad to boot.

Personally, the only thing I have to report is that I'm older than I used to be, a fact that was hammered home all too recently. I was taking a whiz at the club, and trying to read the sports page that Julio so kindly mounts on the wall over the urinal, when I realized my eyesight has degenerated, to the stage that I need my reading glasses to go to the bathroom. Worse than that, even with them on, if I stand far enough away to be able to read, I can't pee far enough to reach the porcelain. Such is life.

Well, that's everyone up to date with us, so I guess I'll talk to y'all next year, in the newsletter. Remember; don't think of visiting us, even if your house is on wheels. I have Willard the Wonder Dog trained to go for the throat of any creature who shares our genes.

Chapter Nine
Idiot's Delight

A Weighty Matter

I heard that bears lose a third of their body weight during hibernation, so this winter I thought I'd give it a try. Alas, so far, it's been a disaster.

I turned my den into the Institute of Sofa Research, where I've been reclining virtually motionless—half-man, half-mattress—with remote in hand. As a result, I've become positively bulbous.

You know you're out of shape when you sit in a rocking chair and can't make it go.

As a player, my winter lifestyle was always fairly sedentary, but it was offset by a hectic playing schedule for the rest of the year. The standing pulse rate of even some of the lumpiest specimens on Tour might surprise you. Heaving luggage around airports and walking six or seven miles a day (often through long grass) will keep the old strawberry ticking and in decent shape, it seems.

My problems are that I don't play golf anymore and the only exercise I get is jumping to the occasional conclusion, or violently swerving past the salad bar on my way to the dessert trolley.

There is always one pivotal moment when you realize you are more than a little overweight, and for me it came the other day as I was wandering through one of our CBS production trailers. I like to study everyone else's jobs, as I eventually plan to take over the entire broadcast industry and start my own religion (whoops, didn't mean to mention that, but what the heck).

Anyway, sneaking around in full covert snoop mode, I heard the mellifluous tones of another finely honed athlete—the dearly departed Bentley Wright—who was warbling about some Ryder Cup rookie. I spun around to face the guilty monitor, knocking over a full can of Diet Coke with my gut, only to be rewarded with the sight of me at the 1991 Ryder Cup.

I was windswept, long-haired, thin, and athletic. An uninvited thought blundered into my head. That was six years and twenty pounds ago. Now, I'm winded, short of hair, fat, and pathetic.

I'm going to be forty next year and something must be done before my birthday cake collapses under the weight of the candles.

All is not lost, however. I'm accustomed to losing weight, and quickly, too. My weight has yo-yoed between 155 and 205 pounds in the last fifteen years and I've got the strange wardrobe to prove it.

No, I'm not talking about my rhinestone-studded posing pouch with the matching thigh-length Wellington boots, no sir. That would be an entirely different column.

I have a strange variety of sizes. I own a pair of trousers that the Artist Formerly Known as Prince would struggle to get into. (So that's how he hits those high notes.) Come to think of it, I only got into them once myself.

I also have a few huge pairs, some of which, sadly, are too small for me at the moment. I own every size in between, too, all because I refuse to go on wimpy diets. You know—the ones where you eat sensibly, exercise, and lose weight gradually over a long period of time.

What I prefer to do is wait until I can't stand it any longer, when I'm so bloated I almost faint while tying my shoelaces. At that point, I waddle out and spend way too much money on pants that are way too small.

In my opinion, blackmail, like a couple of other vices, is not a sin if it is self-administered. These I call my "target pants" (no, I do not buy them at Target). I can nearly always identify the target pants in my closet, even from a distance, as many of them still have the price tags attached.

However, simply buying ill-fitting clothing does not a thin person make, so next comes the diet and exercise, both of which must, in my case, be overdone drastically.

In my exercise world, Forrest Gump would be a slacker. I work on a slow jogging pace of up to five to twelve miles daily and combine this with a diet of PowerBars, coffee, ibuprofen, alcohol, and, if I'm feeling really dedicated, the occasional cigarette.

This fairly makes the pounds drop off, I can tell you, although I would consider it a little too severe if it weren't for the alcohol. A man needs his sustenance, to be sure, and in the great Gaelic tradition, it is better to have whiskey and no food than food and no whiskey. Amen.

Now, you have the picture. I do this until the pants fit, at which point I go straight back to eating like a pig again, which is the only fun part of the whole exercise.

At this stage, I'd like to mention that I feel it would be extremely unwise for any of you folks at home to try this. Remember, I am a highly trained professional with twenty years of experience. And, by the way, if there are any bran-munching, granola-hugging, mountain-bike types out there who feel like writing to tell me the damage I'm doing to my body, forget it.

Call me old-fashioned, if you must, but I firmly believe that there is no point lying in the hospital, dying of nothing.

At any rate, at least I can do something about my self-inflicted obesity. What bothers me even more is a discovery I made this morning—my first gray chest hair!

Now, hold on a minute, I'm thinking. This evil game has dealt me more than a few silver ones on my head, which I don't mind at all. They only serve to make me look more interesting, hard though it may be for you to believe.

From the neck up, I'm going to look like Curtis Strange, which is a good thing. But I can't bear the thought of the little gray buggers heading south, presumably toward their final resting place!

Hair Club For Men here I come…or, perhaps I should lay off the electric soup and eat healthy. I wonder?

Prepping for Augusta

It's that time of the year again. I'm sneezing every 4.3 minutes, and I'm on the Fatkins diet, so I won't look like Chris Farley in a necktie for my headshot at Augusta. I'm not sure about this high-protein, low-carbohydrate deal. The whole potato-deprivation thing is cruel and unusual punishment for an Irishman, and also, I'm having difficulty with the lack of fiber. It's like giving birth to a shillelagh once a week.

But enough of my personal struggle against the forces of human nature—it's almost time for the world's greatest golf tournament. I know there are a couple of weeks to go, but everything else on the run into the Masters seems to fade into irrelevance for me, as I prepare myself for the great event.

I'm kind of like Tiger when I prepare for a major.

That last sentence was such a monumental load of crap that it deserves to either stand alone like a paragraph, or be deleted. I'll leave it up to you. You're my jury here, and you can choose to disregard it if you want, but the truth is, I do treat the Masters very differently to the regular tour events we cover at CBS.

For a start, I never get invited to play the golf course at any other event. On the Sunday before the Masters, the announcers play Augusta National, so that we can familiarize ourselves with the subtle changes that occur every year. I know, I know, but somebody has to do it. I'm just waiting for that inevitable Sunday afternoon when our leader finds himself in a huge, gouging, 45-degree spade mark on the downslope at fifteen, a divot that has "Lundquist" tattooed all over it. I'd have to lie like a berber carpet.

The other thing that we are asked to do, by way of preparation, is putt on our respective greens before play on all four days of the tournament. That way, we have no excuse for reading one incorrectly. Damn! I'm looking forward to watching Bill Macatee 15-putt the fourteenth, and being carted off on a green stretcher, foaming at the mouth. Folks, these are the toughest greens in the world. I would bet, if I were allowed to place the ball thirty feet away on each green, that an average 10-handicapper would not two-putt more than four or five times out of eighteen, and probably wouldn't get more than one first putt dead. Yeah, yeah, you can disagree all you want, but you're never going to find out. You'll just have to take my word for it. Ha, ha. Suffer.

Of course, I'll be zipping it, sucking it up, clenching desperately, and drinking decaffeinated all week. That goes without saying. I can alter my style to suit the moment, which at Augusta is considerably more serious than anywhere else. If you don't believe me, just look at the players' faces. This one means more than any other to them, as it should.

To answer the question I am most commonly asked, no, McCord will probably never work there again. And yes, we miss the idiot. But if he were to even attempt to alter his style, there would be about thirty seconds of silence, followed by the sound of his head exploding. It just wouldn't work. Not on this particular week.

Fashion Statement

Gary McCord turned fifty recently and his long-suffering wife, Diane, put together a very special video for him, featuring, among other things, some of the more embarrassing moments of his career. It turns out that he was sponsored for a while by Lawrence Welk and even appeared on his television show, which brings me to my subject this month: Fashion in golf—or lack thereof.

On Mr. Welk's show, my cosmic colleague was youthful, puffy-cheeked, and positively resplendent in a pair of white, skin-tight polyester flared pants with a pair of four-inch-high, white patent leather clod-hoppers to match.

Also, he had not yet acquired his trademark mustache, so all in all he looked like a guinea pig on stilts. I thought, "Man, does he look ridiculous."

Little did I know that my own wife had a similar shock in store for me on my fortieth birthday. Some of what my video had to offer was pretty spooky to watch, I can tell you. In my first years as a pro, I made a pretty obnoxious fashion statement.

The first real four-round professional tournament I won was the 1980 Irish Professional Championship at Royal Dublin. In the last round, I wore a pair of pants somewhat similar to those that were found around the ankles of the King on the bathroom floor at Graceland.

They were polyester, of course, and so voluminous that any change of direction had to be negotiated carefully for fear of lassoing the ankles and falling over. In those days, I was a strapping 230 pounds, with thighs like a rhino, so in the twilight the inevitable chafing produced enough static to make it seem as if bolts of lightning were shooting out from between my mighty loins. (Well, perhaps that's stretching it a bit.)

Combine all this with the seven-inch collar points on the shirt and the remnants of a highly ill-advised perm, and you have a mental picture of the 1980 Irish Professional Champion.

It looked as if that morning, I had covered my naked body with glue and flung myself into Liberace's closet. Then, while driving to the golf course, I must have flattened a black poodle, which I obviously felt would look good on my head.

My friends, if this footage ever finds its way into CBS's hands, life as I know it is over.

Realizing that, compared to me, McCord didn't look that bad, I decided to delve further back into some old photograph albums. A dog-eared shot of my high school golf team was a rip-snorter and again the pants dominated. In 1974, I was a pimply sixteen-year-old who apparently had no qualms about wearing the kind of red-and-white gingham check that would guarantee I never got a girlfriend.

They were horrific in a "somewhere-in-Little-Italy-there-is-a-tablecloth-missing" kind of way. I cannot believe my mother let me leave the house wearing them. The only solace I could find was in the fact that we were living in the 1970s and my teammates looked equally absurd.

I can't help but think that the decades of the 1960s, '70s, and '80s were the lowest point in golf fashion, which is an oxymoron if I ever wrote one. However, golfers didn't always look so geeky and you only have to look a little further back to find evidence.

Old photographs of the likes of Byron Nelson, Ben Hogan, and Sam Snead reveal dapper, elegant men in pleated oxford trousers and snappy brogues. They wore form-fitting, short-sleeved crewnecks and a variety of jaunty lids.

And, then came Arnold Palmer, with his thighs bulging through his drain-pipe pants, the only man I know who has more hair now than he did in the 1950s. Arnie made tight pants look great, even with an inch of sock showing. He had a flat belly, knotted forearms, and a lean and hungry look.

When the 1970s came along, golf went plaid. High-waisted, beltless slacks infested our pro shops, making it impossible to retrieve a scorecard from the hip pocket, unless you went for it over your shoulder.

The white patent belt was almost compulsory and shirt collars were so long and pointed they became extremely dangerous in high winds. They could put your eye out, for heaven's sake.

Still, out of this mayhem came the relative calm of the 1980s, or so I thought until I saw the video of my first overseas victory—the 1984 ICL International in Pretoria, South Africa. I birdied the last to sneak past Nick Price. This time, your reluctant hero was clad in pink linen pants, a white shirt, and was sporting a ponytail held up with a matching pink ribbon. I remember I had about six different colored ribbons to match my various trousers. What the hell was I thinking? I mean, fourteen years later, it strikes me there were television cameras and people watching me.

Frankly, I think it's about time we revamp the golf look and if it weren't for the variety of walking tackle out there, I'd say shorts were the answer. Unfortunately, all you'd have to do is let the pros wear them once and you'd see every variety of legs-from the hippo-like seam-ripper to the should-be-hanging-out-of-a-bird's-nest type who has to take three paces before the shorts start to move. I don't know about you, but I don't want to see this on television.

I would much rather see a return of the short-sleeved crewneck and I believe Jesper Parnevik is striding in the right direction in his ankle stranglers. He experimented with different widths before settling on the drain pipes he now sports. (He tried even narrower ones, but found that every time he farted, his shoes flew off, so up a notch he went.)

Fashion, like beauty, is in the eye of the beholder and time has a keen way of stripping away the veneer of how good we thought we looked at the time. Fortunately, it's only in hindsight that we look ridiculous; although personally, I can't believe I was stupid enough not to feel ridiculous at the time.

Check this space again in twenty years' time, if you are spared, and I'm certain we'll be laughing at what we are wearing now; although, as spiffy as I look right now, I can hardly see how.

Man and Beast

Much of my decidedly ill-spent youth was spent on the golf course with a very special friend. Daly was my first golfing pooch. She was a stray German shepherd pup that I found almost frozen to death under a sheet of rusting corrugated metal behind the maintenance shed at Balmoral Golf Club in Belfast. I was the eighteen-year-old assistant pro to the 1947 British Open champion, Fred Daly, for whom my new companion was named.

She was emaciated, mangy, and had a ratlike, hairless tail. Come to think of it, in those days, she and I had a lot in common. She was so pitiful that I just had to take her home. I was driving my mom's car to and from work and on the way home that evening, the little dog looked balefully at me from the passenger seat and promptly barfed up the garbage she had been living on since God knows when.

My mom's car was never the same, but neither was our home because after a few months of love and care, the scabby little runt developed into a slender, graceful, and doe-eyed canine beauty queen, with a glorious, bushy tail. Never was a dog so loved.

Her intelligence was astounding, largely, I think, because she was "golf trained" from day one. My dad and I taught her to sit by the tee markers and wait until everyone in the group had hit. Only then was she permitted to take off like a bullet in the rough to flush out hares and rabbits. She would disappear for a while but was always present on the next tee, sitting sphinx-like, waiting patiently for play to begin once more.

In her later years, she even figured out when someone had hit it far enough off line that she should wait to see if he would play a provisional! I have never told anyone this for fear of ridicule, but I suspect she may also have, on occasion, driven my father home after a late night at the club (or at least navigated).

With these memories in mind, I set off some months ago to the pound with my five-year-old son, Rory. I wanted my kids to grow up with a pup. After looking into about one hundred cages, Rory picked out a bleary-eyed, parvo-infested, snot-nosed creature that looked like a cross between a gerbil that someone had inflated with a bicycle pump and a Bermuda divot. Oh, and judging by its tail, there might have been a squirrel scurrying 'round in its family tree.

Rory was adamant that the pup should be called "Derek," but after some tough negotiations, we settled on "Wilfred." Hey, I tried, okay? Today, some ten months and numerous vets' bills later, Wilfred is truly not exactly what you would call magnificent, but he is the only member of my family who is always pleased to see me.

I am fully convinced that the only creatures of the earth that are capable of unconditional love are parents and dogs. I now have Wilfred trained to such an extent that when I take him for his morning constitutional, as regular as clockwork he will heave his little Havana on our neighbor's lawn. "Good boy, Wilfred! Good boy!"

The other day, I decided it was time for his first golf lesson, so both he and I were quite upset when I was told that he could not accompany me onto the golf course. It was obvious that if Wilfie boy was to get the exercise that he needed, he would have to come running with me in the mornings.

So, I geared up for the experiment by buying one of those retractable leashes and the following morning, I slipped the handle into the pocket of my running shorts and away we trotted. We'd gone about three hundred yards down the street when out of the blue Wilfie stopped stone-dead to examine an enemy land mine.

I was oblivious to his maneuver and ran on, regardless. When the leash reached its maximum length, I fell over, suddenly bare-assed on the sidewalk, my shorts around my ankles. Poor Wilfie, who had been nose down, lost in concentration, suffered a partially blocked left nostril and a badly sprained left ear. So much for that idea.

Dammit, I think you should be allowed to walk your woofer on the golf course. Dogs are a common sight on the courses of the British Isles, and they are also an extremely good excuse for coming home late. "Sorry, dear, but Spanky ran off and it took me forever to find him."

In my opinion, the fifteenth club in the bag should be the pooper scooper (if you play Pings or Callaways, their lob wedges work remarkably well). Properly trained dogs should have the right of way on the golf course.

After all, you probably spend so much time being miserable out there, wouldn't it be nice to have a companion that was filled with unbridled joy? Even if you're in a cart, there is no reason Muttley shouldn't ride along with you.

Of course, I'm a dog lover. It's not that I don't like cats, but more that I don't like it when they like me. If I visit a house with a resident feline, the darn thing normally ends up on my lap making a noise like a small-block V8 and tenderizing the flesh of my upper thighs with its claws.

"Oh, don't mind Digby," the host bleats. "That's just his way of saying, 'Hello.'" Yeah, right. I know that if I try to remove Digby, however gently, there goes a good pair of slacks. If the window were open, Digby would discover my way of saying, "Good-bye."

During the Swiss Open some years ago, I had occasion to walk off the seventh tee at Crans sur Sierre, a golf course that doubles as a ski run in the winter. To get an erect stance, you have to wear one shoe on your right foot and the other on your left knee.

To my left, I noticed a cat playing with an unfortunate small rodent. It was a stoat, I believe, and for you who are rodentially challenged, a stoat is somewhat like a weasel, except that whereas a weasel is weasually recognized, a stoat is stoatally different. Ha ha ha! (I've waited since the fifth grade to see that line in print.)

But, wait! I've digressed and not for the first time, either.

Because I am a good Samaritan, I shooed away the cat, enabling the unfortunate little rodent to dart into its burrow, a few feet away. Feeling smug, I sauntered off down the fairway, only to hear the plaintive squeals of varmint torture once more a few seconds later. I spun around to see that the vile feline had indeed retrieved my furry little friend from his hole and was cat-boxing with the stoat's head—a right and a left, a left and a right, with claws extended.

When I could stand it no longer, I sized up a ten-yard shot up the hill, which I timed perfectly. I caught Tibbles clean in the catflap with the old Etonic instep and away she flew, yowling in a tight spiral straight into a hedge some ten feet away. This cat did not, I repeat, did not land on its feet. It took off like a rocket, clearly none the worse for wear, but with a little less taste for stoat-bashing, I dare say.

(At this stage, my two playing partners were waiting for me on the green, presumably wondering what the hell I was doing. This story clearly helps explain why I am now a broadcaster instead of a rich, successful, championship player.)

Now, all cat lovers out there, calm down, please. Do not send the ASPCA out to harass my family or the editors of *Golf Magazine*.

For the record, I am perfectly aware that the torture of small, defenseless animals is part of a cat's nature. The kicking of cats who are conducting such torture is part of my nature.

I have the attention span of a gnat, a creature which, unlike man's best friend, is frequently found on the golf course, despite considerably less acceptable behavior. I mean, when a dog is going to bite you, at least you can see it coming.

My Wilfie never bites; in fact, he would lick my face no matter what I might shoot. Can any of you say that about your regular golf partner? Don't answer that!

New York, Hole by Hole

I just got back from my very first book signing in New York City, and I'm glad to report that everything seems to have returned to normal in the capital of the world. No one was warm and fuzzy. No one seemed afraid, and grown men weren't hugging each other in the streets either. Well, they were in the theater district, but that's normal, too.

Every time I go to New York City, within minutes of arrival, I turn into a New Yorker. I just can't help myself. Chuck Will, who was a legendary associate director of golf at CBS sports, once said that there are three kinds of assholes, and he's from Philadelphia, so he knows an asshole when he sees one. Chuck said you have your common asshole, your flaming asshole, and then, the top of the line, your gaping asshole. (The latter is the kind of asshole of whom you often see pictures in publications like the *Robb Report*, or *Cigar Aficionado*.) I maintain that everyone in New York City fits into one of these categories. They must, to avoid being sucked in by the vortex created by all the other assholes.

For example, when the sign says WALK, and the wee white man appears, you walk, right?

Wrong, unless you want to die. Better than that, they have traffic cops who regularly blow whistles and wave traffic through red lights and the wee white man, when the crossing is full of pedestrians. Now me, I have my three-and-a-half-year-old daughter on my shoulders, and She Who Must Be Obeyed on my arm. I'm in the middle of the road, and a cab is making a left turn. He actually touches my right knee with his front fender, and leans on his horn, so I stop and glare at him. Nobody else even seems to notice. The driver mouthed an obscenity and gave me the finger, so I made a production of stepping back, and sarcastically waving him past. Acting like I was the biggest asshole in the city, he drove on, so I gave the rear wing of his cab a solid kick. Then, my three-and-a-half-year-old daughter and my wife give him the finger. I was so proud.

"Meet the Asshole family, buddy! We're from Dallas, Texas, but we're equally at home in New York!"

On Fifth Avenue, at the Barnes & Noble, it was time for the book signing. They'd set me up on the basement floor, with a podium and microphone, and a table and chair at which I could sit and sign books for the multitude of people who simply had to have it. Also, there were about thirty empty chairs in front of me, for the people who would want to hear me talk about it. And there wasn't an asshole in sight, except for one homeless guy who had torn the plastic wrapping off a *Playboy* and was sitting down in the back, presumably engrossed in one of the articles. (Actually, he did get a book signed, but I'm pretty sure he stole it). No problem, I like homeless people, especially when they have a dog. The dog always has the same expression on its face. "Hey buddy, just how long is this friggin' walk gonna last?"

Apart from the homeless guy, I knew the Christian name of everyone I could see. I bet John Grisham was never able to say that at one of his book signings. Ha! One up for me.

Fortunately, it started raining outside, so a bunch of people were driven into the store, where they had set me up right next to the Self-help for Assholes section, so I had kind of a semi-captive audience. Then, on the PA system they announced that the Q&A and book signing was about to start, and introduced me as a, "Golfcaster," so I got a couple of extra assholes from the Fishing section too. I thanked everyone for showing up, and gave a rough description of what they could expect if they bought *A Nasty Bit of Rough*. Nobody could think of a question, and there was an awkward period of silence as I stared out at a sea of assholes wearing blank expressions. I suspected they were all thinking, "I wonder who this asshole is?"

My publisher broke the ice by asking me a question about Tiger Woods, which I answered, and all of a sudden, you could see the attitude of the crowd change. They sat up.

"Wait a minute," they were thinking. "This asshole knows Tiger Woods!"

For the next hour, the theme of the book signing was, "Screw your novel, asshole, we want to hear about Tiger." Typical. I go all the way to New York to publicize my book, and that asshole

Tiger hijacks the whole episode.

But the upside of it was living proof that the Tiger Effect has been beneficial to everyone in golf. Nearly all of them bought at least one book, even the fishermen, who knew that Tiger likes to drag creatures out of the water by their lips. Half of these assholes wouldn't have shown up if it weren't for the fact I was able to tell them something they didn't know about Tiger. As usual, I made most of it up.

I had a wonderful three-day visit to New York City. It's the most vibrant, energetic, colorful place in the world for me, and I absolutely adore it. As we made our way out of midtown over the bridge toward La Guardia Airport for the flight home, I looked out the back window of the town car (which was being piloted by some insane Serbian asshole) at Manhattan's skyline. It struck me that if this great nation is a fighter, then Manhattan is the chin, which juts out defiantly. It's not perfect, and it's true, there are a couple of teeth missing. But in this town, no one stays down. It's not about buildings; it's about the people who use them, and the attitude of the people of New York City is back. These are people who have the guts to find humor in any situation, even the events of 9/11. That confirms for me what I already suspected. They are unbreakable.

A couple of missing teeth are eminently fixable, but it's going to cost us dearly. This town is full of dentists, and you know how much those assholes charge.

Rhythm of the Times

Hey! Golf is back with a vengeance, and it's cool again. It seems to me that the game went through a tepid spell in the 1970s. Hardly surprising with all the bad hair, flared pants, and plaid.

But then came the 1980s, and golf stayed warm in solidarity with the music industry, which was assaulting our eyes and ears with the likes of Boy George, Duran Duran, and Kajagoogoo. Uh-huh, I know what you're thinking. Not cool.

Not that I feel the music industry is in great shape at the minute, either. I'm afflicted with an emetic boy-band blues and Britney biliousness every time I turn on the radio. But for some reason the game of golf has pulled itself out of the warm spell, and is appealing to a wider audience than ever before.

Changes in the attitude toward dress code are a big help, I'm sure. For decades, a golf shirt has been a golf shirt, and I for one am glad to see a return to the old crew-neck tee of the 1950s and 1960s, even if the collar is a little lower. Now we have Tiger, Duval, and many others dressing in a socially relevant fashion, in outfits that, without the logos at least, would be equally acceptable at a rock concert or in a nightclub. In fact, these days some of the performers at that rock concert might be similarly attired.

After Arnie, who made the game really cool in the '50s, a lot of big stars liked to play golf—you know, Bing Crosby, Bob Hope, Dean Martin, etc.—but it seems to me that they held more appeal for the older generation.

At that time, the people who were the equivalent of today's rock stars were busy either dying in plane crashes or overdosing on the toilet. But some of today's rock stars are now keen on golf. Quite a lot of them actually, if the AT&T Pebble Beach is anything to go by.

If somebody had handed Alice Cooper a persimmon driver

twenty-five years ago, he probably would have beaten the nearest chicken to death with it. If you had kidnapped any self-respecting rock star and left him out on a golf course with a set of clubs, he would have snorted the nearest out-of-bounds line, hot-wired a cart, and died in a head-on blazing wreck with one of the course marshals.

Nowadays, the aforementioned Mr. Cooper is a really good six handicap and Hootie and the Blowfish are mad keen on golf, as are the guys from Creed. Vince Gill could beat me, Celine Dion can play in at least two languages, Glenn Frey swipes at it frequently, Cameron Diaz would win any hole she played simply by bending over to tee the ball up, and Carson Daly is a golf nut. It's not like all these people are getting on in years either; some of them are in their twenties.

So what the hell happened to turn some of our hippest and least square people off drinking, drugs, fornication, and trying to commit suicide by way of general enthusiasm—as did so many normal famous people in the sixties and seventies? Maybe on the fairways they find respite from the craziness of their lives, but I think there might be a more recent development that has more of them punishing the pill. (Bear with me here for a moment, because I haven't even come close to thinking this one through.) In order to find the real reason for golf's popularity today, perhaps we have to cast our addled minds back into our dark, prehistoric past. Imagine, say, for instance, a mammoth hunt during the last ice age. (Like I said, hang in there. Eventually this will make sense.)

There is a group of hunters, huddled around a paltry fire, roasting a turnip, discussing how they can improve their hunting technique. The tribe had always been vegetarian, until an incident some years earlier in which a small caveman had startled an enormous bull mammoth in the act of mating. The great beast had charged, and somehow the unfortunate man had become lodged in its throat and choked it to death.

The tribe suddenly found themselves with enough meat to tide them through the ice-age summer, which was really freaking freezing that year. More importantly, they had discovered a way to kill a mammoth. They just picked the smallest surviving tribe member, tossed him at an enraged mammoth, and hoped to get lucky.

It was a flawed plan, and was not considered in any way a cool activity, especially by the more diminutive of our ancestors, but every now and then they would get lucky, and then afterward, very, very constipated for a few months. Then it was back to the old nuts and berries.

The breakthrough came when a small, nerdy-looking caveman named Erk suggested that it might be an idea to use a bigger version of one of the sharpened sticks they had been using to skewer and hold the mammoth meat/turnip over the fire to skewer the mammoth while it was still alive.

The idea was met with ridicule by the rest of the tribe, whose chieftain, Ugga, lost no time in pointing out to Erk that, as he was the smallest surviving member—and next in line for the old mammoth heave-ho—he obviously came to the campfire with something of a personal agenda. It should have been something of a paradigm shift, but way back then, no one knew how to pronounce paradigm, so nothing shifted for Ugga, who was secretly a little miffed that the boys had rebuffed his idea for a cure to the constipation problem, which had also involved the sharpened sticks.

However, Ugga was not the head honcho because he was dumber than the rest—in fact, far from it. He was also the drummer for the tribe, and I suppose, in a way, an early rock star. Later that evening he was beating the mammoth skins for the ladies, and wallowing in their adoration, when one of his sticks broke during a particularly violent paradiddle. (Which incidentally, is the word right next to *paradigm* in the dictionary.)

The broken stick shot straight up into the night sky, and as Ugga stared up into the blackness for some sign of it, it suddenly speared straight downward into his left eye socket, killing him stone, motherless dead.

The next thing you know, the rest of the tribe is standing around scratching their overhanging eyebrows, and we have a new head Homo sapiens—namely, Erk. Also, the word spread fairly quickly that there was a cool, new, fun, and ultimately, rewarding way to perform a feat which had, up until that point, been nerdy and dangerous. Of course, before they knew it, mammoths were extinct.

I rest my case, which I fully admit is completely ridiculous. But it's a simple fact of evolution, even in golf, that if something better comes along, people will naturally gravitate toward it. In reality, golf has always been a very cool game, and the current upsurge in its popularity has been caused, at least in part, by a public awareness campaign spearheaded by Tiger and a younger, more athletic, and better-looking professional cast.

The game looks more exciting, because, as a direct result of technological advancement, it is more exciting. These days, the holes are cut on impossibly sloping, lightning-fast, wafer-thin peninsulas on devastatingly difficult golf courses. With the equipment of yesteryear, players couldn't find today's flags if you gave them each a Geiger counter, yet I'm continually reading that because of all this new equipment, the game is becoming too easy. I beg to differ. Because of these harder golf courses, I believe golf is becoming more difficult.

This is about the ability to applaud a good idea, even if it isn't yours. Throughout the ages, there have always been naysayers every time somebody manufactured something new and improved. But the development of clubs that make a very difficult, frustrating, and sometimes downright silly pastime both easier to pick up and more fun to continue is of paramount importance to the evolution of the game.

A hundred years ago, golfers looked at the old wooden-shafted, wooden-headed play clubs of centuries gone by and wondered how on earth their golfing predecessors managed to get any enjoyment out of a game played with such crude artifacts. It was hard for them to imagine how the beautiful modern equipment of their day, which was so much easier to play with, could possibly be improved upon.

What were they thinking? I'll tell you what they were thinking: The same thing I was when I took up the game thirty years ago. I was playing with tiny, steel-shafted blades, and a laminated driver that looked like a bran muffin on a stick. My grips were shiny leather on a cork underlying, and they felt so bad that, on a frosty morning, I lost dental work if I caught one near the heel. But even then, I couldn't imagine how we could make better golf clubs than were currently available. But we did, didn't we?

A hundred years from now, the average space-age hacker may look at the graphite and titanium of today as just another step along the road that led to whatever technological marvel he is presently using to dig lumps out of planet Earth, or Uranus, or wherever. I have no doubt it will be the same age-old, often futile, but captivating pastime.

It will be an effort to get a small white orb into some kind of a crater, which I fervently hope will still be no smaller than 4 ¼ inches in diameter.

Guardians of the Game

Well, here we go again. In its infinite wisdom, the USGA has decided the game has become too easy and, as usual, equipment is to blame. Naughty manufacturers.

Personally, I still find the game quite difficult and until they invent a club that makes the hole bigger, I say let every player everywhere have at it. The USGA seems to have forgotten that 99.9 percent of golfers need all the help they can get.

So what if the scores on the PGA Tour are getting lower? Athletes are running faster every year and I don't hear anyone suggesting that we should stick lead up their shorts to slow them down. These pompous outbursts of verbal flatulence from golf's ruling bodies are becoming irritating to me, so I thought I'd ask the opinion of a man who I consider the highest authority in all of golf. The gentleman in question is Major General (Ret.) Sir Richard Gussett, known to his friends as "Dickie." He presides over the most exclusive golf course in the world, a club so secretive that its whereabouts are unknown to all but a select few.

Scrought's Wood refused the British Royal charter back in the 1850s, citing the fact that they wouldn't want to be associated with people who behaved like royalty—a move which, while it seemed like madness at the time, now looks prophetic, to say the least. They also refused to have anything to do with the Royal and Ancient, believing themselves to be the true guardians of the Rules of Golf, a position that they insist they hold to this day and rightly so, say I.

No new members have been accepted into the club since 1960 and, due to attrition, there are only nineteen members remaining. The criteria required for membership are incredibly difficult to meet. They include a blood oath of secrecy, the ability to consume vast quantities of single malt Scotch, and a wife who thinks you died some years ago.

It is my fervent hope that, if I am spared to reach the qualifying age of sixty, I will be allowed the privilege.

The club's one concession to modern technology at Scrought's Wood is a satellite dish because the members worship the game like a religion and subsequently record and review every broadcast of every event.

Uncle Dickie and a couple of his cronies were watching the U.S. Open last year when the USGA ran its commercial, "We didn't give birth to the game, but we've been its legal guardian for the last one hundred years." That sent a few good swallows of Guinness back out through some noses, I can tell you, and ruined a couple of magnificent handlebar mustaches.

Old-fashioned they may be, but unenlightened they are not, so it is with great pleasure and the kind permission of the man I am proud to call "Uncle Dickie" that the following correspondence is reproduced:

Davey, my boy,

So nice to hear from you and thank you for inquiring about your Auntie Myrtle. Ninety years old last week and the old boiler is still fit enough to drain a bottle of Bushmills' in a single sitting, bless her.

She sends her love. Now to business, old chap. You are indeed correct to be worried about the latest ominous rumblings from the bowels of the USGA. As always, any change they make will be for the worse.

In the name of all that's right and drawing back to the fairway, just who the hell do they think they are? Don't they realize that there were only two Rules in the original game? "Thou shalt play the ball as it lies"; and "Thou shalt play the course as thou findest it."

These two Rules gave birth to some of the greatest technological developments in the sport, all of which were totally necessary. These latest clubs are simply a part of the evolution of the game and must be protected at all costs. We have lost too much already.

Take, for instance, Hamish McShug's patented splatterguard niblick (circa 1835), which was rendered obsolete when the Royal Asses poked their noses in and deemed the cow pat an immovable obstruction. Of course, you and I know the cow pat is always immovable, especially when you are trying to get it out of your britches, hence Hamish's splatterguard. Even then, if you let it dry and use a stiff brush, you're whistling Dixie, as they say over there in Yankee land.

But listen old chap, there may yet be a silver lining to this cloud of hot air.

Personally, I feel this latest attempt to halt the natural evolution of the game may result in something of a peasants' revolt and perhaps we here at Scrought's Wood will finally have our say and sanity will prevail.

There may be thirty-five clubs in my bag, but every one of them is vital. They have about an equal chance of taking my oversized driver as they do parting me from my rutting iron because they are totally and equally necessary to my game.

You remember the rutting iron, don't you, Davey boy? (It's not what you think, you evil-minded little bugger.) Let's say your ball has found itself in a wheel rut. Your standard niblick simply won't do the job to extricate it. Hence, the rutting iron.

Just imagine if we at the Wood took our rightful place as guardians of the sacred game. The Bible has but ten rules, so why the hell should a simple game have thirty-four with a six-hundred-page book of decisions?

Here's our decisions book: "Hit it and stop whining." That should speed up play. A golf course is a canvas, my boy, upon which the best and worst players may create their masterpieces.

One must always remember: A low score is never an insult to the golf course, but rather a compliment to the player.

Davey, we here at the Wood are delighted with your progress in the USA. Your broadcasting position serves us well by giving you the opportunity to make average golfers aware of how this sacred game should be played, despite what the so-called "ruling bodies" may say. I wouldn't trust them to rule a straight line. So, be vocal, dear boy, and make us proud. In twenty years' time, perhaps you will, as a member of the "Holy Wood," take your seat on the committee that will restore the game to its original glory.

Or, perhaps you will sit in the clubhouse and drool, like Bertie Featherstone did for years before he popped his clogs two weeks ago. Old Bertie was the second death we've suffered in recent weeks, the first being Penfold, our beloved greenkeeper, who you will remember as the "Sod Father." He was laid to rest in the staff plot behind the thirteenth green. As is our custom here at Scrought's Wood, three bottles of thirty-year-old McCallan's single malt—deducted, of course, from Penfold's last check—was poured over his grave.

Naturally, we drank it first.

As for Squadron Leader Featherstone, old Bertie wanted himself stuffed and placed for all eternity upon his customary barstool in the snug. The only difference that we've noticed thus far is that he has stopped drooling and falls off considerably less often. Also, his breast pocket makes a frightfully good ashtray.

Well, that's the news for now, so toodle pip, my boy, and don't be a stranger.

Yours sincerely,
Gussett of the Wood

Wish Upon a Star

I had yet to visit only four states in this great country, one of which was South Dakota, so a little while ago I was pleased when my agent told me he had booked me a speaking engagement in Sioux Falls for the Make-a-Wish Foundation. The date was the Monday after the International at Castle Pines, and I figured it would be an easy gig. They were picking me up in a private jet in Denver, taking me right to the doorstep in Sioux Falls, and later that same evening, flying me over the Canadian border to Sarnia, Ontario, where the next day I had another commitment.

The weirdest thing was that they were paying me a great deal of money for the pleasure of my company. I know I've said it before, but I love this country. I do about thirty of these speaking engagements a year, and it has never ceased to amaze me how anyone, never mind moi, could get away with such a scam. I had no idea, however, how much of an epiphany I was in for.

For a not-so-famous celebrity such as myself, a charity day is usually a little different from a corporate outing in that everybody I encounter is pleased to meet me and glad that I took time out of my busy schedule to help raise money for a worthy cause. Many times, the good people who attend are under the mistaken impression that the guest speaker is there out of the goodness of his heart. An already inflated ego is liable to burst a seam in such an environment, particularly when there's a jet and a limousine thrown into the bargain.

Everything was going swimmingly that fateful evening, and I met some great people at the cocktail reception before the dinner. As usual, I hoodwinked most of them into thinking I was witty, charming, and devastatingly windswept, with just a hint of vulnerable little boy for the ladies. I had a couple of glasses of claret to loosen up the old yodeling tackle before I spoke (okay, seven), and when Tom Hanson, the chairman of the South Dakota chapter, introduced me, my heart was light as I skipped up to the podium to regale the faithful with my best stuff.

Damn, but I was good, too. I only wish I could have been down among the crowd, listening to myself. It was with a sense of having done a job well that I sat back down at the main table to, as my malaprop-inclined Aunt Jean would have said, "A standing ovulation."

Then, it happened.

Up until that point, I had been aware of what the Make-a-Wish Foundation did, but like the parents of most healthy children, I had never made much of a conscious effort to dwell upon the subject.

Such thoughts are simply too painful. There were a few sick children and their parents there, and one of the moms was scheduled to speak next.

Her daughter, Jordan, stood beside her, and unlike me, both were obviously nervous about performing in front of an audience. I started to squirm in my seat, feeling for the mom as she started to speak. She talked about Jordan's rheumatoid arthritis, the treatment, and how other kids poked fun at her child because of the effect that some of the powerful drugs had had on this beautiful little girl's appearance. All of a sudden I was twisting my napkin under the table, and choking up. I made another discovery—I can suck, but my eyeballs can't. Jordan's mom went on to thank us all for a trip to New York, the spending money, and two visits to FAO Schwarz. Even better than that, they had the chance to talk to other parents, many of whom endure the unimaginable agony of watching their babies slowly fade away.

You have to be strong, I thought to myself as I blew my nose on a linen napkin, and then wiped my eyes. Yeah, I know, I did it in the wrong order, and got snot on my eyebrows. Tom Hanson grasped my wrist under the tablecloth and smiled at me. Some people deal with this every day of their lives.

Then, it was Jordan's turn to speak. She took the microphone from Mom, and for a moment I thought I was going to be all right. Then she thanked us all for the trip of her life. It was something she would never have been able to do had it not been for our generosity.

It was right about then that I knew I had to go back to the stage. Here was a little girl, not much older than my youngest boy, Rory, about whom I had recently heard some good news. Rory did not have rheumatoid arthritis, but a less serious form of the disease. For me, waiting for the results of my little boy's tests was the worst form of torture, and my sense of relief had been overwhelming. Now, I was listening to a little girl and her mom, both of whom had received the news I had dreaded, and they were telling me how lucky they were that I had come to see them in my private jet.

I felt like a guy wearing a big white pointy hood at a Nation of Islam meeting, but nobody in the room appeared to notice. I stumbled back up there after Jordan was done and did my best to talk again, and this time I sucked like a turbocharged Dirt Devil.

I gratefully accepted Kleenex from those near enough the stage to offer as I stumbled through a makeshift apology, and all of this from a career cynic who, up until this point in his life, had cried only when he picked up a check or spilled a drink. I told them that I was the luckiest person in that room because that night I had been given something that I had never even been smart enough to wish for: a chance to do something that would make me feel good forever.

I told them that they could keep their money and engrave my name on their guest list for as long as anyone would pay to hear my nonsense. Never mind the jet, I would crawl on my hands and knees over broken glass from Denver to Sioux Falls to hear Jordan say she had fun or to meet someone as courageous as her mom. Hell, I might even fly there in Clampett's single engine plane. (Actually, check that, I'll take the broken glass.) For me, this was like meeting Jesse Owens and getting to kick Hitler in the nuts, all in one go. It was me who received the gift that night, for I got back perhaps the most important of my senses: my sense of proportion.

I know that golf has had a bad rap over the years for being elitist and racist, but it's hard to make that case about professional golf, or the ordinary Joe who loves to play. This article is not about me; it's about the kind of people who play golf, watch golf, and love golf. People like that racist pig Fuzzy Zoeller, who has given hundreds of thousands of dollars and countless days over the years to the Boys and Girls Clubs of America. Payne Stewart would have given his ass away, if he hadn't been one of those white men who looked like his tush had fainted, and God only knows how many young lives Tiger Woods is touching.

Over the years, the Buy.com, Senior, and PGA Tours have given a combined total of $473 million to charities. Last time I checked, that was close to half a billion. The NBA donates all the money from player fines, but even those guys couldn't behave badly enough to come within a bad week for the Bill Gates of the PGA Tour. It's good to be a part of this game.

That night, I asked for an autograph from Linda Bergendahl-Pauling, whose little boy, Scott, was the first Make-a-Wish kid. Scott was diagnosed with leukemia, but always wanted to be a policeman when he grew up. Thanks to the men and women of the Phoenix Police Department, he got to be a motorcycle cop for one precious day, badge and all. And then he died.

Linda signed her book, Little Bubble Gum Trooper, for me, a book that so far I have not been strong enough to read, but when I have, I think I will have taken one step along the path that will lead to an understanding of what it takes to be a real hero. I already know it has nothing to do with putting a little ball into a hole in the ground, although there is clearly something about that pastime that makes a difference.

Credits

Chapter One: Who am I? And Why am I here?

The Guy on the Fairway	Golf Magazine, June 1997
The Hairy One	Golfonline.com, November 29, 2000
The Invisible Man	Golf Magazine, April 2002
Dinner Is Served	Golf Magazine, December 2000

Chapter Two: Game Theories

Carrying On	Golf Magazine, February 1998
Caddie Firings and Stupid Rules	Golfonline.com, April 21, 1999
Hypocritical Headache	Golf Magazine, September 2002
That Was Ugly	Golfonline.com, October 18, 2000
Members of the Club	Golf Magazine, April 1998
Try This Silly Season Event	Golfonline.com, December 10, 2001
Going Mad	Golf Magazine, June 2000
The Kingdom of Fandom	Golf Magazine, July 1998
Neither Wind nor Rain	Golf Magazine, December 1997
Girls in the Boys' Club	Golf Magazine, February 2003

Chapter Three: My Less Than Finest Hours

Queasy Ryder	Golf Magazine, October 1997
Passages, Port-l-lets, and Pepto-Bismol	Golfonline.com, June 2, 1999
Scratching an Itch	Golf Magazine, February 2001
Letting Loose	Golfonline.com, May 15, 2002
Out-of-Mind Experiences	Golf Magazine, October 1999
A Very Bad Day	Golfonline.com, June 28, 2000
Warning: Stoned Hippos	Golf Magazine, April 1999
Working Vacation	Golfonline.com, July 5, 2001
Taking Complete Relief	Golf Magazine, February 1999
Walking Wounded	Golfonline.com, October 24, 2001
Humanity Stripped Naked	Golf Magazine, October 2001

Chapter Four: The Wages of Idiocy

Chapter Five: A Confederacy of Idiots

Chapter Six: Pet Peeves

Chapter Seven: A Tour of the Tour

Chapter Eight: A Hallowed and Formidable Tradition of Idiocy

Chapter Nine: Idiot's Delight